Palgrave Key Concepts

Palgrave Key Concepts provide an accessible and comprehensive range of subject glossaries at undergraduate level. They are the ideal companion to a standard textbook making them invaluable reading to students throughout their course of study and especially useful as a revision aid.

Key Concepts in Accounting and Finance
Key Concepts in Business Practice
Key Concepts in Criminal Justice and Criminology
Key Concepts in Cultural Studies
Key Concepts in Drama and Performance (second edition)
Key Concepts in e-Commerce
Key Concepts in Human Resource Management
Key Concepts in Information and Communication Technology
Key Concepts in International Business
Key Concepts in Innovation
Key Concepts in Language and Linguistics (second edition)
Key Concepts in Law (second edition)
Key Concepts in Leisure
Key Concepts in Management
Key Concepts in Marketing
Key Concepts in Operations Management
Key Concepts in Philosophy
Key Concepts in Politics
Key Concepts in Public Relations
Key Concepts in Psychology
Key Concepts in Social Research Methods
Key Concepts in Sociology
Key Concepts in Strategic Management
Key Concepts in Tourism

Palgrave Key Concepts: Literature
General Editors: John Peck and Martin Coyle

Key Concepts in Contemporary Literature
Key Concepts in Creative Writing
Key Concepts in Crime Fiction
Key Concepts in Medieval Literature
Key Concepts in Modernist Literature
Key Concepts in Postcolonial Literature
Key Concepts in Renaissance Literature
Key Concepts in Romantic Literature
Key Concepts in Victorian Literature
Literary Terms and Criticism (third edition)

Further titles are in preparation
www.palgravekeyconcepts.com

Palgrave Key Concepts
Series Standing Order
ISBN 1–4039–3210–7

(outside North America only)

You can receive future titles in this series as they are published by placing a standing order. Please contact your bookseller or, in the case of difficulty, write to us at the address below with your name and address, the title of the series and the ISBN quoted above.

Customer Services Department, Macmillan Distribution Ltd
Houndmills, Basingstoke, Hampshire RG21 6XS, England

Key Concepts in Psychology

Julie Winstanley

palgrave
macmillan

First published 2006 by
PALGRAVE MACMILLAN
Houndmills, Basingstoke, Hampshire RG21 6XS and
175 Fifth Avenue, New York, N.Y. 10010
Companies and representatives throughout the world

PALGRAVE MACMILLAN is the global academic imprint of the Palgrave
Macmillan division of St. Martin's Press, LLC and of Palgrave Macmillan Ltd.
Macmillan® is a registered trademark in the United States, United Kingdom
and other countries. Palgrave is a registered trademark in the European
Union and other countries.

ISBN-13: 978-1-4039-4873-1
ISBN-10: 1-4039-4873-9

This book is printed on paper suitable for recycling and made from fully managed
and sustained forest sources. Logging, pulping and manufacturing processes are
expected to conform to the environmental regulations of the country of origin.

A catalogue record for this book is available from the British Library.
Library of Congress Cataloging-in-Publication Data

    p. cm
    Includes bibliographical references and index

Printed in Great Britain by the MPG Books Group, Bodmin and King's Lynn

For Mo,
Who filled my childhood with so many special times.
Thinking of you always, but especially so at Christmas.

Contents

Boxes and figures

Boxes

Figures

Tables

Introduction

This book is designed to provide easy and quick access to the dominant key terms used within the many areas and branches of psychology. Each key concept has been linked with further resources, such as research papers and websites, to an extent that reflects its degree of importance to psychology. This enables the users to further enhance and deepen their knowledge base of the area by searching other appropriate information sources. In providing links to websites, I have attempted to contact all sources for permissions as well as to ensure that the websites will remain online and available for access for as long as possible. It is inevitable that some sites may be moved or removed, and this will be continuously addressed and websites updated in subsequent editions.

As the book's title suggests, I have attempted to identify and highlight the key concepts within psychology. I have provided definitions for each term, and directed readers towards resources for further study that reflect its relative importance within psychology. There are many more terms that may not be specifically included here and, depending on the area of psychology you are working or studying in, there may be much debate about what actually are the 'key concepts' of psychology. In selecting the terms to include, I have attempted to provide an overview of psychological concepts that draw on and reflect the many different debates, perspectives, branches and approaches within the field. Inevitably, on future reflection there will be key concepts that perhaps I will feel I should have included, but again this will be addressed in future editions. Please refer to the index however, as it may be that the topic you are seeking is not a specifically listed key concept but is covered and defined in relation to other entries. So it is always worth checking out the index and reference lists in the back of the book.

Cross-referencing is also used widely throughout the book, with highlighted text denoting further reading on each specific concept. For example, you may wish to find out more about attachment, so the highlighted text in the entry on 'attachment theory' would refer you to Bowlby, maternal deprivation and Ainsworth. This enables you to make quick and easy links between areas and theories of psychology. This is excellent if you are in the process of writing an essay that asks you to compare and contrast different views of attachment, as it enables you to construct a debate without having initially to waste valuable time sourcing many books and papers.

If this is your first introduction to psychological terminology and language, you will realize quite quickly that it can seem almost like a new and foreign tongue, which can be quite confusing at times. My aim for this book is to make the language easier to learn by providing simple, direct definitions that link and connect you to other key concepts related to each particular term, and to further sources of information. You will often find that in psychology some words can have more than one meaning (fixation is a case in point), which can cause confusion at times. In an attempt to provide clarity, the book separates such contrasting definitions in a clear format to allow easier understanding.

The book *Key Concepts in Psychology* provides a valuable resource for exam revision, especially in jogging memories around key concept areas such as statistics, research, key theories and theorists, and areas of psychology. These concepts have been listed separately in the sections at the end of the book; this makes revision easier as the terms are more accessible and the lists themselves can be used as quick and easy memory tests. You can test yourself, or with friends you can test each other by reviewing each concept on the list and checking whether you can remember what each term means.

Finally, I have included a section named key acronyms in psychology, as psychology has a tendency to be dotted frequently with acronyms for key terms, theories and psychological tools. There is also a list of phobias and their 'real' names, which I have included for interest and for those who perhaps work or study within a clinical setting (take a look, there are some quite unusual and interesting fears out there). In such clinical settings it may be useful to be aware of some of the phobias that you may encounter as a psychologist.

Lastly *Key Concepts in Psychology* is designed to progress with you as you undertake your studies or work in psychology. It is a valuable resource for those studying A-levels who need an introduction to the key psychological concepts, those embarking upon or continuing undergraduate degree courses, or even those at postgraduate level who may need to refresh their knowledge.

Psychology has in the last decade become increasingly popular and is fast becoming an integral component of many courses in allied areas such as health, social care, nursing, social work, business studies and early-years education. If you are studying in such areas this book will be extremely useful in providing you with an casy understanding of psychology. If you are working in areas such as clinical or educational psychology, or in professions such as nursing, social work, teaching, health care and management, this book can also be used to refresh your knowledge or to deepen your understanding.

I hope that you enjoy reading *Key Concepts in Psychology*, that it becomes a valuable resource guide which is highly relevant to your studies or work, and that its use extends throughout your studies and career in psychology.

Julie Winstanley

Acknowledgements

While writing this book has been an interesting and enjoyable experience, it has also been a daunting and sometimes frustrating process. Psychology by its very nature is full of conjecture and contrasting viewpoints, and even within established theories there is always room for debate and critique. As a result it has been difficult at times to decide, from so many terms, what the key concepts should be, while simultaneously attempting to reflect the diversity and difference within the many areas of psychology. I am aware that in an area where there are so many perspectives and debates, there will always be different opinions on this point. Therefore, let me now apologise for omitting any concept that you would have liked included.

I would like to thank all the many people, associations and companies that have provided permissions to have their weblinks and material included within this book. Their positive responses have enabled a rich and diverse range of resources to be included, which will undoubtedly be of a great help to students and readers. I would like to offer a personal thanks to Dr Eric Chudler of Washington University, USA, who has been a great help.

On a personal note I am indebted to my colleagues and friends who have offered comments and criticism that have helped to fire and fuel the writing process. Thanks especially to my children, Tegen, Branagh, Bailey and Poppie, who at times had to play second fiddle to my 'fifth child', the computer, as I was consumed for what seemed like days, weeks, perhaps months on end in the writing of this book.

To the readers, I hope this book aids you in your journey through psychology, but please excuse any mistakes or errors, as undoubtedly somewhere within there are bound to be. I hope that ultimately this book will help you to foster further interest in, and generate a healthy critique of psychology and the 'human condition'.

Abnormal (atypical) behaviour

This is a form of behaviour that deviates from what society considers to be indicative of normal behaviour. Abnormal behaviours usually contravene the moral rules and social codes (set by society) about how people are expected to function within particular situations. Any deviations from these '**social norms**' are considered abnormal; such behaviour can often be distressing and disturbing to the individual and those around them.

Rosenhan and Seligman (1989) suggest that there are seven main features or characteristics associated with abnormality. These are: suffering, **maladaptiveness**, vividness and unconventionality, unpredictability and loss of control, irrationality and incomprehensibility, observer discomfort and violation of moral and ideal standards.

There are however many contrasting viewpoints adopted within the different psychological approaches as to the nature and origins of abnormal behaviour. For example:

- **Behavioural** approaches identify abnormal behavioural patterns as arising from the 'learning' and '**reinforcement**' of **maladaptive responses** to different kinds of **stimulus**, originating from **classical** and **operant conditioning** processes and modelling. For example, an individual may imitate the behaviour of members of his/her family, setting a pattern which is then reinforced by the praise given by family members. If this behaviour is to act aggressively in the presence of police officers, then this socially learnt behaviour would be viewed as abnormal and could be distressing to the individual involved.

See **Bandura.**

- Biological approaches take the view that abnormal behaviour is due to internal, innate factors that are inherent in the person's physiological and biological make-up. For example, behaviours that may be seen as abnormal, such as **schizophrenia** or

depression, may be caused by biochemical changes in the **brain**, hormonal changes and/or physiological problems.

- **Cognitive** approaches take the view that abnormal behaviour is caused by 'faulty' cognitive, mental functioning, such as the onset and development of irrational or negative thought processes and assumptions about the world and our experiences. For example, an individual may develop a negative thought that leads to an assumption that the world is going to end in the next week, and so undertake a series of 'abnormal', irrational behaviours, such as leaving his/her job and going into social isolation.

- **Humanistic** approaches view abnormal behaviour as occurring when people are prevented in some way from developing to their potential, when their self-growth is somehow limited and restricted and they are unable to meet their self-goals or expectations. For example, an individual may want to be a primary school teacher, but because of financial problems and childcare commitments may feel forced to stay in a job he or she does not enjoy. This inability to move towards one's goals may lead to **depression** and social withdrawal and may be construed as abnormal behaviour.

  See **self-actualization theory.**

- Psychodynamic approaches take the view that abnormal behaviour is caused by unconscious and unresolved psychological forces and conflicts that the person has no conscious awareness of. Such forces quite often originate from childhood experiences and repressed thoughts and emotions. For example, an individual may have suffered a traumatic or upsetting event at four years old that he or she has repressed and no longer has conscious awareness of. This could lead to an unresolved psychological conflict that may manifest itself in the form of abnormal behaviour.

  See **Freud, psychoanalysis.**

- Sociocultural approaches take the view that abnormal behaviour is a product of social and cultural factors and pressures. In dysfunctional families, abnormal behaviour patterns may be encouraged and reinforced through 'reward', and the social stress systems that are experienced may create further problems and exacerbate the continuance of abnormal behaviour. For example, a family may have a poor view of the value of education and so promote in their children 'negative' **attitudes**

A

and behaviours such as non-attendance and/or non-engage ment in studies. The children then may gain reward for such abnormal behaviours and – particularly where this is combined with the social stress of parents who expect their children to behave in a particular way – they may feel impelled to behave in such a manner.

- **Biopsychosocial** approaches such as **diathesis-stress models** identify abnormal behaviour as having originated primarily through biological, psychological or sociocultural forces, which are then triggered and perpetuated by experiencing psychological **stress**. Such a model therefore can be seen as an interactive model of abnormal behaviour, being seen as occurring through the interaction of biological, psychological and sociocultural factors with the experience of stressful life events and psychological **stress**. For example, an individual may have experienced a physical illness that has made him/her weak and tired; when this is combined with social stressors such as financial worries, the individual may become socially withdrawn, depressed and anxious.

See **abnormal psychology, attitude, behaviourism, biopsychology, brain, classical conditioning, depression, diathesis-stress models, humanistic psychology, maladaptiveness, operant conditioning, reinforcement, schizophrenia, social norms, stimulus, stress.**

Bedi, R. P. (1999) Depression: an inability to adapt to one's perceived life stress? *Journal of Affective Disorders,* **54** (1–2), 225–34.

Lewinson, P. M., Joiner, T. E. and Rohode, P.(2001) Evaluation of cognitive diathesis-stress models in predicting major depressive disorders in adolescents. *Journal of Abnormal Psychology,* **110** (2), 203–15.

Sarason, I. G. and Sarason, B. R. (2004) *Abnormal Psychology: The Problem of Maladaptive Behaviour.* London: Prentice Hall.

Sue, D., Sue, S. and Sue D. (1994) *Understanding Abnormal Behaviour.* Boston: Houghton Mifflin.

www. sciencedirect.com/science (Search online at Science Direct for journal articles).

www. apa.org/journals/abn (American Psychological Association, *Journal of Abnormal Psychology* webpage).

Abnormal psychology

Abnormal psychology is concerned with scientifically examining and highlighting the 'causes' and factors associated with **abnormal behaviour**. In using scientific **research** methods, psychologists attempt to explain and predict why individuals experience and engage in **abnormal behaviours**. The fundamental aim of such investigation is to be able to control, predict and prevent the onset of **abnormal behaviours**.

See also **abnormal behaviour, addiction, antisocial behaviour, research.**

Davidson, G. C.(2003) *Abnormal Psychology.* London: John Wiley.

Getzfield, A. R. *(2006) Essentials of Abnormal Behaviour.* London: John Wiley.

Kring, A. M., Davison, G. C., Neale, J. M. and Johnson, S. (2006) *Abnormal Psychology: Study Guide*, 10th edn. London: John Wiley.

Rosenhan, D. L. and Seligman, M. E. P. (1989) *Abnormal Psychology.* New York: W. W. Norton.

Thomas F. Oltmanns, T. F., Martin, M., Neale, J. M. and Davison, G. C.(2006) *Case Studies in Abnormal Psychology*, 7th edn. London: John Wiley.

www. sruweb. com/~walsh/ablinks.html (Professor Walsh's Clinical and Abnormal Psychology Links on the WWW Department of Psychology, Salve Regina University, Newport, Rhode Island United States).

www. wwnorton. com/abnormal (*Abnormal Psychology* student website).

Absolute threshold

The absolute threshold, often referred to in psychophysics, is the lowest strength, point or intensity of a sensory stimulus at which it can be sensed, observed and detected, for example, light, taste, smell or noise. As the absolute threshold can differ from subject to subject (according to **variables** such as age, other sensory input and situation), experiments to determine human sensory perception of stimuli are strictly regulated. These experiments are undertaken in strict experimental conditions where 'other' sensory stimuli can be excluded, so ensuring **fixation** on the **stimuli variable** can be achieved. An example of this is seen in research on hearing that uses experimental conditions to remove other sound stimuli. Such research has found the average human absolute threshold for sound intensity to be approximately 1,000 hertz.

A

In everyday life our ability to detect at this absolute threshold level is challenged, as many similar sensory stimuli compete simultaneously for processing. For example, in a silent room we may hear a clock ticking 20 feet away; in a crowded noisy hall we may be unable to hear our own watch ticking. If we have not tasted sugar for a year, we may be able to taste one teaspoon of sugar in three gallons of water; if however we have just eaten a chocolate bar we may unable to sense the sugar in the water.

Hence, the ability for humans to perform within their absolute threshold limits is dependent on the amount of sensory stimuli that can be processed at any one time. Performance levels can be linked to demand: the greater the demand by sensory stimuli, the longer a signal will take to detect; the lower the demand, the nearer to the absolute threshold people can perform. To determine an absolute threshold level, the stimulus must have been detected and noticed in at least 50 per cent of presentations.

See **automatic processing, experimental condition, perception, research, stimulus, variables.**

Galantner, E. (1962) Contemporary psychophysics. In R. Brown (ed.), *New Directions in Psychology*. New York: Holt, Rinehart & Winston.

Accidental sample

See **sample.**

Accommodation

Accommodation has a variety of meanings within psychology. For example:

- It is a concept usually associated with Jean **Piaget**'s (1896–1980) stage theory of (children's) cognitive development. **Piaget** argued that a child's intellectual development occurred in a series of processes or stages, each stage marking a change in the child's cognitive abilities. He viewed children as active in building their own mental capacities for understanding and interacting with the world around them.

  Accommodation is the process in which 'old' mental structures, knowledge or **schemas** are adapted and modified to incorporate the new information, objects, actions and situations that the child has experienced. Accommodation enables new **schemas** to be created and existing ones to be expanded upon. This allows the child to become more efficient in meeting the demands of the social world. Accommodation can be described as the way in which a child has to adjust his or her way of thinking to accommodate the realities of external objects and the social world. For example, a child may be faced with a 'new' and novel problem, and by interacting and experimenting with this problem the child may find a solution (see **conservation**). In solving this problem the child has accommodated the new knowledge into his or her existing **schemas**, so that if faced with the same problem again, the new or modified **schema** will immediately 'solve' the problem. Thus a problem is no longer a problem.

- In biological and **cognitive psychology**, accommodation is also a term used to define how a nerve cell (**neuron**) decreases

A

its tendency to fire (**action potential**) when it is continuously stimulated with an electric current.

- In studies of visual **perception**, accommodation is a term used to describe how the change of the curvature of the lens of an eye can bring an object into sharp focus. If the lens if less convex, objects far away come into clearer focus and if more convex, objects closer by, become clearer.

See **action potential, assimilation, cognitive psychology, conservation, neuron, perception, Piaget's theory of cognitive development, schema.**

Atherton, J. S. (2004) *Teaching and Learning: Assimilation and Accommodation.* UK: online. Available at:
www.learningandteaching.info/learning/assimacc.htm.
Geert, P. V. (1998) A dynamic systems model of basic developmental mechanisms: Piaget, Vygotsky, and beyond, *Psychological Review*, **105** (4), 634–77.

Acculturation

Acculturation is the process by which people adapt to and learn the social codes, rules and morals of the society into which they have been born or have come to live. Acculturation thus, can be seen to exert a dramatic effect upon human behaviour and **abnormal behaviour,** and is often defined in relation to a deviation or non-acceptance of such cultural '**norms**'.

See **abnormal behaviour, individualism, norms.**

Berry, J. W. (1997) Acculturation strategies. In A. Baum, S. Newman, J. Weinman, R. West and P. R. Dasen (eds), *Culture and Cognition: Readings in Cross-Cultural Psychology*. London: Methuen.
Davis, C. and Katzman, M. A. (1999) Perfection as acculturation: psychological correlates of eating problems in Chinese male and female students living in the United States' *International Journal of Eating disorders*, **25** (1), 65–70.

A

Action potential

This refers to a change in a **neuron**'s cellular membrane, which creates an electrical nerve impulse or signal that travels in a wave-like manner down the **axon** of the **neuron**.

The action potential acts as a transmitter by which information can be sent quickly throughout the nervous system. To be able to transmit the information, the action potential needs to be able to move. It manages this by initiating a chain reaction that produces a wave of activity that is propelled down the **axon**. The action potential has an all-or-nothing characteristic, which means there either is or is not an action potential.

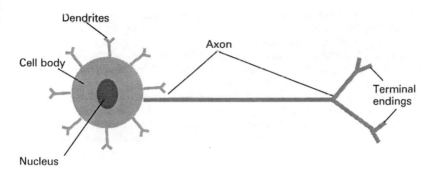

Figure 1 Action potential

See **axon, neural network, neuron, neurotransmitter, neuron.**

Pinel, J. P. J. (2005) *Biopsychology: And Beyond the Brain and Behavior.* CD-ROM. Boston: Allyn & Bacon.
http://faculty.washington.edu/chudler/ap.html (Dr Eric Chudler's website full of interesting information on the brain and neural networks).

Action slips

These are actions or sequences of behaviours that occur but were not intended. They are usually caused by absent-mindedness or attentional failure. Action slips appear to occur more frequently in highly repetitive or practised activities, such as driving. For example, have you ever been driving to the supermarket on a Saturday morning only to find you have taken the wrong road and are heading to work instead? This has happened because driving is a highly practised activity that requires little **attention**, and because of the lack of **attention**, you have taken the more familiar journey (to work).

Action slips occur in activities in which we would expect to make fewer errors because they are familiar. These slips appear to occur because of the type of attentional control processes we use when undertaking such activities. In new and less familiar activities we use conscious attentional control; as the activity becomes more familiar, we switch to **automatic processing**. When using **automatic processing**, we can make errors because we lack the close attentional control and monitoring that we can only gain in conscious attentional control processing.

See **attention, automatic processing, memory.**

Hay, J. F. and Jacoby, L. L. (1996) Separating habit and recollection: memory slips, process dissociations, and probability matching. *Journal of Experimental Psychology: Learning, Memory and Cognition,* **22** (6), 1323–35.

A

Reason, J. T. (1979) Actions not as planned: the price of automisation. In G. Underwood and R. Stevens (eds), *Aspects of Consciousness*, Vol. 1: *Psychological Issues*. London: Academic Press.

Reason, J. T. (1992) Cognitive underspecification: its variety and consequences. In B. J. Baars (ed.), *Experimental Slips and Human Error: Exploring the Architecture of Volition*. New York: Plenum.

Smallwood, J., Davies, J., Heim, J, Finnigan, F., Sudberry, M., O'Connor, R. C. and Obonsawin, M. (2004) Subjective experience and the attentional lapse: task engagement and disengagement during sustained attention. *Consciousness and Cognition*, 13, 657–90. Available online at: www.stir.ac.uk/staff/psychology/ro2/candc2004a.pdf#search='action%20slips'

Actor/observer bias

The actor/observer bias can occur when people are attempting to make sense of the causes behind their own or others' behaviour.

The actor/observer bias suggests that when we are the actor (doing the behaviour) we tend to attribute **situational** factors (things external to us) in attempting to make sense of our behaviour.

In contrast, when we are the observer (observing the actor) we have a tendency to explain the causes of other people's behaviour in terms of **dispositional** factors (something inside the person).

For example, you (the actor) are walking along the street and fall over. You (the actor) attribute your own behaviour (falling) to **situational** factors: the pavement being uneven or weather conditions making the street slippery.

You (the observer) are observing the other person (the actor) as he falls over in the street. You (the observer) attribute the other person's falling to **dispositional** factors: the actor's clumsiness or careless nature.

A possible reason for this bias is that you (the actor) have more privileged knowledge about the event, your past behaviour and disposition in comparison to that of the observer.

See **attribution, attributional biases, fundamental attribution error, self-serving bias, situational attribution, dispositional attribution.**

Jones, E. E. and Nisbett. R. E. (1971) *The Actor and the Observer; Divergent Perceptions of the Causes of Behaviour.* Morristown, NJ: General Learning Press.

Nisbett, R. E., Caputo, C., Legant, P., and Maracek, J. (1973) Behaviour as seen by the actor and as seen by the observer. *Journal of Personality and Social Psychology*, 27, 154–64.

ACT* system

This refers to the 'adaptive control of thought' system of **memory**. It is a model of information processing and human cognition put

A

forward in 1976 by John Anderson. ACT* distinguishes three types of **memory** structures: declarative, procedural and working. Declarative **memory** contains knowledge about facts and things, while procedural **memory** is knowledge about how to perform actions. Both are types of long-term **memory** and together they both represent the stored knowledge used by the ACT* system. The working **memory** contains all the information the system can currently process. Here, declarative **memory** can be stored and **retrieved** from long-term **memory** as well as transferred from sensory information into declarative knowledge. The working **memory** uses the procedural **memory** to establish what actions to take. If the information in the working **memory** 'matches' the production rules (ways to act) contained within the procedural **memory**, it can be recognized and an action may be undertaken.

> See **Atkinson and Shiffrin, memory, retrieval.**

Anderson, J. R. (1976) *Language, Memory and Thought*. Hillsdale, NJ: Erlbaum.

Anderson, J. R. (1983) *The Architecture of Cognition*. Cambridge, MA: Harvard University Press.

Anderson, J. R. (1990) *The Adaptive Character of Thought*. Hillsdale, NJ: Erlbaum.

Anderson, J. R. (1993) *The Rules of the Mind*. Hillsdale, NJ: Erlbaum.

Lebiere, C. and Anderson, J. (2005) *A Connectionist Implementation of the ACT-R Production System*. Available online at: http://act-r.psy.cmu.edu/papers/Lebiere_Anderson93.doc

Adaptation

Adaptation in its simplest form means an individual or organism being flexible rather than rigid, and so able to change and adapt appropriately to its environment and in any given situation.

- Evolutionary theory depicts the process of adaptation as occurring when genetic variation or **mutation** produces an organism that is physiologically and behaviourally more able to adapt to its environment. Through this process of **natural selection**, organisms that are more adaptive are more likely to survive in their environment. These adaptive individuals are likely to be competitively stronger than less advantaged individuals, which increases their chances of successfully reproducing and generating offspring who will also possess advantageous genetics.
- In studies of **perception**, adaptation refers to the adjustments made to the sensitivity of the sensory system, which have a tendency to increase the ability to discriminate under particular

A

conditions. For example, our eyes adapt (by expansion of the pupil) to be able to retain good vision when light is reduced or it is dark.

See **Darwinism, mutation, natural selection, perception, theory of evolution,**

Darwin, C. (1859) *On the Origin of Species by Means of Natural Selection, or the Preservation of Favoured Races in the Struggle for Life*. London: Murray.
Hagen, E. (1999) The functions of postnatal depression, evolution and human behaviour, *Elsevier Press*, 20, 325–59.
www.talkorigins.org/origins/faqs-evolution.html (The Talk Origins archives).

Addiction

Addiction is regarded as the possession of a type of **habit** that is very difficult to stop and involves reliance on a particular chemical or substance, such as alcohol or heroin. Breaking the **habit** can be very difficult as the person will have developed a strong physiological and/or psychological need for the substance. The addict feels unable to resist the substance even though he or she is aware that taking it may have adverse and unpleasant consequences. An addict who experiences an abrupt deprivation of the substance can experience a range of unpleasant withdrawal symptoms such as nausea, heart palpitations, **anxiety** and **depression**. The varieties of symptoms differ in nature and severity according to the **habit**. Common addictions are alcoholism, drug addiction, gambling, smoking and overeating.

The withdrawal problem that addicts experience is often referred to as dependency. Dependency means that the addict has come to need the substance to avoid the withdrawal symptoms that are associated with the **habit**. Defining addiction can be difficult as there are debates as to whether addiction is entirely psychological, or if an addiction is only present if there are specific physical changes in the body that make the drug vital for normal functioning.

Sometimes addicts may develop a tolerance for a particular chemical, which means that they need increased amounts of the substance to achieve the desired effect. Continuation of similar doses results in a diminishing effect due to various processes within the body, such as **habituation** that reduce our **response** to the chemical on repeated exposure. Some of the different approaches to understanding and studying addiction are:

* *Biological or 'disease' models of addiction*
  These models assume that there is an underlying biological cause that makes or predisposes a person to become an addict. Such an approach takes the view that there is something inher-

ently wrong with these people and that it is not their fault: they are sick and their addiction is a disease or illness.

Goodwin et al. (1973) found evidence that in some addicted people there is an inherited predisposition to become an addict, and suggested that this means some people could become more easily or quickly addicted than others. Goodwin et al. claimed, however, that this does not mean that everyone with this predisposition will go on to develop an addiction. Moreover, this does not explain all cases of addiction, as there are many addicts who have no family history of addiction.

Goodwin (1979) has suggested that addicts such as alcoholics have an inability to discriminate blood alcohol level (BAL), which leads them to be less aware of the effect of drinking and to drink more without sensing their condition. Alternatively, Schuckit (1984) proposed that alcoholics inherit a different style of metabolising alcohol, such as producing higher levels of acetaldehyde due to drinking, which propels them to drink more.

Such a biological model suggests that a biological abnormality resulting from the impairment of healthy neurochemical or behavioural processes causes an alcoholic's desire for another drink to increase after taking one drink. According to such a model, alcoholism and addiction are incurable diseases and the best that can be hoped for is to achieve remission. A biological approach views addicts as being addicts for life and holds that the only way of managing the addiction is abstinence from the substance or 'thing' the person is addicted to.

- *Moral model*
  The moral model locates addiction at the level of the individual, a product of human weakness and/or defects of character. Such a model, as suggested by Peele (1987), does not accept that there is any biological basis or cause for addiction. The model attributes an individual's addiction to a lack of will-power and moral strength, and so has little sympathy for the addict. As this is a 'blaming and failure' model, it is considered to have little therapeutic value. However, elements of the moral model, especially a focus on individual choices, have found enduring roles in other approaches to the treatment of dependencies, as seen in the psychosocial and sociological models in learning how to cope and manage the life stressors that may exert an effect on the addiction.
- *Genetics versus environment (**nature–nurture debate**)*
  The roles of both genetics and environment in creating

A

addicts have been intensively studied in the area of alco-holism. Studies such as Goodwin et al. (1973) have attempted to separate genetic from environmental factors by comparing adopted children of alcoholics with adopted children of non-alcoholic biological parents, and have claimed a three to four times higher alcoholism rate for those children whose biolog-ical parents were alcoholic. Vaillant's (1983) **research,** however, did not confirm this genetic link with alcoholism; his findings revealed that children with alcoholic relatives were no more likely to be alcoholics than those without alcoholic relatives. Vaillant did suggest however that it was possible that environmental factors exerted an effect on alcoholism, as the findings did not distinguish inherited disposition from environmental factors. Vaillant found that non-genetic factors such as ethnicity seemed to exert a major influence on alco-holism, noting that Irish-Americans in a Boston **sample** were seven times more likely to be alcoholics than Bostonians with Mediterranean roots.

- *Sociological models*
It has been suggested (Peele, 1987) that social pressures and stressors can produce higher levels of inner tension such as guilt, stress, suppressed aggression, conflict and sexual tensions, all of which can lead to higher rates of heavy drinking and drug use. This model suggests that the primary role of an addict's alcohol and/or drug use is to serve as a coping mechanism aimed at reducing **anxiety**. Within this model, societies that are permis-sive of and/or encourage drug or alcohol use have higher rates of problem drinking, drug use and addiction. This model also exam-ines the influence of social pressures exerted by the media and **social representations** on television of drug and alcohol use.

   Treatment for the addict under this model would involve promoting change in society. Change at such a level however can be slow, and for an individual who has problems in his or her life due to an addiction, change at such a level may offer no immediate help.

- *Psychosocial approaches*
A **diathesis-stress**/vulnerability-stress model of addiction views individuals as possessing a psychological predisposition (diathesis, particular personality traits or characteristics) that, when given a particular range of social stressors can lead an individual into addictive behaviour. Individuals can go through their entire lives and never develop any kind of addiction, but

someone who is affected at a critical time by a specific stressor or combination of stressors may be more inclined to develop an addiction. If the individual begins drinking alcohol or taking drugs even occasionally and then continues to increase consumption, he or she may develop a **dependency** on the substance. It is the specific combination of time, person and event that would lead to the development of addiction. The idea is that it is not the event or the person that is important; it is the interaction between person and event that is most crucial to the addiction.

See **abnormal behaviour, abnormal psychology, anxiety, depression, desensitization, diathesis-stress, habit, habituation, nature–nurture debate, personality, research, response, sample, social representations, trait theories of personality.**

Butters, J. (2002) Family stressors and adolescent cannabis use: a pathway to problem use. *Journal of Adolescence*, 25, 645–54.

Cunningham, J., Koski-Jannes, A., Wild, T. and Cordingley, J. (2002). Treating alcohol problems with self-help materials: a population study. *Journal of Studies of Alcohol*, 63, 649–54.

Goodwin, D. W. (1979). Alcoholism and heredity. *Archives of General Psychiatry, 36,* 57–61.

Goodwin, D. W., Crane, J. B. and Guze, S. B. (1971). Felons who drink: an 8-year follow-up. *Quarterly Journal of Studies on Alcohol, 32,* 136–47.

Goodwin, D.W., Schulsinger, F., Hermansen, L. et al (1973). Alcohol problems in adoptees raised apart from alcoholic biological parents. *Archives of General Psychiatry, 28,* 238–43.

Le, A. D. (2002) Effects of nicotine on alcohol consumption. *Alcoholism: Clinical and Experimental Research*, 12, 15–16.

Peele, S. (1987) A moral vision of addiction: how people's values determine whether they become and remain addicts. *Journal of Drug Issues,* **17** (2), 187–215.

Schuckit, M. A. (1984). Prospective markers for alcoholism. In D. W. Goodwin, K. T. Van Dusen and S. A. Mednick (eds), *Longitudinal Research in Alcoholism*. Boston: Kluwer-Nijhoff.

Vaillant, G. E. (1983). *The Natural History of Alcoholism: Causes, Patterns, and Paths to Recovery*. Cambridge, MA: Harvard University Press.

Vaillant, G. E. and Milofsky, E. S. (1982). The etiology of alcoholism: a prospective viewpoint. *American Psychologist, 37,* 494–503.

www.camh.net/ (Centre for addiction and mental health, Canada).

www.camh.net/pdf/camh_researchar03pubs.pdf (wide and varied list of research, journal articles, book chapters and books in the area of addiction).

A

Adolescence

Adolescence is often marked in Western culture as a transitionary period, a particular developmental stage, between puberty and **adulthood**. Western theories have attempted to understand adolescence by looking towards a range of psychological and sociological explanations. Developmental psychologist **Erikson** focused upon physiological changes at puberty and upon identity formation. Erickson viewed adolescence as a critical period in which individuals 'tested' out a number of different identities before committing themselves to a secure identity that would take them into **adulthood**. To **Freud,** adolescence was a stage in which **instinctual** urges following puberty created psychological conflict within the mind, leading to emotional imbalances. This 'storm and stress' model identifies adolescence as the period in which individuals must disengage from their families so that they can take their place in the adult world.

Social psychologists in contrast have focused on external rather than internal factors, such as changes in expectations and social roles that can have impacts upon an adolescent's life. This view explores social pressures and stresses on adolescents, so that the transition to **adulthood** is seen more as an adjustment to stress and pressure than as due to innate emotional conflicts. Adolescence as a particular developmental stage does not translate so easily into other cultural views, which often regard adolescence as a particular 'rite of passage' that denotes a child's transition into **adulthood**.

See **adulthood, Erikson, Freud, individualism, instinct.**

Erikson, E. (1968) *Identity: Youth and Crisis*. New York: Norton.

Phoenix, A. (1991) (1991) *Young Mothers*. Cambridge: Polity.

Morrow, V. (2003) Moving out of childhood. In J. Maybin, and M. Woodhead (eds), *Childhoods In Context, Book 2*, ch. 7, 268–312. Milton Keynes: Open University in association with John Wiley.

Journal of Research on Adolescence. The Official Journal of the Society for Research on Adolescence, B, Bradford Brown (ed.), Blackwell publishers. Available quarterly. Available online at: www.blackwellpublishing.com/journal.asp?ref=1050-8392

www.s-r-a.org/ (Society for Research on Adolescence, United States).

A

Adoption studies

These studies are used to explore the role of genetics in influencing an individual's behaviour. Studies have focused on examining the behavioural characteristics of adopted individuals in comparison to both their biological and adopted parents. If the individuals are shown to share similar behaviours and characteristics with their biological parents, then it can be suggested that genetics have exerted a greater influence than environmental factors on their behaviour. Therefore nature can be viewed as exerting a greater impact upon behaviour than nurture. Adoption studies have been used to study the role of genetics in behaviours and disorders such as alcoholism, **depression** and **schizophrenia**.

See **depression, genotype, nature–nurture debate, phenotype, schizophrenia, twin studies.**

Capron, C. and Duyne, M. (1989) Assessments of effects of socio-economic status on IQ in a full cross-fostering study. *Nature*, 340, 552–54.

Daniels, D. and Plomin, R. (1985) Origins of individual differences in infant shyness. *Developmental Psychology*, 21, 118–21.

Horn, J. M. (1983) The Texas Adoption Project: adopted children and their intellectual resemblance to biological and adoptive parents. *Child Development*, 54, 266–75.

Loehlin, J. C., Horn, J. M. and Willerman, L. (1989) Modelling IQ change: evidence from the Texas Adoption Project. *Child Development*, 60, 893–904.

Adulthood

Adulthood is viewed as the point at which an individual or organism has achieved maturity through attaining its full size and strength. Different psychological theorists have focused upon different aspects of development in determining when humans enter adulthood. Western theorists have explained adulthood in terms of individuals having achieved a particular stage of development.

- **Piaget** suggested that when humans have reached the **formal operational stage** of intellectual development, adulthood had begun.
- **Freud** suggested that adulthood was signified when individuals entered the **genital stage** of **personality** development.
- In contrast many cultures celebrate the onset of adulthood with highly ritualized procedures, which mark physical or chronological changes in individuals, such as the onset of menstruation or attainment of a particular age. In Latin America, the *Quinceanera* is a ceremony that marks the transition of 15-year-old girls into adulthood and womanhood. It is particularly celebrated among Central and South American migrant communities in the United States. The *Quinceanera* involves a thanksgiving mass, in which the 15-year-old arrives at church in a full-length dress, accompanied by handmaidens and boy escorts. After the mass there is a family party, where the girl has the first dance with her father, then with other escorts until she is finally raised up on the shoulders of the young men. There is also a ceremonial cutting of a cake. The whole ceremony is very similar to a traditional Western 'white' wedding, but is used to

A

denote a girl's move into adulthood. Contrastingly, the Xhosa tribe (from which Nelson Mandela originates) in South Africa mark the transition of teenage boys into adulthood by a rite of passage in which they undergo a ceremonial circumcision followed by a period of exclusion in the bush.

> *See* **adolescence, formal operational stage, Freud, genital stage, personality, Piaget.**

> Erikson, E. (1968) *Identity, Youth and Crisis*, New York: Norton.
> Mandela, N. (1994) *Long Walk to Freedom*, London: Little, Brown and Company.
> Maybin, J. and Woodhead, M (2003) *Childhoods in Context*, Milton Keynes: John Wiley in conjunction with Open University Press.

Afferent neurons

These are nerve cells that are responsible for transmitting information, in the form of nerve impulses from the senses (ears, nose, eyes) to the **central nervous system (CNS).** In the **CNS**, nerve impulses can be processed and understood. Afferent neurons function in the opposite manner to **efferent** (or motor **neurons**), which send information from the **CNS** to the body's muscles and glands.

> *See* **action potential, central nervous system, efferent neurons, neural network, neurotransmitter.**

> www.surch.co.uk/-/Neuron.html (information from Surch about neurons).

Affiliation needs

Affiliation needs are an individual's need to pursue the company of others. An individual's need to affiliate is identified as a source of **motivation** for engaging in certain behaviours and undertaking social interactions. However the reasons influencing that need for affiliation may differ. There are a variety of reasons why people may display affiliative needs:

- To fulfil their need for **attention**. In seeking the company of others they may experience being the centre of **attention**, and thus satisfy that need.
- To decrease or remove **anxiety**. Being in the company of others may serve as a source of information and guidance, which may serve to reduce **anxiety** or the social involvement may provide needed emotional support.
- To address and diminish feelings of loneliness that an

A

individual experiences as a consequence of having no, or an inadequate social network and friends.

See **anxiety, attention, motivation, self-actualization theory.**

McClelland, D. (1988) *Human Motivation*, Cambridge: Cambridge University Press.

Aggression

Aggression is a behaviour in which the sole function or purpose is to harm, hurt or injure another individual or organism, whether psychologically or physically. This behaviour has been theorized to be in part innate, but has also been identified within **research** as a **response** to frustration or social and cultural factors. Different types of aggression have been identified by psychologists, including:

* Person-oriented aggression, in which the main goal is to cause harm and hurt someone else.
* Instrumental aggression, in which the main goal is to attain some desired reward or outcome, such as a child gaining the toy. Here aggression is a **response** to enable the individual to attain the desired outcome.
* Proactive aggression is seen as a display of aggression that is initiated by an individual's desire to reach a desired outcome.
* Reactive aggression is viewed as an individual's reaction to somebody else's aggressive actions.

Researchers such as Mead (1935) and Gorer (1968) who undertook anthropological studies explored cross-cultural factors in aggression. Findings suggested that cultural and social factors played a major role in individual aggressive behaviour.

Studies have also been undertaken to examine the effect of gender on aggressive behaviour. Researchers such as Eagley and Steffan (1986) found that there was only a small tendency for men to act more aggressively than women. It has been suggested that the male hormone testosterone plays a role in making men appear to be more aggressive than women. Hawke (1950) found that men who had been castrated as punishment for aggressive sexual crimes revealed lower testosterone levels and displayed less aggression. Subsequently, when testosterone levels were increased in these men, there was a return to aggressive behaviour.

In the **frustration–aggression hypothesis** suggested by Dollard et al. (1939), aggression is viewed as a **response** to a frustrating event or experience.

A

See **antisocial behaviour, frustration–aggression hypothesis, research, response.**

Dollard, J., Doob, L. W., Miller, N. E., Mowrer, O. H. and Sears, R. R. (1939) *Frustration and Aggression*. New Haven, CT: Yale University Press.

Gorer. G. (1968) Man has no 'killer' instinct. In M. F. A. Montague (ed.), *Man and Aggression*. Oxford: Oxford University Press.

Eagley, A. H. and Steffan, V. J. (1986) Gender and aggressive behaviour: a meta-analytic review of the social psychological literature. *Psychological Bulletin*, 90, 1–20.

Hawke, C. (1950) Castration and sex crimes. *American Journal of Mental Deficiency*, 55, 220–26.

Mead, M. (1935) *Sex and Temperament in Three Primitive Societies*. New York: Morrow.

Simmons, R. (2002) *Odd Girl Out: The Hidden Culture of Aggression in Girls*, New York: Harcourt.

http://en.wikipedia.org/wiki/Aggression (information on aggression from Wikipedia).

Ainsworth (strange situation technique)

Ainsworth, Mary (1913–1999), developed a rigorous method of measuring individual differences in an attempt to understand how securely infants had become attached to their caregivers. Ainsworth conducted studies in countries such as Uganda and United States, using a method known as the strange situation technique (Ainsworth and Bell, 1970). It uses structured **observation** to observe and assess how securely or insecurely attached infants are responding to their caregivers. To determine this, they devised a method of categorizing and coding infants' observed behaviour, according to three **attachment** styles (avoidant, secure, ambivalent), by adopting the following 'strange situation' methods:

a) The caregiver and child are introduced to a room with toys.
b) Caregiver and child are left alone and the child can explore and investigate the toys.
c) A stranger comes into the room and chats with the caregiver. The stranger gradually approaches the child with a toy.
d) The caregiver leaves the room leaving the child alone with the stranger to interact.
e) The caregiver returns to the child and comforts him/her.
f) The caregiver leaves, again leaving the child with the stranger.
g) The stranger tries to interact and engage with the child.
h) The caregiver returns to the child.

All sessions apart from the first one lasted three minutes.

A

Following **observation**, the children's **attachment** styles can be coded into three categories of **attachment** style behaviour:

- Avoidant infants (type A): these children do not focus on the caregiver as they play with toys and investigate the room, and they do not seem concerned by her absence.
- Securely attached infants (type B): these children tend to explore the unfamiliar room; they become quiet and subdued when their caregiver leaves, but greet her positively when she returns.
- Ambivalent infants (type C): these children often reveal intense distress when the caregiver leaves and is absent, but on the caregiver's return they tend to reject her pushing her away

See **attachment theory, Bowlby, maternal deprivation, observation.**

Ainsworth, M. D. S. (1979) Attachment as related to mother-infant interaction. In J. G. Rosenblatt, R. A. Hindle, C. Beer and M. Busnel (eds), *Advances in the Study of Behaviour, 9*. Orlando, FL: Academic Press.

Ainsworth, M. D. S. (1982) Infant–mother attachment. *American Psychologist*, 34, 932–37.

Ainsworth, M. D. S. and Bell, S. M. (1970) Attachment, exploration and separation: illustrated by the behaviour of one year olds in a strange situation. *Child Development*, 41, 49–67.

Ainsworth, M. D. S., Bell, S. M. and Stayton, D. J. (1971) Individual differences in strange situation behaviour of one year olds. In H. R. Schaffer (ed.), *The Origins of Human Social Relations*. London: London Academic Press.

Ainsworth, M. D. S., Blehar, M. C., Waters, E. and Wall, S. (1978). *Patterns of Attachment: A Psychological Study of the Strange Situation*. Hillsdale, NJ: Erlbaum.

Connell, J. P. and Goldsmith, H. H. (1982). A structural modeling approach to the study of attachment and strange situation behaviors. In R. N. Emde and R. J. Harmon (eds), *The Development of Attachment and Affiliative systems*. New York: Plenum.

Holmes, J. (2001) *The Search for the Secure Base: Attachment Theory and Psychotherapy*, Hove: Brunner-Routledge.

http://en.wikipedia.org/wiki/Attachment_theory (information on attachment theory from Wikipedia).

A

Allele

Allele is an abbreviation of the term allelomorph. Alleles are two forms of a **gene** that occupy a specific position on a **chromosome**. Each **gene** is responsible for determining an individual's observable characteristics or **phenotype**, such as eye or hair colour. The **genotype,** the genetic composition of alleles will determine the organism's **phenotype**. When the alleles are the same, an individual is described as being homozygous, and will exhibit the observable

trait (for example, hair colour), carried by both alleles. If the alleles are different, the dominant allele will determine the **trait** (colour of hair) and this individual is described as heterozygous.

See **chromosomes, gene, genotype, phenotype, trait theories of personality.**

Altruism

Altruism is often referred to in **social psychology** and social biology as a form of behaviour exhibited by an individual that benefits another individual or set of individuals, either in terms of direct advantages or by increasing their ability and chances to reproduce and survive. Altruistic behaviour is always undertaken at some form of cost or risk to the benefactor.

Altruistic behaviour in animals appears to conflict with **Darwin's** (1859) theory of **natural selection**, which portrays animal behaviour as being **motivated** to increase (not reduce) the chances of reproduction and survival. According to Krebs and Davies (1993), there are four main reasons that may offer an explanation as to why animals engage in altruistic behaviours:

- **Kin selection**: if an individual offers help to its close relatives it can actually increase its genetic representation within future generations.
- Reciprocity: in offering help to another individual, the 'giver' may expect help in return.
- Mutualism: two individuals may both engage in altruistic behaviour and both gain from the alliance.
- Manipulation: an individual may be misled or falsely guided in some way to engage in an altruistic act.

Batson's (1987) empathy–altruism **hypothesis** suggests that there are links between empathy, altruistic and unselfish behaviour. Batson suggests that we exhibit two emotional reactions when we observe someone in distress:

- Empathic concern: we sympathise with the individual's distress and are **motivated** to reduce it.
- Personal distress: we are concerned with our own discomfort and are **motivated** to reduce it.

See **Darwinism, hypothesis, kin selection, motivation, natural selection, reciprocal altruism, social psychology.**

Batson, C. D. (1987) Prosocial motivation: is it ever truly altruistic? In L. Berkowitz (ed.), *Advances in Experimental Social Psychology*, 20. New York: Academic Press.

A

Darwin, C. (1859) *The Origin of Species*. London: Macmillan.
Krebs, J. R. and Davies, N. B. (1993) *An Introduction to Behavioural Ecology*. Oxford: Blackwell.

Ambiguous figures

These are images where the **stimulus** or image has no clear figure–ground relationship. The **stimuli** can be perceived in more than one way; for example in Rubin's figure, the viewer can flip between viewing two faces or a vase, depending on whether the viewer is focusing on what he perceives to be the figure or the ground. This is however not an illusion as some people believe; it occurs simply because the viewer can only cognitively process and perceive one interpretation at any one time. Perceptual illusions and ambiguous figures have fascinated the Gestalt branch of psychology in particular, as Gestalt theorists suggest that they indicate that the mind is actively involved in interpreting (rather than passively recording) the perceptual input. Other images are the **Necker cube**, Mach illusion, Schroder's staircase and young girl/old woman figure. See Figure 2 below for an example.

> *See* **field dependence, field independence, Gestalt psychology, object recognition, stimulus.**

Li, T. H. and Klemm, W. R. (2000) Detection of cognitive binding during ambiguous figure task by wavelet coherence analysis of EEG signals, *Proceedings of the 15th International conference of Pattern recognition*, Barcelona, Spain. Available at: www.research.ibm.com/people/t/thl/myhtml/parafilter/papers/eeg2.pdf.
www-rci.rutgers.edu/~cfs/305_html/Gestalt/Illusions.html (examples of ambiguous figures to explore).

A

Which is it: black figure on a white background or a white figure on a black background?

Figure 2 An ambiguous figure

Amygdala

This is a cluster of cells, an almond-shaped brain structure located in the limbic system, at the base of the inside of each temporal lobe of the **brain**. Studies such as those of Kluver and Bucy (1939) revealed the importance of the amygdala in regulating the experiencing and control of emotions such as aggression, rage, arousal and sex drive, and its involvement in **motivation**, long-term **memory** and feeding. Kluver and Bucy's study found that when the anterior temporal lobe (in which the amygdala is situated) of monkeys was removed, they became less aggressive, expressed little fear and were more sexually active. This form of behaviour became known as the Kluver–Bucy syndrome and is related to damage to the amygdala; in humans this can occur through head injuries or tumours.

See **brain, memory, motivation**.

Kluver, H. and Bucy, P. (1939) Preliminary analysis of functions of the temporal lobes in monkeys. *Archives of Neurology and Psychiatry*, 42, 979–1000.

LeDoux, J. E. (1995) Emotion: clues from the brain. *Annual Review of Psychology*, 46, 209–35.

Muller, J. (1997) Functional inactivation of the lateral and basal nuclei of the amygdala by muscimol infusion prevents fear conditioning to an explicit conditioned stimulus and to contextual stimuli. *Behavioral Neuroscience*, **111** (4), 683–91.

http://web.sfn.org/Template.cfm?Section=AboutSFN (The Society for Neuroscience includes information on research and developments in all areas of brain development).

www.sfn.org/content/Publications/BrainBriefings/fear.html (information from the Society for Neuroscience on fear and the amygdala).

Anal stage

This is a **psychosexual stage** in **Freud**'s **psychoanalytic** theory of **personality** development. **Freud** depicted the anal stage as being experienced by an infant between the ages of 18 months and three years. In this stage **Freud** suggests pleasure is derived from expelling or retaining urine and/or faeces.

The major focus at this stage is on toilet training, when children acquire an understanding of when, where and how going to the toilet is appropriate. Children at this stage begin to notice the pleasure and displeasure experienced with bowel movements. They also discover their own ability to control such movements through toilet training, which makes them realize the power they can exert over their parents, as they begin to take control (or not) over their bowel

A

movements. They choose to either grant or **resist** their parent's wishes by deciding to control the retention and expulsion of faeces.

The stage is separated into two distinct stages, the anal expulsive and anal-retentive stages, which if unresolved can lead to anal fixation and relevant **personality** development:

* Anal-expulsive **personality**: the child will derive pleasure and success from the expulsion of faeces if the parents have been too lenient and have been unable to instil society's 'norms' of behaviour about toilet training. Individuals with this fixation tend to be excessively sloppy, disorganized, irresponsible, slapdash and defiant.

* Anal-retentive **personality**: the child will experience **anxiety** over bowel movements and take pleasure in purposely withholding such functions when the parents, during toilet training, give excessive pressure and punishment concerning the child's performance. Individuals who are fixated within this stage tend to be overly concerned with being clean and have a dislike and intolerance of individuals who they perceive as being unclean and disorderly. Those **personality** types tend to be stingy, passive-aggressive, controlling, withholding, obstinate and conforming.

See **anxiety, Electra complex, Freud, genital stage, latency stage, Oedipus complex, oral stage, personality, phallic stage, psychoanalysis, psychosexual stages, resistance.**

psychology.about.com/library/weekly/aa111500a.htm (about information pages on Freud).

Anchoring

Anchoring is a process defined in terms of **social psychology** and **social representations** theory. It is a process that allows individuals to transform unfamiliar objects or events into something more familiar that they can make sense of. Individuals come to make sense of 'things' according to existing knowledge, categories and/or **schemas**.

In making judgements we often need a starting point, an anchor from which we can make mental adjustments. For example, we find out that the population of Bristol is 400,000. We ask someone whether the population of Bristol is more than 100,000 and ask someone else whether the population is less than 1,000,000; they will both say 'Yes'. If we ask them to estimate Bristol's population, the person who starts from 100,000 might guess 350,000 and the person who starts from 1,000,000 might guess 650,000. Individuals rely on the anchor point and adjust toward the correct answer.

Greenberg and Ruback (1991) in a mock-jury study found that when participants were instructed to think about the harshest sentence for a defendant, they used this as an anchor point, from which only small adjustments were made. Thus, a harsh sentence was passed on the defendant. Participants asked to consider the most lenient sentence similarly used this as an anchor point, and gave a lenient sentence.

See **heuristics, social psychology, social representation, schemas.**

Chapman, G. B. and Bornstein, B. H. (1996) The more you ask for, the more you get: anchoring in personal injury verdicts. *Applied Cognitive Psychology,* 10, 519, 526–27.

Greenberg, M. S. and Ruback, R. B. (1991). *Social Psychology of the Criminal Justice System*. Dubuque: Kendall/Hunt.

Whitley, B. E. and Greenberg, M.S. (1986). Role of eyewitness confidence in juror perceptions of credibility. *Journal of Applied Social Psychology,* 16 (5), 387–409.

Anderson

See **ACT* system.**

Androgynous/Androgyny

The term androgynous is often used to define an individual who appears to possess what society views to be representative of both 'typically' male and female characteristics. Such people are thus regarded as displaying behaviours and/or characteristics that prevent classification into traditional 'norms' of masculine and feminine gender identities because they are seen to display a mixture of both 'gendered' features.

Bem's (1974, 1976, 1977, 1993, 1995) work has had a significant impact upon the understanding of sex role orientation. Bem explored the nature of gender roles, creating the Bem Sex Role Inventory (BSRI) in which individuals can be measured for the possession of both masculine and feminine **traits**, and so can be rated for masculinity, femininity and androgyny. Bem's (1974) theory of psychological androgyny held the view that masculinity and femininity are separate, but individuals who possessed both masculine and feminine characteristics (who were androgynous) were very effective and well-functioning individuals. Bem (1974, 1977) suggested that a mixing of both masculine and feminine **traits** in an

A

individual could actually be more adaptive and beneficial than the possession of a **stereotypical** gender role. Bem (1977) also suggested that feminine and masculine qualities hold equal value within society, a claim that has been challenged by Hare-Mustin and Maracek (1988) as they argue that society actually values masculine qualities more than feminine ones. They also claim that Bem's (1974) theory is an example of **beta bias,** which has the effect of minimizing or ignoring sex differences.

See **beta bias, gender bias, stereotyping, traits.**

Bem, S. L. (1974) The measurement of psychological androgyny. *Journal of Consulting and Clinical Psychology*, 42, 155–62.

Bem, S. L. (1976). Sex typing and the avoidance of cross-sex behavior. *Journal of Personality and Social Psychology*, 33, 48.

Bem, S. L. (1977). On the utility of alternative procedures for assessing psychological androgyny. *Journal of Consulting and Clinical Psychology, 54,* 196–205.

Bem, S. L. (1993). *The Lenses of Gender: Transforming the Debate on Sexual Inequality.* New Haven, CT: Yale University Press.

Bem, S. L. (1995). Dismantling gender polarization and compulsory heterosexuality: should we turn the volume down or up? *Journal of Sex Research,* 32, 329–334.

Eisenstein, H (1983) *Contemporary Feminist Thought*. Boston: GK Hall.

Hare-Mustin, R. T. and Maracek, J. (1988) The meaning of difference: gender theory, post-modernism and psychology. *American Psychologist*, 43, 455–464.

www.ifac.org.au/index.cgi) (International Foundation for Androgynous Studies).

ANOVA

Analysis of **variance** (ANOVA) models are very powerful **parametric** methods that are used for testing the level of **significance** of differences between **sample means** when there are two or more conditions, or when several independent measures are concerned. There are different types of ANOVA, such as one-way ANOVA, multi-factorial ANOVA and repeated-measures ANOVA that can be used for different purposes. For example, by using ANOVA we can examine the effects of both temperature and oxygen levels on plant growth in one experiment, rather than running two sets of separate independent experiments.

See **mean, parametric tests, sample, significance, variance.**

Coolican, H, (2004) *Research Methods and Statistics*. Bristol: Hodder and Stoughton.

www.psychstat.missouristate.edu/introbook/sbk27.htm (an introduction to statistics by Dr David Stockburger).

Antisocial behaviour

This is regarded as any behaviour that is disrespectful, antagonistic or harmful within any group or society. The term 'antisocial' is **subjective**, as what is considered to be antisocial in one group, society or culture, may be viewed as the 'norm' in another. Antisocial behaviour therefore, can be understood as such only if it falls beyond or outside the anticipated, laid-down **social norms** or codes of conduct of the groups, society or culture that the individual exists within.

For example, smoking in communal areas such as in offices and restaurants in New York, United States and Ireland is perceived as being antisocial and has now been made illegal. However within cultures such as the tribal groupings of New Guinea and Jamaica, smoking is considered to be a communal **social norm**.

See **group dynamics, social norm, subjectivity.**

http://news.bbc.co.uk/1/hi/health/4575551.stm (BBC news late edition 'Antisocial behaviour "inherited"', 24 May 2005).

Anxiety

Anxiety is a psychological feeling of fear and apprehension that an individual experiences, which is usually associated with physical symptoms such as increased heart and pulse rates, sweating, blushing and nausea. Anxiety can be seen as a normal, short-lasting **response** to particular internal or external **stimuli**, or can be long lasting in which case it may be viewed as abnormal.

In relation to anxiety, fear is understood to be the actual thought, in terms of social **phobia**, the fear of making a fool of oneself, or in obsessive compulsive disorder (OCD), of contamination. In contrast, anxiety is seen as the **response** to these thoughts, the fearful thoughts triggering the **flight or fight** reaction, which causes the physical symptoms such as pounding heart, shaking and quickened pulse.

The State–Trait Anxiety Inventory (STAI) designed by Spielberger et al. (1980) is a self-report assessment device that measures an individual's levels of anxiety, including separate measures of state and **trait** anxiety. State anxiety is defined as a transitory emotional state or condition of an individual that is characterized by **subjective**, consciously perceived feelings of tension and apprehension and by heightened physical activity. State anxiety can change over time and in intensity. In contrast, **trait** anxiety is defined as a relatively stable individual proneness to anxiety, and refers to a general tendency to respond with anxiety to perceived threats in the environment.

A

There are many treatments and therapies that have been developed to help individuals to overcome and learn to manage feelings of anxiety. These include drug therapy (mild tranquillizers), client-centred therapy (Rogerian), **cognitive behaviour therapy**, behaviour therapy that uses techniques such as **flooding**, exposure, systematic **desensitization** and **aversion therapy**, psychotherapy and **hypnotherapy**.

See **aversion therapy, cognitive behaviour therapy, depression, desensitization, fight–flight response, flooding, hypnotherapy, list of phobias, phobia, response, stimulus, subjectivity, trait theories of personality.**

Andrade, L, Gorenstein, C, Vieira Filho, A. H, Ting, T. C and Artes, R. (2001) Psychometric properties of the Portuguese version of the State–Trait Anxiety Inventory applied to college students: factor analysis and relation to the Beck Depression Inventory. *Brazilian Journal of Medical Biological Research*, **34** (3) 367–374. Online at www.scielo.br/scielo.php?script=sci_arttext&pid=S0100-879X2001000300011

Eysenck, M. (2000) Psychology, A Student's Handbook. Hove: Psychology Press.

Spielberger, C. D, Vagg, P. R, Barker, L. R, Donham, G. W. and Westberry, L. G. (1980) Factor structure of the State–Trait Anxiety Inventory. In: I. G. Sarason and C. D. Spielberger (eds), *Stress and Anxiety*, Vol. 7. Washington, DC: Hemisphere.

www.anxietynetwork.com/ (The Anxiety Network International).

www.adaa.org/ (Anxiety Disorders Association of America).

Applied psychology

Applied psychology is a general term used to define the various strands of psychology that link and use **research** findings to inform and enhance applied psychological practice. It is a term that can be applied to branches such as **clinical, counselling, educational, forensic, health** and **occupational psychology**.

In fields such as **clinical** and **counselling psychology**, **research** into mental disorders and health is used and applied within healthcare and social care settings with the aim of helping individuals to address, overcome and cope with their difficulties.

In **educational psychology**, **research** attempts to address issues such as 'how' children learn best, why problems in learning occur, and the best ways to address adjustment and behavioural difficulties in school. Applying such **research** findings within education enables both teachers and parents to understand the best ways of aiding children in their learning.

In **forensic psychology**, problems associated with criminal behaviour, investigation and legal processes are addressed to allow different approaches and methods of addressing crime to be applied.

A

In **health psychology**, **research** findings and psychological knowledge are applied to the development of better methods of preventing and treating illnesses and providing health care.

In **occupational psychology**, **research** examines ways of enhancing the best performance and conditions for employees at work, and is applied to address the problems that can arise in the workplace in such organizations.

> *See* **clinical psychology, coaching psychology, counselling psychology, educational psychology, forensic psychology, health psychology, occupational psychology, research.**

> American Psychological Association, S. Zedeck (ed.), *Journal of Applied Psychology*, published bi-monthly. Available at: www.apa.org/journals/apl/ www.bps.org.uk (The British Psychological Society).

Asch (effect)

Asch, Solomon (1907–96), was an American psychologist who pioneered studies in **conformity** (1951, 1956) that were based on the work of Sherif (1935). In Asch's original study (1951), 18 pairs of cards were shown to participants seated around a table. In each pair, one card was a 'standard test line', and on the other card were three lines of differing lengths. Each of the participants was asked to select which line on the three-line card best matched the single 'test line'. The best match was always obvious, as the test was deliberately made easy to ensure that individuals when tested alone, and hence not subject to **conformity** pressure, would have virtually a zero chance of answering wrong. All except one of the participants were accomplices of the researcher, and on 12 out of the 18 occasions when participants were shown the cards, the accomplices would answer unanimously wrong. The 'real' participant would be left to answer until last, so that Asch could explore the effects of **conformity** pressure on the sole participant's decision. If the participant's answer conformed with the majority answer of the group, going against the individual's own logic, Asch suggested that the individual had conformed to group pressure. Asch found that around 37 per cent of the 'real' participants' judgements had been conforming responses in which the participant had gone along with the unanimous vote and pressure of the others.

> See **conformity, group dynamics, game theory.**

> Asch, S. E. (1951) Effects of group pressure on the modification and distortion of judgements. In H. Guetzkow (ed.), *Groups, Leadership and Men*. Pittsburgh: Carnegie.

A

Asch, S. E. (1956) Studies of independence and conformity: a minority of one against a unanimous majority. *Psychological Monographs,* **70** (416), whole issue.

Sherif, M. (1935) A study of some factors in perception. *Archives of Psychology*, 27, (187).

www.psych.upenn.edu/sacsec/ (The Solomon Asch Center)

www.qeliz.ac.uk/Psychology/Asch.htm (information on Asch's studies)

Assimilation

This is a term used within **Piaget's theory of cognitive development**. Assimilation refers to the process in which infants can modify and enhance their own learning and knowledge by incorporating new information from the social world into their already existing **schema**s or knowledge structures. Put simply, the interpretation of the social world is modified to fit the child. For example, an infant may already possess a **schema**, possess knowledge about a set of wooden building blocks. The infant may know that he or she can pick them up and drop them and then they fall. The infant may pick up a block and drop it, but then the block hits another and makes a noise. This is a novel experience, in which new knowledge has been acquired: that the blocks can make a noise when falling on each other. This new information is then 'assimilated' into the existing **schema**/knowledge relating to building blocks, so that this new understanding can be used and further built upon by the child. It is a process that enables the child to build, reflect and progressively continue to further his or her learning.

See **Piaget's theory of cognitive development, schemas.**

www.piaget.org/ (The Jean Piaget Society).

Journal of Cognitive development, P. Bryant (ed.), Elsevier. Available at: www.elsevier.com/wps/find/journaldescription.cws_home/620192/description#description.

A

Atkinson and Shiffrin, multi-store model of memory

Atkinson and Shiffrin (1968) put forward a theory, the multi-store model of memory, which proposed that memory consisted of a number of memory stores and goes through a series of three stages:

* Sensory memory is our ability to retain impressions of external sensory information, (information gained via any of our senses) for a short period, from one to two seconds after the sensory item has disappeared. Information is held in our sensory stores,

occurring outside our conscious awareness in an automatic process.

- Working or short-term memory is often referred to as 'active' or 'primary' memory. This part of our memory can retain a limited amount of information for a limited amount of time, usually 30–45 seconds. Information stored in short-term memory stores may have been gained from recently processed sensory information, **retrieved** from long-term memory or may be due to recent mental processing by, for example, converting one form of information into another (such as processing mental calculations or reading). Short-term memory is the mode in which information can be stored for a while, processed and **retrieved** from long-term memory.
- Long-term memory refers to a memory that may last from days to years in the long-term store. Short-term memories are seen as being able to become stored as long-term memories through a process known as memory consolidation, which occurs through several retrievals, rehearsals and recalls of the memory.

This model of memory has often been subject to criticism (Warrington and Shallice, 1972) due to its over-simplistic view that short-term memory is the only place in which long-term memories can be stored and retrieved.

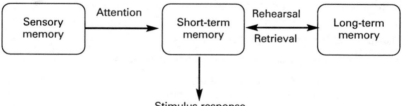

Figure 3 Atkinson and Shiffrin's multi-store model of memory

See **memory, retrieval.**

Atkinson, R. C. and Shiffrin, R. M. (1968). Human memory: a proposed system and its control processes. In K. W. Spence and J. T. Spence (eds), *The Psychology of Learning and Motivation (Vol. 2)*. London: Academic Press.

Eysenck, M. W. and Keane, M. T. (2000). *Cognitive Psychology: A Student's Handbook*. Hove, UK: Psychology Press.

Lee J. L., Everitt B. J., Thomas K. L. (2004) Independent Cellular processes for hippocampal memory consolidation and reconsolidation. *Science*, May 7, **304** (5672), 839–43.

Warrington, E. K. and Shallice, T. (1972) Neuropsychological evidence of visual

A

storage in short-term memory tasks. *Quarterly Journal of Experimental Psychology,* 24, 20–40.

avru1.derby.ac.uk/~kpat/Israel_cognitive/memorystructures.shtml (provides an in-depth overview of the multi-store model of memory and highlights criticism).

Attachment

Attachment is viewed as the development of a strong and enduring emotional bond to another person or persons. Most children as they develop, engage in social interactions with many individuals, but typically only develop attachments to a small number of people.

There are many theories of how attachments occurs:

- Psychodynamic theory: This suggests that infants are initially attached to their mothers because they satisfy their **instinctual** needs of hunger, warmth and comfort. **Freud** (1924) viewed early attachment as occurring while infants underwent the first stage of **psychosexual development**, the **oral stage** that lasted approximately 18 months. In this stage an infant gains much satisfaction from oral experiences, such as sucking the mother's breast. **Freud** suggested that attachment occurred as the mother was seen for the rest of the child's life, as the primary object of love, against which all other love relations would be compared.
- **Social learning theory**: This suggests that children 'learn' to develop attachments through modelling, direct instruction and social facilitation. Children will imitate the behaviour/s shown by their parents, who will direct them to behave in affectionate ways, while offering assistance as necessary.
- Ethological approach: This approach, based on studies of birds, identified a process called **imprinting**, in which a bird for a short period in its life would follow the first moving object it saw. The bird would then continue to follow it, forming an attachment that is virtually irreversible. **Bowlby** (1969) suggested that a similar process occurs in humans.

See **attachment theory, Bowlby, Freud, imprinting, instinct, maternal deprivation, oral stage, psychosexual stages, social learning theory.**

A

Bowlby, J. (1969) Attachment and Love, vol. 1, *Attachment.* London: Hogarth.

Hay, D. F. and Vespo, J. E. (1988) Social learning perspectives on the development of the mother-child relationship. In B. Birns and D. F. Hay (eds), *The Different Faces of Motherhood*. New York: Plenum.

Dollard, J. and Miller, N. E. (1950) *Personality and Psychotherapy*. New York: Mcgraw-Hill.

Freud, S. (1924) *A General Introduction to Psychoanalysis*. New York: Washington Square Press.

http://www.attachmentnetwork.org/links.html (The International Attachment Network).

Attachment theory (Bowlby)

A theory first developed by John **Bowlby** (1907–1990) in 1951. **Bowlby** suggested that an infant possesses an inbuilt, innate, biological need to experience close contact with its primary caregiver, usually the mother, in the first six months of life. These needs, **Bowlby** suggested are normally met by the mother's/caregiver's natural responsiveness to the infant's needs. **Bowlby** theorized that **maternal deprivation** in this critical period could have detrimental effects on psychological development, and if attachments were not formed by the middle of the child's second year of age, then this would result in permanent, irreversible emotional damage in later life.

Bowlby based much of his **maternal deprivation**/attachment theory on the work of Spitz (1945) and Goldfarb (1947), who researched children in several very poor and/or understaffed orphanages. Many of these children by the very nature of the orphanages, received very little warmth or **attention**. Spitz (1945) and Goldfarb (1947) actually provided less support for the **maternal deprivation** hypothesis than **Bowlby** claimed, as the findings can be interpreted in several different ways. It is difficult to determine whether the findings were due to the absence of the mother or poor institutional conditions, or indeed a combination of the two.

Bowlby (1944), attempting to highlight the effects of **maternal deprivation** on human behaviour, also conducted studies with juvenile delinquents. Rutter (1981) challenged **Bowlby**'s findings (based on such studies) of the effect of **maternal deprivation** on child development. Rutter suggested that the findings could have been due to privation and not deprivation. Rutter claimed that the juvenile delinquents **Bowlby** had studied had experienced several changes of home and of caregiver and so had probably never developed a close bond with anyone (privation). This challenged **Bowlby**'s claim that emotional damage could occur through deprivation, through separation from the primary caregiver after a bond had formed.

See **Ainsworth, attention, Bowlby, maternal deprivation**.

Bowlby, J. (1944) Forty-four juvenile thieves: their characters and home life. *International Journal of Psycho-Analysis*, 25, 19–52 and 107–27.

Bowlby, J. (1951) *Maternal Care and Mental Health*. Geneva, World Health

A

Organization; London: Her Majesty's Stationery Office; New York: Columbia University Press. Abridged version: *Child care and the growth of Love* (2nd edn, 1965), Harmondsworth: Penguin.

Goldfarb, W. (1947) Variations in adolescents adjustment of institutionally reared children. *American Journal of Orthopsychiatry*, 17, 49–557.

Holmes, J. (1993). *John Bowlby and Attachment Theory*, London: Routledge.

Rutter, M. (1981) *Maternal Deprivation Reassessed*, Harmondsworth: Penguin.

Spitz, R. A. (1945) Hospitalism: an enquiry into the genesis of psychiatric conditions in early childhood. *Psychoanalytic Study of The Child*, 1, 113–117.

www.chetwynd.staffs.sch.uk/courses/bowlby.htm (provides a good range of material around attachment theories, Bowlby and Ainsworth).

www.qeliz.ac.uk/Psychology/bowlby.htm (discusses Bowlby's maternal deprivation theory and includes a fun quiz).

www.attachment.edu.ar/bio.html (a biography of John Bowlby).

Attention

Attention can be understood in a number of ways. It can be viewed as concentration, but is usually seen as the ability to focus upon one aspect of information in the environment so further processing can take place.

Attention therefore, is continuous focus and concentration upon an event, activity, action, object, thought or **stimulus**. Attention thus causes an individual's information processing systems to handle, and interpret, vast amounts of information gained from an individual's own **memory** stores or through sense organs.

Eysenck and Keane (1995) suggested that there are two types of attention:

* Focused attention: when an individual is in a situation in which he or she attempts to attend to just one **stimulus** input while ignoring all others.
* Divided attention: when an individual attempts to attend to two or more **stimulus** inputs at the same time.

How attention works and the processes involved has also been explored by examining **action slips**, through understanding what causes an individual to fail to attend or to pay attention within particular situations.

Cherry (1953) suggested focused auditory attention. Cherry wanted to explain why individuals are able to follow one conversation even when several people may be talking at once. Cherry found that individuals were able to do this by making use of the physical differences between different auditory messages, selecting the one of interest and not attending to the other speaker's voices. Physical

A

differences included the intensity of the speaker's voice and the sex and position of the speaker.

Broadbent's (1958) filter theory of attention proposed an information processing theory of attention in which information gained from the environment is processed through a series of systems. These particular processing systems then select and transform the information in various ways. **Broadbent** considered that various items of information from the environment being presented to an individual at the same time were placed initially within a sensory buffer, which holds the information for a short while until it is attended to or until it disappears from the system. This theory echoed Cherry's (1953) findings, in that unattended messages are rejected and receive little processing.

Treisman (1964) suggested the **attenuator model of attention**, which suggests the processing of unattended information is reduced or attenuated through the possession of a 'leaky filter'.

See **action slips, attenuator model of attention, automatic processing, Broadbent, memory, stimulus.**

Broadbent, D. E. (1958) *Perception and Communication*. Oxford: Pergamon.
Broadbent, D. E. (1982) Task combination and selective intake of information. *Acta Psychologica*, 50, 25–290.
Cherry, E. C. (1953) Some experiments on the recognition of speech with one or two ears. *Journal of the Acoustical Society of America*, 25, 97–979.
Eysenck, M. W. and Keane, M. T. (1995) *Cognitive Psychology: A Student's Handbook*. Hove, UK, Psychology Press.
Treisman, A. M. (1964) Verbal cues, language, and meaning in selective attention. *American Journal of psychology*, 77, 206–19.

Attenuator model of attention

This model was proposed by Anne Treisman (1964), who suggested that individuals are able to perceive a range of information even when they appear not to be paying attention. She argued that within the first stage of attention, when stimuli are selected for further processing, information that is rejected is not lost but is instead weakened (attenuated). The rejected information does not reach actual conscious thought but does receive some processing. The mechanism that allows this process to occur is called the attenuating filter.

See **attention, Broadbent, stimulus.**

Deutsch, J. A. and Deutsch, D. (1963) Attention: some theoretical considerations. *Psychological Review*, 70, 80–90.
Treisman, A. M. (1964) Verbal cues, language, and meaning in selective attention. *American Journal of Psychology*, 77, 206–19.

Treisman, A. M. 1993. The perception of features and objects. In A. Baddeley and L. Weiskrantz (eds) *Attention: Selection, Awareness and Control. A tribute to Donald Broadbent*. Oxford: Clarendon University.
http://webscript.princeton.edu/~psych/PsychSite/fac_treisman.html (information on Treisman's publications and background).

Attitude

Attitude defines an individual's consistent thoughts or feelings towards a thing, person, object or issue, and is likely to determine how the individual would react towards it. Attitudes often relate to an individual's belief systems, values and personal 'ideals', and can underpin the value or disregard that an individual may place on particular objects, issues or people.

Attraction theories

These theories attempt to explore why individuals invest and partake in particular social and interpersonal relationships and often focus on examining the formation of romantic relationships.
Social psychologists have particularly examined the role of:

* Physical attractiveness: studies such as Walster et al. (1966), Walster and Walster (1969) and Murstein (1972) have found that physical attractiveness is one of the major determinants as to whether an individual will wish to develop a romantic or platonic relationship with another.
* Similarity: studies such as Murstein (1972) have revealed that individuals are likely to engage in relationships in which they regard themselves to be of comparable attractiveness. From this the matching **hypothesis** (Huston 1973) was suggested: that individuals are more likely to engage in relationships where they regard themselves as being equally matched in physical attractiveness.
* Frequency of interaction and proximity: many theorists have suggested that individuals are more likely to develop relationships with people they are exposed to frequently (Zajonc 1968) or live in close proximity to (Festinger et al. 1950). Warr's (1965) study, however, revealed that frequency of interaction could also produce disliking for an individual.
* Evolutionary function: this sociobiological theory argues that attraction and relationship formation may be seen to serve some evolutionary function. Wilson (1975) suggests that attraction may be understood as a survival efficiency in which

A

bargaining occurs between men and women, which then defines their sexual relationship. Relationships are entered into as men need to perpetuate their **gene** pool by impregnating as many women as possible, and women want to form stable long-lasting relationships to ensure the safety and perpetuation of her offspring. This theory suggests that attraction and relationships are based and formed from sexual attraction and reproduction needs. However there are many criticisms of such a deterministic and **reductionist** approach as it disregards **free will**, the choice not to have children, presumes heterosexuality and can be seen to perpetuate gender **stereotypes**. It can also be seen to legitimise male promiscuity and sexual unfaithfulness as innate and beyond the control of the man.

See **free will versus determinism, gene, hypothesis, theory of evolution, reductionism, relationship theories, stereotyping.**

Festinger, L., Schachter, S. and Back, K. W. (1950) *Social Pressures in Informal Groups*. New York: Harper.

Huston, T. L. (1973) Ambiguity of acceptance, social desirability and dating choice. *Journal of Experimental Psychology*, 9, 32–42.

Murstein, B. I. (1972) Physical attractiveness and marital choice. *Journal of Personality and Social Psychology*, 22, 8–12.

Walster, E., Aronson, V., Abrahams, D. and Rottman, L. (1966) The importance of physical attractiveness in dating behaviour. *Journal of Personality and Social Psychology*, 4, 508–16.

Walster, E. and Walster, G. W. (1969) *A New Look at Love*. Reading, MA: Addison Wesley.

Warr, P. B. (1965) Proximity as a determinant of positive and negative sociometric choice. *British Journal of Social and Clinical psychology*, 4, 104–9.

Wilson, E. O. (1975) *Sociobiology: The New Synthesis*. Cambridge, MA: Harvard University Press.

Zajonc, R. B. (1968) Attitudinal effects of mere exposure. *Journal of Personality and Social Psychology*, 9, 1–27.

www.colostate.edu/Depts/Speech/rccs/theory08.htm (information by Mendy Johnson on attraction theories).

A

Attribution

Attribution is the understanding, projection or **perception** of the causes that underpin a particular behaviour. These causes or attributes include external **situational** factors and personal **dispositional** factors. For example, your psychology lecturer turns up 'unusually' late for the lecture; you make a **situational attribution** that perhaps they are late for work because they have been stuck in traffic. A different lecturer who is often late, is again late for the lecture; this time however you make a **dispositional attribution** (based on prior knowledge) that they are perhaps laid back, lazy and/or perhaps arrogant. The attributions we make therefore are affected by the amount and types of information available to us.

See **attributional biases, dispositional attribution, fundamental attribution error, perception, situational attribution.**

Attributional biases

When we attempt to make a judgement about the causes of our own or other people's behaviour we are making an **attribution.** In making an **attribution** our **brain** examines and processes information gained from **situational** factors (social, environmental) and **dispositional** factors (**personality**, nature).

Unfortunately when we make **attributions** our **brain** often takes short cuts in processing all the information available to us. This is termed the cognitive miser effect; the **brain** is conserving its energy by processing **attributions** in the most cost-effective manner. This often leads people to form wrong or misleading **attributions**, or as some may say 'jumping to the wrong conclusions'.

There are three particular types of **attributional biases** that can lead people to form wrong or misleading **attributions** in explaining behaviour. These are:

- The **fundamental attribution error (FAE):** when individuals make **attributions** about others' actions, they tend to overemphasize **dispositional** factors about the actor and underemphasize **situational** factors.
- **Actor/observer bias:** individuals often attribute their own successes to **dispositional** factors and failures to **situational** factors, and conversely attribute others' successes to **situational** factors and failures to **dispositional** factors.
- **Self-serving bias:** individuals tend to attribute their own failures to **situational** factors and their successes to **dispositional** factors.

See **actor/observer bias, attribution, brain, causal schemata model, cognitive dissonance, correspondent inference model, co-variation theory, dispositional attribution, fundamental attribution error, personality, self-serving attributional bias, situational attribution.**

Ross, L. D., Amabile, T. M. and Steinmetz, J. L. (1977) Social roles, social control, and biases in social perception: biased attributional processes in the debriefing paradigm. *Journal of Personality and Social Psychology*, 35, 485–94.

A

Audience effect

This refers to how an individual's behaviour and performance can be affected when being watched by others (an audience). **Research** reveals contradictory findings: sometimes the audience effect can improve an individual's performance (social facilitation) and sometimes it can reduce his or her performance (social inhibition).

See **conformity, social psychology, research.**

Zajonc, R. B. (1965). Social facilitation. *Science*, 149, 269–74.
Zajonc, R. B. and Apsely, D. K. (2000) *Unraveling the Complexities of Social Life: A Festschrift in Honor of Robert B. Zajonc (Decade of Behavior)*. Washington, DC: American Psychological Association (APA)
Zajonc, R. B (2003) *The Selected Works of R. B. Zajonc*. London: John Wiley.

Authoritarian personality

Possession of an authoritarian personality in an individual is shown when that person is overly respectful of authority, adheres to convention, rules and regulations, and shows hostility to any group that appears to threaten or challenge those beliefs and conventions. Adorno et al. (1950) identified the authoritarian personality after **research** in which he interviewed individuals with such personality **traits**. Adorno et al. (1950) observed that such individuals tended to:

- idealise their parents, viewing them as wholly virtuous
- had been subject to a very strict upbringing
- withheld a repressed hostility to their parents.

See **research, social psychology, trait theories of personality.**

Adorno, T. W., Frenkel-Brunswick, E., Levinson, D. and Sanford, R. (1950) *The authoritarian personality*. New York: Harper.
www neuro-doc com/articles/somatic html (an article by M. A. Berger and P. G. Bernad on somatic fixation and the authoritarian personality).

Autobiographical memory

See **memory.**

A

Automatic processing

Automatic processing is a form of information processing, a mental operation that occurs without conscious thought, control or awareness. It occurs in well-rehearsed and practiced behaviours such as driving, riding a bike or reading. The Stroop effect (Kahneman and

Henik, 1979) is a good example of automatic processing; participants are shown colour words (blue, red, green) but the words are
each written in a different colour (blue is written in red ink, green in
blue ink). Participants are then asked to name the ink colour of the
word, they tend to experience difficulty as they have a tendency to
name the word rather than the ink colour. This is taken as evidence
of automatic processing, as participants find it easier to read the
word, rather than recall the ink colour.

See **attention, attenuator model of attention.**

Kahneman, D. and Henik, A. (1979) Perceptual organization and attention. In M.
Kubovy and J. R. Pomerantz (eds), *Perceptual Organization*. Hillside, NJ:
Lawrence Erlbaum.

www.itee.uq.edu.au/~cogs2010/cmc/chapters/Stroop/slide0.html (take the
Stroop effect test).

Aversion therapy

Aversion therapy is a method of **behaviour modification** that is
used in an attempt to eradicate unwanted or undesirable **habits**,
such as cigarette smoking. It is a form of treatment based on aversive conditioning. Unpleasant or painful **stimuli** such as electric
shocks, or drug-induced **responses** such as nausea are linked with
the unwanted behaviour, through the process of association. This
leads the individual to develop a behavioural **response** to the **habit**
that he or she will not want to repeat and so the **habit** is less likely
to be repeated. There are however important **ethical** issues to
consider about a form of treatment that can cause high levels of
discomfort and distress.

See **behaviour modification, ethics, flooding, desensitization, habit,
response, stimulus.**

Roth, A. D. and Fonagy, P. (2005) *What Works for Whom: A Critical Review of
Psychotherapy Research*. New York: Guildford.
Salkovskis, P. M. (1996) *Frontiers of Cognitive Therapy*. New York: Guildford.

A

Axon

An axon is a long fibre extending via a **neuron**, which transmits
impulses usually down the cell body towards the axonal terminals,
where the impulse can then be transmitted to another **neuron** via a
synapse.

See **action potential, brain, neural network, neuron, neurotransmitter,
synapse.**

Bb

Baddeley

See **memory** (working).

Balance theory

This theory promotes a **cognitive** consistency theory of **attitude** change and person **perception** and was first proposed by Heider (1946). It suggests that individuals will strive to maintain consistency in their **attitudes** to themselves, others and events in their lives and social world. Heider suggested that the relationships between person, other and events are either balanced or unbalanced. For example, if you take the standpoint of being against abortion and then discover that a new work colleague is pro-abortion and actively campaigns for women's right to terminate unwanted pregnancies, this would pose a problem. The relationship you choose to develop, or not to develop with your new work colleague would depend on whether a balance could be achieved. You might find that it would be impossible to like a person who takes such a different view of abortion rights. The only way to achieve cognitive balance would be either to dislike your work colleague or to change your own **attitude** to abortion rights, thus restoring cognitive consistency and balance.

> *See* **attitude, cognitive dissonance, cognitive psychology, equity theories, exchange theory, perception, relationship theories, social psychology.**

Bandura

Bandura, Albert (1976) developed the **social learning theory** of behaviour in which he suggested that all behaviour was learnt through interaction with the social world, modelling, imitation and **reinforcement**. He is most famous for the Bobo doll experiment (1973) in which he tested children's **responses** and behaviours to a

Bobo doll after they had watched adults acting aggressively and hitting the doll. Bandura found that children would imitate and model the adult's behaviour and that they would also hit and act aggressively towards the doll. This led him to propose that aggressive behaviour is a learnt behaviour, shaped through the processes of behaviour modelling and **observational learning**. He concluded that individuals learn patterns and styles of behaviour through watching, observing and modelling the ways other people behave.

See **behaviour modification, behaviourism, frustration–aggression hypothesis, observational learning, reinforcement, response, social learning theory.**

Bandura, A. (1962). *Social Learning through Imitation.* Lincoln, NE: University of Nebraska Press.

Bandura, A. (1965) Influences of models' reinforcement contingencies on the acquisition of initiative responses. *Journal of Personality and Social Psychology*, 1, 589–93.

Bandura, A. (1973) *Aggression: A Social Learning Analysis*, Eaglewood Cliffs, NJ: Prentice-Hall.

Bandura, A. (1999). Moral disengagement in the perpetration of inhumanities. *Personality and Social Psychology Review*, 3, 193–209.

Bandura. A., Caprara, G. V., Barbarenelli, C., Pastorelli, C. and Regalia, C. (2001) Sociocognitive self-regulatory mechanism governing transgressive behavior. *Journal of Personality and Social Psychology*, 80, 125–35.

www.criminology.fsu.edu/crimtheory/bandura.htm (information about Bandura by Margaret Isom).

www.plebius.org/encyclopedia.php?term–Bobo+doll I experiment (information by PsychDaily on the Bobo doll experiment).

Beck Depression Inventory (BDI)

The BDI is a **questionnaire** used in psychology predominantly as a self-report scale for indicating whether an individual is likely to be experiencing **depression**. It consists of 21 items, each describing a behavioural characteristic of **depression**, alongside four to six self-evaluative statements from which an individual is asked to choose the statement that is most suitable. There is a four-point scale for most items ranging from 0 to 3, on which individual scores are measured. On two items (16 and 18) there are extra evaluative statements to choose from, to indicate either an increase or decrease of appetite and sleep. A total score of 0–13 is considered minimal range, 14–19 is mild, 20–28 is moderate and 29–63 is severe. It was designed by Beck et al. in 1961. There are many forms of the BDI, including several computerized forms, a card form (May et al. 1969;

B

cited in Groth-Marnat, 1990), the 13-item short form and the more recent BDI-11 (Steer et al. 1990).

See **depression, DSM IV, questionnaire.**

Beck, A. T., Ward, C. H., Mendelson, M., Mock, J. and Erbaugh, J. (1961) An inventory for measuring depression. *Archives of General Psychiatry, 4*, 561–71.

Groth-Marnat G. (1990) *The Handbook of Psychological Assessment*, New York: John Wiley.

Richter, P., Werner, J., Heerlien, A., Kraus, A. and Sauer, H. (1998). On the validity of the Beck Depression Inventory; a review. *Psychopathology*, **31** (3), 160–168.

Shannon, S., Schwartz, R, George, R. and Panke, D. (2004) Convergent validity of the Beck Depression Inventory for youth. *Psychological Reports, part 2,* **94** (3), 1444–6.

Steer, R. A., Rissmiller, D. J. and Beck, A. T. (2000) Use of the Beck Depression Inventory–11 with depressed geriatric patients. *Behaviour Research and Therapy*, **38** (3), 311–18.

www.swin.edu.au/victims/resources/assessment/affect/bdi.html (information on BDI by Victim's web).

Behaviourism

Behaviourism is a branch of psychology, which was founded in 1913 by the American psychologist John Watson (1878–1958). It focuses on explaining human behaviour in terms of **stimulus–response**, in relation to the laws of **cause and effect**. Behaviourism views all behaviour as being determined by the environment and a product of **social learning** and **reinforcement**. The behaviourists are on the nurture side of the **nurture versus nature** debate, theorizing that all behaviour is learnt from the environment after birth. Behaviourism takes a scientific, experimental approach to understanding behaviour, suggesting that psychology should only investigate the laws and products of learning. It should therefore only focus upon the **objective** study of observable behaviour and not on thought and cognition. Behaviourists suggest that 'fact' cannot be gained through seeing into people's thoughts and minds, as people may lie or be mistaken.

B

See **Bandura, cause and effect, classical conditioning, nature–nurture debate, objectivity, operant conditioning, Pavlov, reinforcement, Skinner, social learning theory, stimulus–response learning.**

Skinner, B. F (2006) *About behaviourism*. London: Pimlico.

Staddon, J. E. R. (2000) *The New Behaviourism: Mind, Mechanism and Society*. Hove: Psychology Press.

www.questia.com/library/psychology/other-types-of-psychology/behaviorism.jsp (links to many research articles from Questia).

Behaviour modification (therapy)

This is a form of therapy in which the principles of **behaviourism** and **social learning theory** are integrated to develop methods of teaching individuals to overcome **maladaptive** or unwanted **habits** or behaviours. It originates in the belief that any unwanted behaviours have been learnt or conditioned in the first place and that by replacing such unwanted behaviours with more positive forms (through the use of conditioning principles) the individual's life and health can improve. Behaviour modification tends to use a reward and punishment strategy, following a **stimulus–response** technique. This method is often used within areas such as childcare and education to promote and encourage academic achievement and co-operative behaviour (just think of the smiley faces and gold stars that denote 'good' work or behaviour).

There are many types of behaviour modification therapies, such as exposure or **flooding**, systematic **desensitization**, **token economy** and **aversion therapy**.

See aversion therapy, behaviourism, desensitization, flooding, habits, maladaptiveness, social learning theory, stimulus–response learning, token economy.

Bijou, S. W. and Ruiz, R. (1981) *Behavior Modification: Contributions to Education*. Hillsdale, NJ: Lawrence Erlbaum.

Staats, A. W. (1996) *Behavior and Personality; Psychological Behaviorism*. New York. Springer.

www.autism-treatments.co.uk/html/behaviour-modification.php3 (information on autism).

Bell-shaped curve

This is a frequency that resembles the outline of a bell. It is also called the normal probability distribution or the Gaussian distribution. The bell curve simply plots and displays the **data**, revealing that the **data** has a **normal distribution**. This means that most of the values in a set of **data** are close to the 'average', while relatively few values tend to be at one extreme or the other. For example, if we wanted to find out how many times a day children brushed their teeth, a **normal distribution** would show that on average children brushed their teeth a similar number of times, with a few children brushing less or more often than average.

See data, measures of dispersion, normal distribution.

www.robertNiles.com/stats/stdev.shtml (for picture and information about bell-shaped curve).

B

Beta bias

This is a term used to define any **research** or theory that disregards or diminishes the differences between men and women. Beta bias theories tend to ignore the value of asking questions about women's lives, instead assuming that insights gained from examining men's lives, can equally apply to women. It has been claimed that some psychological theories, such as **Kohlberg**'s **theory of moral development** (1963) are beta bias, as the findings were based only on male participants. Gilligan (1982, 1977) challenged **Kohlberg's** claim that men tended to be at a higher level of **moral development** than women by studying and highlighting the differences in men and women's **moral development**.

> See **gender bias, Kohlberg, moral development, research.**

> Gilligan, C. (1977) In a Different Voice: Women's Conceptions of the Self and of Morality. *Harvard Educational Review*, 47, 481–517.
> Gilligan, C. (1982) *In a Different Voice: Psychological Theory and Women's Development*. Cambridge, MA: Harvard University Press.
> Hare-Mustin, R. T. and Maracek, J. (1988) The meaning of difference: gender theory, postmodernism and psychology. *American Psychologist*, 43, 455–64.
> Kohlberg, L. (1963) Development of children's orientations toward a moral order. *Vita humana*, 6, 11–36.

Biased sampling

> See **sampling.**

Big Five model of personality

> See **five-factor model of personality.**

Binomial distribution

This is used in **inferential statistics** to determine the probability of an event occurring within any given number of independent occurrences. Each occurrence of the event is random; no repetition of the event will generate any knowledge or an insight into the likelihood of outcomes of the next event. An example is determining the probability of how many times a dice would roll a six in 100 occurrences. It is used within the binomial test that is also known as the Bernoulli trial.

> See **inferential statistics.**

> www.mywiseowl.com/articles/Binomial_distribution (information from Mywiseowl. com on the Binomial distribution).

B

Biological model of abnormality

See **abnormal behaviour.**

Biomedical model

The traditional medical model of health and illness is based on the view that all illnesses, be they mental or physical, are caused by abnormal physiological causes.

See **biopsychosocial model.**

Kemp, D. R. (1994) *Biomedical policy and mental health.* Westport, CT, London: Praeger.

Biopsychology

This is a term used to define the branch of psychology and scientific **research** that explores the effects of biology upon an individual's behaviour, studying in particular the **brain**, physiology and the nervous system.

See **brain, research.**

Pinel, J. P. J. (2005) *Biopsychology and Beyond the Brain and Behaviour.* CD ROM. Boston: Allyn and Bacon.
Wickens, A. P. (2004) *Foundations of Biopsychology.* Englewood Cliffs, NJ: Prentice Hall.

Biopsychosocial model

This model of understanding behaviour, health and illness offers a contrasting view to traditional biomedical models. It attempts to explore the effects upon human behaviour and experience of social, cultural, psychological and biological factors. A biopsychosocial model would not attempt to identify a specific single root cause but explore a variety of possible causes and effects.

B

A form of a biopsychosocial approach to examining women's health originated with Ussher's (2003) work and has been used to explore concepts such as premenstrual tension (PMT) (Ussher 2003, 1997, 1996) and postnatal depression (PND) (Winstanley 2006, 2004). Such **research** has explored women's lives in relation to material (experiences of embodiment), **discourse** (dominant ideologies and meanings inherent and used within particular social systems, cultures and people) and intrapsychic factors (psychological processes and functioning).

See **discourse analysis, research.**

Saleebey, D. (2001) *Human Behaviour and Social Environments. A Biopsychosocial Approach*. New York: Columbia University Press.

Ussher, J. M. (1996) Premenstrual syndrome: reconciling disciplinary divides through the adoption of a material-discursive epistemological standpoint. *Annual review of Sex Research*, 7, 218–51.

Ussher, J. M. (1997) *Body talk: The material and Discursive Regulation of Sexuality, Madness and Reproduction*. London: Routledge.

Ussher, J. M. (2003) The role of premenstrual dysphoric disorder in the subjectification of women. *Journal of Medical Humanities*, 24, 131–46.

Winstanley, J. (2006) *A Material-Discursive-Intrapsychic (MDI) Approach to Understanding Women's Maternal Experiences*. PhD thesis. University of Huddersfield: UK.

Winstanley, J. (2004) A feminist material-discursive approach to understanding women's maternity care experiences and the implications for the development of postnatal depression interventions. Work in progress article in *The Psychologist*, British Psychological Society, **17** (3), 126.

Bipolar disorder

Previously known as manic depression, this is a category of mood disorder that is categorized by experiences and symptoms of both mania and **depression**. Mania is seen as the individual experiencing an intense emotional state characterized by extreme, often inappropriate elation that leads to hyperactivity, racing and/or disruptive thought processes, excessive talking and being easily distracted. **Depression** is a similarly intense emotional state characterized by great sadness and feelings of guilt and worthlessness.

Bipolar disorder is usually formally diagnosed if the following symptoms are extreme enough to create difficulties in functioning or require hospitalization, and if an individual is experiencing an irritable or elated mood and at least three of the following symptoms:

- increased activity
- excessive or unusual degrees of talking
- loss of sleep
- over-inflated self-esteem
- being easily distracted
- engaging in risk-taking behaviours or actions.

See **depression, DSM IV, abnormal behaviour**

Bottom-up processing

Bottom-up processing or **data**-driven processing is a term used within **cognitive psychology** to explain how individuals can recognize, process and perceive information. This explanation of perceptual processing identifies **perception** and understanding as being directly influenced through sensory input, **object recognition** and the visual field. It suggests that any given **stimulus** is perceived and understood after an analysis of its component parts has been undertaken through a series of **pattern recognition** and information-processing stages. Bottom-up processing therefore is processing that is influenced more by external factors than by an individual's experience and knowledge. This contrasts with **top-down processing,** which is influenced more by an individual's existing expectations and knowledge.

Mary had a
a little
lamb

Figure 4 Bottom-up and top-down processing

For example, if you looked at Figure 4 the likelihood is that you read the sentence as 'Mary had a little lamb' and did not notice the extra 'a' in the sentence. This is because your expectation (**top-down processing**) that it is a well-known line of a nursery rhyme (existing knowledge) overrode the actual external **stimulus** information (bottom-up processing).

> *See* **cognitive psychology, data, Gestalt psychology, memory, object recognition, pattern recognition, perception, stimulus, top-down processing.**

Gibson, J. J. (1966) *The Senses Considered as Perceptual Systems*. Boston: Houghton Mifflin.

Gibson, J. J. (1979) *The Ecological Approach to Visual Perception*. Boston: Houghlin Mifflin.

www.rdg.ac.uk/AcaDepts/ll/app_ling/buptdown.htm (information on bottom-up processing by Amos Paran at the University of Reading).

B

Bowlby

Bowlby, John (1907–1990) is best known for his theories and **research** on the importance of the **attachment** bond formed between child and caregiver. Bowlby (1969) theorized that the pattern of an infant's early **attachment** to its caregiver would form the basis for all later social relationships. On the basis of his studies of institutionalized and hospitalized children and evacuees, he hypothesized that when the caregiver (usually the mother) was unavailable or only partially available during the early months of a child's life, the **attachment** process would be interrupted. This failure or inability to form an **attachment** bond (privation) he suggested, could predispose a child to behavioural problems, lead to adverse effects in later life and leave enduring emotional scars.

See **attachment, attachment theory, maternal deprivation, research.**

Bowlby, J. (1969) Attachment and Love, vol. 1, *Attachment*, London: Hogarth.
Feeney, J, A. and Noller, P. (1994) Whither attachment theory: attachment to our caregivers or to our Models? *Psychological Inquiry*, **5** (1), 51–7.
www.psychematters.com/bibliographies/bowlby.htm (a range of reference material on John Bowlby and related topics).
www.attachment.edu.ar/bio.html (biography details of Bowlby).

Brain

The brain is the **central nervous system (CNS)**, which is contained within the skull, but does not include the peripheral nerves. A normal human brain weighs approximately 1,300–1,400 grams and contains

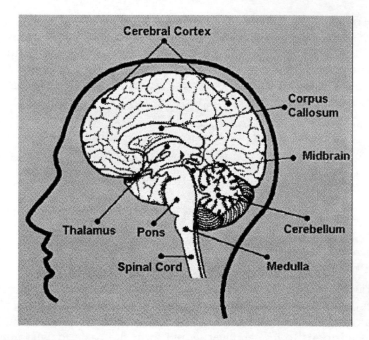

Figure 5 The brain
Courtesy of Dr E. Chudler, Washington University (2005)
faculty.washington.edu/chudler/nsdivide.html

80 billion **neurons** (a sperm whale brain by comparison, weighs 7,800 grams). In mammals, the brain consists of three major divisions: the forebrain, midbrain and hindbrain. The forebrain is subdivided into the telencephalon, whose principle structures are the cerebral cortex, basal ganglia and limbic system and the diencephalons, whose principle structures are the thalamus and hypothalamus. The midbrain is subdivided into the mesencephalon, whose principle structures are the tectum and tegmentum. The hindbrain is subdivided into the metencephalon with principle structures of cerebellum and pons, and the myelencephalon with principle structures of medulla oblongata.

> *See* **central nervous system, neuron.**

> http://faculty.washington.edu/chudler/introb.html (for pictures and more information on the brain).

Brainstorming

Brainstorming is a method of problem solving in which individuals or groups can quickly and spontaneously generate a wide range of possible solutions or thoughts as to how a particular problem may be solved. Brainstorming is a process in which no evaluation of any suggestions is attempted until a later stage, as on-the-spot evaluation could inhibit the free-flowing nature of the approach. Mind-maps are an example of a type of brainstorming technique.

> www.peterussell.com/mindmaps/mindmap.html (pictures and information and about mind maps).

Broadbent

Broadbent, Donald (1958) developed the first major theory of **selective attention** – the filter model of **selective attention** – which attempted to explain why individuals could focus on one thing at a time and exclude other competing **stimuli**. An example is how someone is able to read a book while music is playing. Broadbent designed the **split span** procedure (1954) to investigate this. The procedure involved participants attempting to recall digits presented simultaneously in pairs, with one digit being played to one ear, and the other digit to the other. Participants later were asked to recall the digits in either of two ways:

- 'pair by pair', stating the first pair of digits followed by next pair

B

- 'ear by ear', stating three digits heard in one ear followed by three from other ear.

Broadbent found that participants found it easier to recall 'ear by ear' than 'pair by pair'. This led him to suggest that the ears act as two different channels that participants could only attend to one at a time. Broadbent thus developed the filter model of **selective attention**, which suggested that:

- Two messages when presented simultaneously to the two ears can be processed in parallel by entering a temporary **buffer store.**
- One message is then selected on the basis of physical properties and enters a filter, while the other message waits in the **buffer store.**
- The filter acts as a stopper, a bottleneck that prevents the attentional system becoming overloaded. The message is then analysed for meaning in a limited capacity processor (which can only focus on one input at a time). When this message has been processed, then the second message can undertake processing and move from the **buffer store**.

See **attention, attenuator model of attention, buffer store, selective attention, split span procedure, stimulus.**

Broadbent, D. E. (1954) The role of auditory localisation in attention and memory span. *Journal of Experimental Psychology*, 47, 191–6.

Broadbent, D. E. (1958) *Perception and Communication*. Oxford: Pergamon.

Broadbent, D. E., Baddeley, A. D. and Weiskrantz, L. (1993) *Attention: Selection, Awareness and Control: A tribute to Donald Broadbent*. Oxford, New York: Clarendon.

Broca's aphasia

B

This is experienced when damage has occurred in an area in the frontal lobe of the cortex of the **brain** called Broca's area, which is the centre for speech production. Individuals who experience Broca's aphasia experience difficulties in speaking. They may experience any of the three major speech deficits associated with the condition:

- Anomia: struggling to find the 'right' words, which can cause slowness of speech and a lack of fluency.
- Agrammatism: difficulties in using common, important grammatical words, such as 'the', 'a', 'in' or 'some'.
- Articulation difficulties: being unable to pronounce words correctly.

See **brain.**

www.aphasia.org/ (The National Aphasia Association, United States).

Bruner

Bruner, Jerome (1915–), is a cognitive psychologist who has provided some valuable contributions in the area of cognitive development and its application to education. He suggested (1966) that children's inter-action with the world could increase their cognitive ability to begin to think and understand the world in more complex ways. Bruner was concerned with how knowledge was organized and represented as a child developed and interacted with the world. He proposed three ways of representing knowledge or how children would think:

* Enactive mode: this mode is prevalent in babies who begin to understand and first represent their world through their actions. Have you ever given road directions and noticed how your hands and arms seem to move uncontrollably? This is because knowledge – a representation of the route – has been acquired through action (walking or driving through this route).
* Iconic mode: this mode represents knowledge and thinking gained through the use of imagery, pictures or icons.
* Semantic mode: in this mode, thinking and a representation of the social world is gained through language. Children are now able to group and categorize information that enables their intellectual development to go beyond physical images and the iconic mode. Bruner viewed language as crucial in opening up intellectual development.

Bruner, J. S. (1966) *Toward a Theory of Instruction*, Cambridge, MA: Belkapp.
Bruner, J. (1996) *The Culture of Education*. Cambridge, MA: Harvard University Press.
Gardner, H. (2001) Jerome S. Bruner. In J. A. Palmer (ed.), *Fifty Modern Thinkers on Education: From Piaget to the Present*. London: Routledge.
Smith, M. K. (2002) Jerome S. Bruner and the process of education. *The Encyclopaedia of Informal Education*. Available online at: www.infed.org/thinkers/bruner.htm.

B

Buffer store

A term used in relation to information processing, this is a temporary memory store that holds information for a short period of time, before it is sent elsewhere.

See **memory buffer, Broadbent.**

Bystander effect

This relates to the tendency for individuals and groups of people who have witnessed an incident or emergency to ignore the event. In normal everyday life, individuals experience familiar experiences and events, but when there are unplanned incidents that are unfamiliar and require action, individuals often ignore such events. An individual is overwhelmingly more likely to offer help in an unfamiliar situation if he or she is alone. When individuals are in the company of other 'potential helpers' they are less likely to help.

There are three social processes that have been proposed to explain this effect:

- Social influences: Brickman et al. (1982) found that individuals observe each other when in groups in order to interpret the situation correctly. If they observe other individuals not responding then they will assume that it is not an emergency.
- Diffusion of responsibility: Darley and Latane (1968) found that when there are multiple individuals present, the amount of responsibility is spread; each individual thus feels less responsible and is less likely to take action.
- Audience inhibition: Piliavin et al. (1981) in their arousal/cost–reward model, found that individuals may worry about whether their actions are appropriate and may feel embarrassed about helping. They weigh up the costs and rewards of helping versus not helping, compare possible outcomes of helping – such as personal satisfaction or possible embarrassment – against the outcomes of not helping (possibly feeling guilty but being free from embarrassment).

See **social psychology, exchange theory, relationship theories.**

Brickman, P., Rabinowitz, V. C., Karuza, J., Coates, D., Cohn, E. and Kidder, L. (1982) Models of helping and coping. *American Psychologist*, 37, 368–84.
Darley, J. M. and Latane, B. (1968) Bystander intervention in emergencies: diffusion of responsibility. *Journal of Personality and Social Psychology*, 8, 377–83.
Piliavin, J. A., Dovidio, J. F., Gaertner, S. L. and Clark, R. D. (1981) *Emergency Intervention*. New York: New York Academic Press.

B

Case study

Case study can be argued to be both a **research** approach and a method. As an approach it allows a detailed investigation of the behaviour and experiences of a specific group or individual. Case study **research** as a method uses **ethnographic** techniques that involve accumulating detailed descriptions of the behaviour of the individual(s) conducting the **research** as well as gathering details of the behaviour of those under study. Case study **research** can therefore be seen to adopt reflexive methods and places value on the acquisition of **subjective data** (what individuals feel, think or perceive) as well as **objective data**. Case studies can adopt many different **research** methods, but are often characterized by the use of predominantly **qualitative methods**, such as participant **observation**, focus groups and interviews, rather than scientific tests and measurements (**quantitative methods**).

See **data, ethnography, objectivity, qualitative research, research, subjectivity.**

Yin, R. K. (2002) *Case Study Research, Design and Methods*. London: Sage.
http://www.gslis.utexas.edu/~ssoy/usesusers/l391d1b.htm (information on case study research).

Cattell

Cattell, Raymond (1905–98), an American psychologist who suggested that human **personality** consisted of **traits** (a **trait** being a marked feature or characteristic style of behaviour, such as perfectionism, warmth, liveliness). Cattell in 1946 identified 171 **personality traits**, which he narrowed to 35 surface **traits**, from which could be derived 16 source **traits** that made up an individual's **personality**. Cattell viewed source **traits** as the underlying basic factors of an individual's **personality**. From this theory he developed the Sixteen Personality Factor Questionnaire or 16PF designed to assess 16 different source **traits** associated with 'normal' behaviour. The Cattell 16PF model is probably the most widely used system for categorizing and defining **personality**.

See **Eysenck, five-factor model of personality, personality, trait theories of personality.**

Cattell, R. B. (1946) *Description and Measurement of Personality*. London: Harrap.
www.chimaeraconsulting.com/16pf.htm (information on 16PF by Chimaera consulting).

Causal schemata model

The causal schemata model is Kelley's (1972) second **attribution** theory, building on from the **co-variation theory**. The causal schemata model attempts to understand and attribute causes of individual's behaviour when there is no:

- Consensus: this relates to the extent to which observers behave in the same way towards the same events/experiences and **stimulus** as the person being observed.
- Consistency: this relates to the extent to which the individual being observed has behaved in the same way previously to the same event/experience or **stimulus**.
- Distinctiveness: this relates to the extent to which the individual behaves in the same way to other **stimuli**.

Kelley theorized that when we have none of the above information, or when we do not know the individual being observed, then we can only use our causal schemata. Causal schemata's are general **schemas**, or understandings that individuals possess of how certain kinds of **stimuli**, events, experiences or causes interact with people to exert or elicit a particular type of **response** or effect. Causal schemata are therefore understood to be important in allowing individuals to attribute causes to people's behaviour even when information is unavailable or incomplete.

See **attribution, co-variation theory, schemas, stimulus, response.**

Duval, S. and Duval, V. H. (1983) *Consistency and Cognition: A Theory of Causal Attribution*, Hillsdale, NJ: Lawrence Erlbaum.
Kelley, G. (1972) Causal schemata and the attribution process, in E. E. Jones, D. E. Kanouse, H. H. Kelley, R. E. Nisbett, S. Valins and B. Weiner (eds), *Attribution: Perceiving the Causes of Behaviour*. Morristown, NJ: General Learning Press.

Cause and effect

Cause and effect is a view held predominantly in scientific psychology that for everything that happens there is an identifiable

C

reason or cause, a belief that events do not just happen but that they are manipulated or caused by something. In an experiment, the manipulation of the independent **variable** is seen as the cause and the resulting change in the observed behaviour or event, the dependent **variable** is seen as the effect.

See **behaviourism, experimental psychology, quantitative research, variables.**

Ceiling effect

In statistics, this is an artificial upper limit placed on the value that a **variable** can achieve, which causes the distribution of scores to be **skewed** (scores are clustered/distributed in one particular direction). For example, the distribution of scores will be **skewed** by a ceiling effect if adult participants are given an intelligence test designed for children, allowing all adults to achieve perfect scores.

See **kurtosis, normal distribution, skewed distribution, variables.**

Central nervous system (CNS)

This is the part of the nervous system, which in humans and vertebrates consists of the spinal cord and the **brain**.

See **brain.**

en.wikipedia.org/wiki/Central_nervous_system (information from Wikipedia).
faculty.washington.edu/chudler/nsdivide.html (simple, straightforward and colourful information by Dr Chudler).

Central tendency

See **measures of central tendency, mean, median, mode.**

C

Chi-square (χ^2)

A chi–square (χ^2) test (pronounced kye) is used when testing for associations (differences and correlations) between two categorical **variables.** It is suitable for use with **nominal** (categorical) **data** (frequencies or headcounts within specific categories).

For example, when testing for associations between gender and drink-driving, the chi-square could examine whether being male is associated with being more likely to drink and drive or whether being female is associated with being less likely to do this. Participants could be divided into categories by gender and we could also divide the participants according to whether they have ever been convicted of drink-driving. Essentially the chi-square helps us to understand if membership of one category (gender) is associated with membership of another category (likelihood of being convicted of drink-driving)

To use a chi-square test certain conditions must be met:

- **Data** must be in **nominal** or categorical form.
- Each participant's **data** must belong exclusively to one particular category. No person can belong to more than one category.
- **Sample** size (number of participants) should exceed 20 to prevent making a type I **error**.

See **data, degrees of freedom, errors, hypothesis, inferential statistics, nominal measurements, non-parametric tests, sample, significance level, errors, variables.**

Camilli, G. and Hopkins, D. (1978) Applicability of chi-square to 2 x 2 contingency tables with small-expected cell frequencies. *Psychological Bulletin*, **85** (1), 163–7.
Coolican, H. (2004) *Research methods and statistics in Psychology*. Bristol: Hodder and Stoughton.
http://www.georgetown.edu/faculty/ballc/webtools/web_chi_tut.html (Further information from Georgetown University, USA on the chi-square).

Chomsky

Chomsky, Noam (1928–), is well known for his theories of **language development** and acquisition, suggesting that the ability to manipulate and understand language is innately wired in, that humans are genetically pre-programmed to use language. Chomsky theorized that children acquire language easily because they posses a language acquisition device (LAD), an innate mechanism that is programmed to recognize linguistic features, phonological elements such as vowels and syllables and syntactic structures such as nouns, plurals, verbs and tenses.

See **language development.**

Chomsky, N. (1957) *Syntactic structures*. The Hague: Mouton.
Oates, J. and Grayson, A. (2004) *Cognitive and Language Development in Children*. Oxford: Blackwell.

Chromosomes

Chromosomes are rod-like microscopic structures that exist within the nucleus of every cell of an organism that contains DNA. They encode the **genes** and determine an organism's hereditary characteristics. Chromosomes therefore can determine such things as the sex of an individual, eye and hair colour, and conditions such as Down's syndrome.

Human females possess two X chromosomes, whereas males possess one X and one Y chromosome. If a Y chromosome is absent a human foetus will develop as female.

See **gene, genotype, phenotype.**

Classical conditioning

This was first theorized by **Pavlov** (1927), who was investigating the salivating reflex in dogs, an **unconditioned response** (UCR) that occurred in response to food being administered. **Pavlov** realized that dogs would salivate not just in **response** to food (**unconditioned stimulus**, US) but also to anything else that coincided with the feeding routine, such as the ringing of a bell (neutral **stimulus,** NS). In a classical conditioning experiment, an artificial neutral **stimulus** (such as the bell) is offered consistently just before the natural trigger (US, such as food). Following repeated exposure to the neutral **stimulus**, the dog learns (is conditioned) to respond to the neutral **stimulus**. The dog will now salivate to the ring of the bell. When a learned **response** is acquired, conditioning is said to have occurred, and the neutral **stimulus** is now termed the **conditioned stimulus**.

Before conditioning
Food (UCS) ⟶ Salivation (UCR)
Bell (NS) ⟶ No response

During conditioning
Bell (NS) + Food (UCS) ⟶ Salivation (UCR)

After conditioning
Bell (CS) ⟶ Salivation (CR)

See **behaviourism, conditioned stimulus, operant conditioning, Pavlov, response, stimulus, unconditioned response, unconditioned stimulus.**

Boakes, R. A. (1984). *From Darwin to Behaviourism*. Cambridge: Cambridge University Press.
Pavlov, I. P. (1927) *Conditioned Reflexes*. Oxford: Oxford University Press.
en.wikipedia.org/wiki/Ivan_Pavlov (information from Wikipedia on Pavlov).

C

Clinical psychology

Clinical psychology is one of the major psychological professions and is concerned with the classification, **diagnosis**, nature, treatment and prevention of mental disabilities and disorders. To apply for clinical psychology training in the United Kingdom an undergraduate degree in psychology that meets the British Psychological Society requirements for Graduate Basis for Registration (GBR) is needed. This should be followed by relevant clinically related work experience, for example as an assistant psychologist, health worker, researcher or carer. Following this, application can be made via Leeds Clearing House (address below) for postgraduate courses to undertake doctorate training in clinical psychology. Competition for training places can be quite fierce and it is becoming quite common for applicants now to be studying towards or to hold master's degrees alongside undergraduate degrees.

> The Clearing House
> 15 Hyde Terrace
> Leeds, LS2 9LT

See **diagnosis.**

http://www.leeds.ac.uk/chpccp/ (the clearing house for postgraduate courses in clinical psychology).
http://www.bps.org.uk/careers/careers_home.cfm (information from the British Psychological Society on careers in psychology).

Closed questions

Closed questions, also known as close-ended questions are questions that restrict the respondent to a fixed, limited number of possible answers, typically yes-or-no answers. Do you like cats? Yes or no. Closed questions are used to direct the conversation to a particular subject, to obtain decisions and points of view in specific areas.

See **open-ended questions.**

Coaching psychology

Coaching psychology is a relatively new branch of psychology that focuses on enhancing well-being and performance in both personal life and work domains. It is underpinned by models of coaching grounded in established adult learning or psychological approaches (adapted from Grant and Palmer 2002). Coaching psychology is a field widely applied within Australia and the United States and recognized by the governing psychological associations. In the United Kingdom however, coaching psychology as a specialist branch has only recently been recognized (2004), following the successful proposal of a specialist group of coaching psychologists within the British Psychological Society.

Grant, A. M. (2001). *Towards a Psychology of Coaching*. Sydney: Coaching Psychology Unit, University of Sydney.

Grant, A. M. and Palmer, S. (2002). *Coaching Psychology*. Workshop and meeting held at the Annual Conference of Division of Counselling Psychology, British Psychological Society, Torquay, 18th. May.

Jarvis, J. (2004). *Coaching and Buying Coaching Services: A CIPD Guide*. London: Chartered Institute of Personnel and Development.

Palmer, S. and Whybrow, A. (2004). The brief history of the UK BPS Coaching Psychology Movement: from acorns to oak trees! Paper delivered at the *BPS Special Group in Coaching Psychology Inaugural Conference*, held at City University, London on 15 December.

www.bps.org.uk/sub-sites$/coachingpsy/coachingpsy_home.cfm (The British Psychological Society Special Group in Coaching Psychology home pages).

Coding

Coding is a **research** method used to analyse, interpret and organize **data** and information collected within a study. **Data** is coded through assigning values to it, or through a process of categorization into collective or similar groups or characteristics. For example, participant responses to a **questionnaire** may be coded into yes/no categories or assigned values of 1 for yes or 0 for no. **Data** may be coded into numerical values, for example how many times a participant uses the word 'trust' in an interview, or lines of text (taken from an interview) may be coded into themes of 'trust'. Coding can be used in both **quantitative** and **qualitative research**; however, the way coding techniques are used can vary between these approaches. **Quantitative** approaches tend to focus upon numerical coding into observable measurements, whereas **qualitative** approaches use a variety of **subjective** coding strategies, such as **discourse analysis** (DA), interpretive **phenomenological analysis** (IPA) and thematic analysis.

C

See data, discourse analysis, phenomenology, qualitative research, quantitative research, questionnaire, research, response, subjectivity.

Banister, P, Burman, E., Parker, I., Taylor, M. and Tindall, C. (1994) *Qualitative Methods in Psychology*. Buckingham: Open University Press.

Wetherall, M., Taylor, S. and Yates, S. (2001) *Discourse as Data: A Guide for Analysis*, Milton Keynes: Sage in association with the Open University Press.

Robson, C. (2002) *Real world research*. Oxford, Cambridge: Blackwell.

Cognitive behaviour therapy (CBT)

CBT is a method used to treat particular psychological disorders that integrates cognitive and behavioural therapies:

Behaviour therapy helps to reduce the connections between troublesome situations and the individual's habitual, learnt **responses** to them where these are **responses** such as fear or **depression**, or self-defeating and self-damaging behaviour(s). It also teaches individuals how to calm their minds and bodies so that they can think more clearly, feel better and make better decisions.

Cognitive therapy helps individuals to understand how certain ways of thinking are causing particular symptoms, by creating a distorted picture of what is happening in their lives, making them feel anxious, angry or depressed for no good reason, or provoking them to engage in ill-chosen actions.

CBT therefore attempts to:

* Alter individuals' ways of thinking, changing their thoughts, beliefs, ideas, **attitudes**, assumptions, mental imagery, and promoting more positive ways of directing their **attention** for the better.
* Help people to greet the challenges and opportunities in their lives with a clear and calm mind, helping them to take actions that are likely to have desirable results.

CBT is often used to treat a multitude of disorders such as **depression**, social anxiety, mood swings, insomnia, eating disorders, panic attacks, shyness and obsessive compulsive disorder (OCD).

> *See* **attention, attitude, aversion therapy, depression, psychoanalysis, response, Rogers.**

> www.babcp.org.uk/ (The British Association for Behavioural and Cognitive Therapies).

C

Cognitive consistency theories

Cognitive consistency theories such as the **balance theory, cognitive dissonance** theory and congruity theory attempt to explain **attitude** formation and change by viewing individuals as striving to maintain a consistency between their cognitions, understandings and **perceptions**.

> *See* **attitude, balance theory, cognitive dissonance, perception.**

Cognitive development

See **Piaget's theory of cognitive development.**

Cognitive dissonance

Cognitive dissonance is said to evoke an unpleasant psychological tension in an individual. It was theorized by Festinger (1957) through his work on cognition, which may be defined as a piece of knowledge, such as a person's knowledge about an **attitude**, an emotion, or a belief. Individuals can hold a multitude of cognitions simultaneously. When two cognitions conflict, for example when two **attitudes** are inconsistent with each other ('I like my science teacher, but I don't like his/her views on animal testing'), cognitive dissonance is said to occur. If dissonance is experienced as an unpleasant experience, the individual will be **motivated** by the desire to reduce the negative effects.

Dissonance can be reduced by *changing cognitions*. If two cognitions are conflicting, an individual can simply change one to make it more consistent with the other, or can change each cognition in the direction of the other. For example, in the example above one may change one's **attitude** either to the teacher (coming to dislike him or her) or to animal testing, thus reducing cognitive dissonance and restoring cognitive balance.

See **attitude, balance theory, motivation.**

Festinger, L. (1957) *A Theory of Cognitive Dissonance*. Stanford, CA: Stanford University Press.
Wicklund, R. A. and Brehm, J. A. (1976) *Perspectives on Cognitive Dissonance*. Hillsdale, NJ: Lawrence Erlbaum.
http://en.wikipedia.org/wiki/Cognitive_dissonance (information from Wikipedia).

Cognitive miser effect

See **attributional biases.**

C

Cognitive modelling

This is concerned with attempting to create representations of the functioning, networks, systems and cognitive processes such as **memory, perception, attention** and language acquisition that occur within the cognitive structures of the **brain**. Cognitive modelling often uses computer software packages to demonstrate and highlight the ways in which such cognitive structures function.

See **attention, Chomsky, memory, perception.**

Cooper, P., Yule, P., Fox, J. and Glasspool, D. W. (2002) *Modelling High Level Cognitive Processes*. Hillsdale, NJ: Lawrence Erlbaum.

Cognitive psychology

Cognitive psychology is a branch of psychology that is concerned with the study of all forms of cognition, such as **perception, attention, memory**, thinking, problem solving, decision making, language and information processing. It attempts to explore and understand the way in which cognitive processes work. Such an approach lies in direct contrast to **behaviourism** as it focuses on exploring the innate mental, cognitive basis from which behaviour originates, as opposed to identifying **situational**, environmental and social causes.

See **attention, behaviourism, memory, perception.**

Barsalou, L. W. (1992) *Cognitive Psychology: An Overview for Cognitive Scientists*. Hillsdale, NJ: Lawrence Erlbaum.

Conner, D. B. (1996) From Monty Python to total recall: a feature film activity for the cognitive psychology course. *Journal of Teaching of Psychology*, **23** (1), 33–5. Available online at: www.questia.com/PM.qst?a=o&d=77037915.

Cohort

A cohort is a group of individuals that possess some common experience/s or **demographic traits**, for example being of similar ages, same sex or race, or living in the same geographic location.

See **demographics, trait theories of personality.**

Collectivism

See **individualism.**

C

Comparative psychology

Comparative psychology is concerned with studying the differences in the behaviour of different species; it is sometimes termed animal psychology. The approach attempts to understand the ways in which different species have evolved and the particular processes and mechanisms that underpin and/or regulate their behaviour.

See **imprinting, theory of evolution.**

Hayes, N. (1996) *Principles of Comparative Psychology*. Hove: Psychology Press.

en.wikipedia.org/wiki/Comparative_psychology (information form Wikipedia).

www.apa.org/journals/com/ (Journal of Comparative Psychology. American Psychological Association).

Concrete operational stage

The concrete operational stage is the third stage described in **Piaget's theory of cognitive development**. The theory proposes that children sequentially progress through a series of four stages of **maturation** and interaction with the environment. Each stage of development reflects how children's thought processes transform and build upon the previous stage.

Key aspects of the concrete operational stage (7–11 years) are:

* In this stage children's cognitive abilities allow them to carry out mental operations on the world.
* Children can now understand and logically manipulate relationships between objects and situations.

For example:

Number conservation

a) o o o o o

b) • • • • •

Children within the concrete operational stage can now understand that although row (b) is longer, there are still the same number of dots as in row (a) despite its different appearance.

Children in this stage however, need objects with a concrete, physical presence in the world. They are still unable to logically calculate and deduce solely within their heads.

See **accommodation, assimilation, conservation, formal operational stage, maturation, Piaget's theory of cognitive development, preoperational stage, sensori-motor stage, three-mountain task.**

McGarrigle, J. and Donaldson, M. (1974) Conservation accidents. *Cognition*, 3, 341–50.
Piaget, J. (1952) *The Origins of Intelligence in Children,* New York: International University Press.

C

Conditioned response (CR)

In **classical conditioning,** a CR is a response that is learnt through the process of association, **reinforcement,** modelling or imitation to a conditioned **stimuli.**

See **classical conditioning, behaviourism, Pavlov, reinforcement, Skinner, stimulus, unconditioned response, unconditioned stimulus.**

Conditioned stimulus (CS)

In **classical conditioning** a neutral **stimulus** (NS), such as a bell, will transform into a CS after repeated occurrences of the NS being followed by **unconditioned stimuli**, such as the presentation of food. Through learning, the new CS will elicit the same response (salivation) as the UCS.

See **behaviourism, classical conditioning, conditioned response, Pavlov, Skinner, stimulus, unconditioned stimulus.**

Confidence interval

Confidence intervals are used to express the results of statistical tests as they can provide more information than simply a statement of the p (probability) values alone. The confidence interval (a range where values are grouped according to frequency distribution) calculated from the **mean** and **standard deviation** for which there is a level of probability (usually set at 0.95 or 0.99) that includes the value of a population parameter. A 95 per cent confidence interval indicates that you can be 95 per cent certain that it contains the true population value as it might be estimated from a much larger study. The width of the confidence interval gives us information about how uncertain we are about the unknown parameter. A very wide interval may suggest that more **data** should be collected before anything very definite can be said about the parameter.

See **data, mean, standard deviation.**

en.wikipedia.org/wiki/Confidence_interval (information from Wikipedia).

C

Conformity

Conformity is a form of social influence in which individuals conform to group 'norms' of behaviour or pressure, even though the individuals have not been specifically asked by individuals within the group to comply. Kelman (1958) identified three forms of conformity:

- Compliance involves conforming to the majority group whether or not you agree with them.

- **Identification** occurs when an individual conforms to society's demands and the expected behaviours associated with a particular social role.
- **Internalization** is present when individuals conform because they agree with the beliefs and views of the people who are attempting to influence them.

Moscovici (1976) suggested that many researchers such as **Asch** had placed too much emphasis on the role of majority groups on influencing the minority. Moscovici suggested that it was also possible for the minority to influence the majority through the process of conversion. Conversion involves convincing the majority that the minority's views are correct.

See **Asch, identification, internalization, social impact theory, social psychology, social identity theory.**

Kelman, H. (1958) Compliance, identification, and internalization: three processes of attitude change. *Journal of Conflict Resolution*, 2, 31–60.

McCurdy, D. W. and Spradley, J. (2005) *Conformity and Conflict: Readings in Cultural Anthropology*. Boston: Allyn & Bacon.

Milgram, S. (1963) Behavioural study of obedience. *Journal of Abnormal and Social Psychology*, 67, 371–8.

Moscovici, S. (1976) *Social Influence and Social Change*. London: Academic Press.

pespmc1.vub.ac.be/CONFORM.html (information from Principia Cybernetica web).

Consciousness

Human consciousness is defined as being in the normal mental and physical state of being awake and alert. It is characterized by an individual experiencing **perceptions**, thoughts, emotions and an awareness of the outside world, and possessing self-awareness. In different psychological theories consciousness is viewed in more specific ways:

- **Psychoanalytic** theory identifies consciousness as being the level in which the **ego** functions and it is the decision-making, logical part of the mind.
- **Cognitive psychology** identifies consciousness as being an aspect of **attention.**

See **attention, cognitive psychology, ego, perception, psychoanalysis.**

http://consc.net/chalmers/ (information on consciousness from Professor Chalmers, Australian National University).

Conservation

Conservation is a term introduced by **Piaget** (1896–1980) to encapsulate the knowledge of how physical quantity remains unaffected despite changes in its appearance, as long as nothing is added or taken away. **Piaget** developed the conservation task to support his claim that young children think differently at different life stages. When water is poured from a short wide jug into a tall thin jug, young children think that because the water level in the tall thin jug is higher then there must be more water. **Piaget** suggested that when children could understand that in fact there is no change in quantity, that they have entered the **concrete operational stage** of development. Children who had not made this change in thinking, **Piaget** claimed, were in the **preoperational stage** of development and displayed an **egocentric** understanding of the world. This is a stage in which their understanding of the world is overtly based on their own **perception** of the environment and they have a tendency to focus on only one aspect of the situation. In the conservation task, children at this stage cannot understand that there is the same amount of liquid because they have focused on only one dimension of the experiment, height or width. This is called centration, as the child has centred on only one feature of the situation.

See **accommodation, assimilation, concrete operational stage, perception, Piaget's theory of cognitive development, preoperational stage.**

Constructivism

Constructivism is a doctrine that proposes that human experience, understanding, **perception, memory** and other mental structures are continuously and actively constructed and acquired by the mind. This theory contrasts with forms of **determinism** and **biopsychological** approaches, as it does not accept that such mental structures are innate or passively acquired. Different branches of constructivism include radical constructivism, originating with **Piaget**'s work, which theorized that children construct mental structures, knowledge and understanding through their own actions and interactions with the social world. Social constructivism, originating with Berger and Luckman (1966), explored the manners in which individuals come to share interpretations of the social world.

See **biopsychology, determinism, memory, perception, Piaget's theory of cognitive development, social constructionism.**

C

Berger, P. and Luckman, T. (1966) *The Social Construction of Reality*. New York: Garden City
Burr, V. (1995) *An Introduction to Social Constructionism*. London: Routledge.
www.constructivism123.com (Society for Constructivism in the Social Sciences).

Content validity

See **validity.**

Control condition

A control condition in an experiment serves as a comparison or baseline measurement against which to measure the effects of the experimental group. For example, a drug company is testing the effects of a new drug in treating Alzheimer's disease. The study needs to compare participants with Alzheimer's disease who receive the drug against a **matched group** that is not receiving the drug. The control group is given a **placebo** (which contains no drug) and the experimental group is given the drug. As long as each group has been exposed to the same situational factors, any changes in the participants in the **experimental conditions** can be attributed to the drug.

See **control group, experimental psychology, matched group, placebo.**

Control group

This type of group is used as a comparison group when conducting experiments. Control groups are not subject to the manipulation of the independent **variable** (IV); the control group is not subject to the treatment that the experimental group is exposed to. This provides researchers with a baseline measurement of participant behaviour against which they can compare the experimental groups, thus revealing the effects of the independent **variable**.

C

For example in an experiment to identify the effect of a new drink on weight loss, the experimental group is provided with the drink (IV), whereas the control group is given a substitute that contains just water.

See **placebo, placebo effect, variables.**

Correlation coefficient (Spearman's rho)

Spearman's rho is a test of association, which is used to test whether there is an association or correlation between two sets of scores – two sets of **variables** – from each of the participants. **Data** should be **ordinal** and the test will indicate if there is a correlation between the **variables** and if so, what type of correlation this may be. A correlation simply means that there is a relationship between the two sets of **variables** that shows if a trend or pattern exists within the **data**. An example would be a relationship between the number of hours an athlete spends training for a race and the athlete's final finishing position in the race.

Spearman's rho (r_s) reveals the strength of the association. If the findings show a perfect positive correlation between the two **variables**, (which rarely occurs) r_s is said to equal $+1$, and a perfect negative correlation is said to equal -1. If $r_s = 0$ then there is no relationship between the two **variables**. The degree to which the **Spearman's rho** varies between $+1$, 0 and -1 indicates the strength and direction (negative or positive) of the correlation coefficient.

For example, a researcher is studying whether there will be association between the amount of hours (from one to ten) that ten athletes have trained the day before a race and their ultimate finishing position in the race. The researcher records and **ranks** the number of hours in training for each participant, as **variable** A, assigning the lowest number of hours trained as one and highest as ten. The finishing positions of the runners are recorded and **ranked** as **variable** B, with the higher **ranks** (ten, nine, eight and so on) being **ranked** with the fastest runners (runners in finishing positions one, two, three) and the lower **ranks** (one, two, three and so on) with slowest runners (finishing positions ten, nine, eight and so on) . The prediction is that there will be some level of positive correlation between the two **variables**, so r_s value is expected to fall somewhere between $+1$ and 0; the closer this value is towards $+1$ the stronger the positive correlation. This would then support the prediction that number of hours training will be associated with the runners' finishing positions.

See **data, ordinal measurements, rank, Spearman rank order correlation, variables.**

Coolican, H. (2004) *Research Methods and Statistics*. Bristol: Hodder and Stoughton.

Correspondent inference model

This model (Jones and Davis 1965) is used within **attribution** theory to depict how individuals use information gained from observing the behaviour of others to infer that they possess specific **traits** that are constant over time. For example, a person may infer that an individual possesses sensitive and caring **traits** if that individual is observed helping an elderly lady across the road. When one uses information (correspondence) to make an inference about another person's stable **traits**, three factors must be noted:

- The observed behaviour should be voluntary, not influenced in any way by the actions of others. Behaviour that is asked for, or forced will not allow insights to be achieved about the real **traits** of the observed person.
- If the behaviour is low in social desirability, (goes against the social 'norm'), we are more likely to view it as a stable **trait**/ characteristic of this individual. For example, a person who shouts out across a quiet street is more likely to be viewed as loud, brash and confident.
- If the behaviour creates non-common effects (effects that seem to result from the individual's behaviour rather than the influence of other people's actions), we are more likely to interpret the individual's behaviour as resulting from a stable **trait**. For example, we view individuals as being more caring and generous if they offer their time voluntarily, rather than being asked by a teacher to help out in their children's school.

See **attribution, co-variation theory, dispositional attribution, situational attribution, trait theories of personality.**

Jones, E. E. and Davis, K. E. (1965) From acts to dispositions: the attribution process in person perception. In L. Berkowitz (ed.), *Advances in Experimental Social Psychology*, 2. New York: Academic Press.

Counselling psychology

C

Counselling psychology is a branch of **applied psychology** that attempts to use psychological principles to help individuals overcome a diverse range of issues, problems and difficult life events, such as bereavement, relationship issues and working with mental health issues. Counselling psychologists explore underlying issues and facilitate an active collaborative relationship that attempts to empower people and promote change. They work within a 'holistic' framework, treating the whole person rather than the symptoms alone, by examining the issues in a wider context of what has given rise to them. Training in the United Kingdom to become a counselling psychologist involves undertaking an undergraduate degree course in psychology or a conversion course, which will entitle graduates to Graduate Basis for Registration with the British Psychological Society (BPS). This is then followed by an accredited course by the BPS in counselling psychology; entry to such courses usually requires the applicant to have a certificate in counselling. For further details please visit the BPS website.

See **applied psychology.**

www.bps.org.uk/careers/areas/counselling.cfm (British Psychological Society information on counselling psychology).

Co-variation theory

This is a type of **attribution** theory developed by Kelley (1967) that suggests individuals take into account three factors when they attempt to determine whether another person's actions or behaviour/s are caused by an internal disposition (**trait** or characteristic) or by the situation. The factors are:

* Distinctiveness: how far the action is specific to the situation.
* Consensus: whether many people would undertake a similar action in the same situation.
* Consistency: how frequently the person would undertake the action in other situations.

See **attribution, causal schemata model, trait theories of personality.**

Kelley, H. H. (1967) Attribution theory in social psychology. In D. Levine (ed.) *Nebraska Symposium on Motivation.* Lincoln, NE: University of Nebraska Press.

Critical social psychology

C

Critical social psychology can be defined as an assortment of approaches that challenge the scientific and positivist traditions adopted by experimental social psychology that promote the 'reality' and existence of objective truths and laws. Approaches within critical psychology include social constructionism, postmodernism, and discursive and narrative approaches to psychology. Its key element is the rejection of the scientific method as the 'best' or only method to gain knowledge, a claim that critical social psychology views as always having an ideological character. Critical psychology adopts an understanding of the social world as being constructed through active human meaning making; the social world is a product of collective individuals' interactions within it. Critical social psychology asserts that the reality of the social world only exists in how people come to make sense of it. Experimental social psychology in contrast, takes a view of the social world as being separate from human experience: the social world has an actual reality/existence that can exert 'real' effects upon human action and behaviour.

Critical social psychology holds that there are many varying shifting knowledges to be gained about the social world and human action, which are culturally and historically mediated. This position challenges experimental social psychology claims that suggest that by examining the underlying laws of cause and effect, specific, universal truths and knowledges about the social world (which transcend time and place) can be gained.

For example, a mother has been feeling sad, weepy, tired and lethargic lately following the birth of her baby. She goes to the doctor who asks her questions about how she has been feeling and the recent events in her life. The doctor diagnoses that she has post-natal depression. From an experimental social psychology approach, the social world, external influences and events (having a baby, lack of sleep, lack of support) alongside biological and hormonal changes are located as possible causes of postnatal depression. In this approach findings are sought from a typical cause and effect relationship that can be used to create a generalized understanding of what postnatal depression is and the 'common' symptoms and experiences associated with it.

From a critical social psychology approach, the mother's under-standing of her experiences are examined in relation to her interactions with the social world. The mother may have come to make sense of her postnatal experiences by looking at the many representations of motherhood on TV and in the media, and by comparing herself to other mothers. She may have then come to understand what she should feel like after having a baby through her interactions with such knowledge. In making sense of her 'self' in relation to such dominant 'ways' and ideologies of how mothers' moods are represented in the postnatal period, a critical psychology approach would suggest that postnatal depression is 'brought into being' through the interactions the mother engages within in her social world. Ultimately her interaction with the doctor may have affected her understanding of postnatal depression, self and postnatal well-being.

See **cause and effect, depression, generalization, qualitative research, social constructionism, social psychology.**

Fox, D. and Prilletensky, I. (1997) *Critical Psychology: An Introduction.* London: Sage. Available at: www.dennisfox.net/critpsy/book.html

C

Stainton Rogers, W. (2003) *Social Psychology, Experimental and Critical Approaches.* Berkshire: Open University Press.

Cue arousal theory

See **frustration–aggression hypothesis**.

C

Darwinism

In 1859 Charles Darwin put forward a **theory of evolution,** which explored the role of heredity, **natural selection** and the evolution of the species.

See **theory of evolution, comparative psychology, natural selection.**

Data

Data are the pieces of information or measurements gathered during the process of a **research** study, which culminates in their analysis and interpretation. Analysis and interpretation may be undertaken by **qualitative** and/or **quantitative methods**. The final interpretation of such data can allow researchers to draw conclusions and produce findings in relation to the event under study.

See **qualitative research, quantitative research, research.**

Debriefing

Debriefing is a technique used when undertaking **research**, to explain to the **research** participants the nature and purpose of the study. The British Psychological Society and American Psychological Association among many other professional bodies, lay out codes of **ethical** conduct for psychologists and researchers, which specify the use of debriefing whenever possible. There are instances however, when debriefing may not be practical or suitable: for example, in **ethnographic** or naturalistic **research** in which **research** participants are not aware of being under study.

See **ethnography, ethics, research.**

Decentration

Decentration is a term suggested by **Piaget**, used within his cognitive development theory, which directly contrasts with the concept of centration. Decentration is the name given to the process by which children become able to perceive the world with greater **objectivity**; when they move away from understanding and perceiving the world in relation to themselves and their own wants and needs.

> See **egocentrism, conservation, objectivity, Piaget's theory of cognitive development.**

Declarative memory

> See **memory.**

Defence mechanism

A defence mechanism is a term originating from **psychoanalysis** to refer to a process by which the **ego** protects itself against the demands and innate desires of the **id**.

In the general fields of psychology and psychiatry, a defence mechanism can be identified as a sense, a feeling, a behaviour or a thought that is triggered in **response** to the **perception** of psychic threat. The defence mechanism therefore, enables an individual to avoid stress or **anxiety**-arousing ideas, and so avoid conscious awareness or conflict.

> See **anxiety, ego, id, perception, psychoanalysis, psychosexual stages, regression, repression, response.**

Degrees of freedom (df)

In statistics the degrees of freedom are the number of values in a final calculation of a probability distribution that are free to vary. It is used in many **significance** tests and tests that produce estimates of **variance**.

> See **significance levels, variance.**

Coolican, H. (2004) *Research methods and Statistics in Psychology.* Bristol: Hodder and Stoughton.

Jiang, J., Shen, Y. and Nielson, P. D. (2002) A stimulation study of the degrees of freedom in reaching and grasping, *Human Movement Science*, **21** (6), 881–904.

seamonkey.ed.asu.edu/%7Ealex/computer/sas/df.html (information on degrees of freedom, courtesy of Dr Chong Ho Yu).

www.creative-wisdom.com/computer/sas/df.html (main website).

D

Deindividuation

This is a psychological condition in which people experience a loss of identity or individuality and feel that they have lost their sense of belonging within a group. It is suggested that deindividuation can lead to a lack of inhibition and feelings of responsibility and to an increase in **antisocial behaviour**. It has been suggested that deindividuation can provide explanations for the occurrence of mob violence.

See **antisocial behaviour, bystander effect.**

Abelson, R. P., Frey, K. P. and Gregg, A. P. (2004) *Experiments With People: Revelations From Social Psychology,* Mahwah, NJ: Lawrence Erlbaum.

Diener, E. (1980) Deindividuation: the absence of self-awareness and self-regulation in group members. In P. B. Paulus (ed.), *Psychology of Group Influence.* Hillside, NJ: Lawrence Erlbaum.

Zimbardo, P. and Leippe, M. R. (1991) *Psychology of Attitude Change and Social Influence.* New York: McGraw Hill Education.

www.ex.ac.uk/~tpostmes/deindividuation.html (information from Dr Postmes, University of Exeter).

Demographics

Demographics are the physical characteristics of a population such as sex, age, marital status, education, family size, occupation and general location.

Dendrites

Dendrites are threadlike extensions near the cell body of a **neuron**, which are designed to receive incoming impulses from other **neurons**.

See **brain, action potential, neural network, neuron.**

Denial

D

Denial is a type of behaviour or **response** that can be seen to act as a **defence mechanism**, a mode by which our conscious mind is protected from experiencing **anxiety** by distorting our **perception** of reality. An individual experiencing denial may choose to deny some aspect of reality. For example, an individual who cannot accept the death of his or her dog may buy a new dog of the same breed, and continue treating the new dog in the same way as the previous one, even giving the new dog the same name.

See **anxiety, defence mechanism, perception, psychoanalysis, repression, response.**

Dependent variable (DV)

See **variables.**

Depression

Depression can be defined as a mood disorder, a state of sadness or gloom in which an individual often experiences a sense of guilt or worthlessness, or feels that life has no meaning. The Diagnostic Statistical Manual classification of mental disorders (**DSM IV** American Psychological Association, 1994) defines two categories of depression:

- major depression (or unipolar disorder).
- **bipolar disorder** previously known as manic depression.

Major depression is the most common form. It is probably the most widespread mental disorder and affects approximately 5 per cent of people.

The formal **diagnosis** of depression in an individual requires that he or she must suffer from the first two symptoms listed below and at least three others on the list:

- depressed or sad mood.
- loss of pleasure and interest in usual activities
- insomnia (difficulty in sleeping), or a desire to sleep all the time
- a shift in energy levels
- weight loss or weight gain and/or an increased or decreased appetite
- tiredness and loss of energy
- low self-esteem, poor self-image and feelings of worthlessness or guilt
- lack of concentration and indecisiveness
- suicidal ideation (thinking about death or suicide).

There are many theories about and explanations for the cause/s of depression. They include:

- Biological theories that locate the causes of depression at a genetic level, stressing that some individuals may have an inherited disposition to experiencing depression. **Research** (Fuchs et al. 2004) has recently found links between **neurotransmitters** such as **serotonin** and noradrenalin and depression. Such biological theories have been heavily criticized however for their deterministic nature and for not

D

acknowledging the role of human agency and social factors in depression.

* Cognitive or psychological theories that have looked towards individuals' irrational or negative thought processes and belief systems that may affect the emotional state of the individual. **Beck** (1976) theorized that depression could be caused in **adulthood** by possessing a cognitive bias towards the negative interpretation of events.
* Social theories that have looked towards stressful social factors, such as moving house, financial pressures and childbirth, as being the cause of depression
* Psychosocial theories that have looked towards models such as the **diathesis-stress model**, a stressful-life-events model that looks at how individuals may become more susceptible to depression if they have particular psychological **traits** or characteristics that make them vulnerable when experiencing particular stressful life events.

There are a range of various treatments for depression, which include:

* Psychological therapies, such as **cognitive behaviour therapy** that attempt to challenge negative and illogical ways of thinking about being depressed, and to help sufferers develop a new, beneficial and positive way of thinking about themselves.
* Biological therapies such as electroconvulsive therapy (ECT), and drug therapies such as anti-depressants are also widely used.

See **abnormal behaviour, abnormal psychology, adulthood, Beck Depression Inventory (BDI), bipolar disorder, cognitive behaviour therapy, diagnosis, diathesis-stress model, DSM IV, neurotransmitter, research, serotonin, trait theories of personality.**

American Psychiatric Association (1994). *Diagnostic and Statistical Manual for Mental Disorders*, (4th edn.), Washington: APA Press.

Beck, A. T (1976) *Cognitive Therapy of the Emotional Disorders*. New York: New American library.

Becker, J. and Kleinman, A. (1991) *Psychosocial Aspects of Depression*, Hillsdale, NJ: Lawrence Erlbaum.

Fuchs, E., Kole, M., Michaelis, T. and Lucassen, J. (2004) Alterations of neuroplasticity in depression: The hippocampus and beyond. *European Neuropsychopharmacology*, **14** (3) 481.

Hara Estroff, M. (1999) Depression: Beyond serotonin. Psychology Today. 32 (2), 30.

www.soslg.ac.uk/roads/subject-listing/World-cat/psychdis.html (information from Social science Information Gateway).

D

Descriptive statistics

Descriptive statistics are the most basic of statistics and use mathematical measures to summarize and describe **data** so that they can be more easily interpreted. They are used in the first instance to get a feel for the **data**; in the second they are used within the statistical tests; and in the third to indicate the error associated with the results. Descriptive statistics include:

- **measures of central tendency** (which describe how the **data** cluster together around a central point) such as the **mean, mode** and **median**
- **measures of dispersion** (which indicate whether the scores are spread out or similar) such as **variance, standard deviation** and **range**.

The **measures of dispersion** use the various **measures of central tendency** in determining the spread of scores.

See **data, mean, measures of central tendency, measures of dispersion, median, mode, range, skewed distribution, standard deviation, variance.**

Desensitization

Desensitization refers to the reduction in sensitivity to an object, action or **stimulus**. For example, an individual may react strongly on first hearing a sudden noise, but after hearing it a few times may become less and less responsive.

See **addiction, flooding, stimulus.**

Determinism

D

Determinism suggests that human behaviour can only be understood through the understanding that everything that happens has a definite cause. It goes against the concept of an individual's capacity for **free will**, as **free will** does not have a definite account and cannot be scientifically observed and predicted. Determinism is associated with experimental and **biopsychology** approaches and many different psychologists therefore take the deterministic approach; behaviourists especially suggest that nearly all behaviour is the product of our environment. Psychodynamic theorists also believe in determinism as the root basis of human action, suggesting that behaviour is caused by an individual's **instinctual** desires, psychological conflicts and **motivational** systems.

See **biopsychosocial model, free will versus determinism, instinct, motivation, nature–nurture debate.**

Developmental psychology

Developmental psychology is a branch of psychology that is concerned with the study of mental changes, both cognitive and emotional, and development that take place over an individual's lifespan. Developmental psychology is strongly associated with theorists such as **Piaget** and **Chomsky**, whose focus has been on child development and the term 'child psychology'. Terms such as 'gerontology' and 'lifespan psychology' have been created to refer to the study of later development.

See **Erikson's psychosocial development stages, Chomsky, Freud, Kohlberg's theory of moral development, Piaget's theory of cognitive development, Vygotsky, zone of proximal development.**

Bremner, G, and Slater, A. (2003) *Introduction to Developmental Psychology*. Oxford: Blackwell.
Chomsky, N. (1986) *Knowledge of Language: Its Nature, Origin, and Use*. New York: Praeger.
Winston, R. and Livingston, T. (2005) *A Child of our Time*. London: Bantam.

Deviation

In relation to statistics, deviation is the extent to which a score or scores differ from the **mean**.

In relation to **social** and **abnormal psychology**, deviation can be seen as a departure from the social or moral 'norms' in any given society, culture or group.

See **abnormal behaviour, abnormal psychology, antisocial behaviour, mean, social psychology, standard deviation.**

D

Diagnosis

Diagnosis is the term given to the classification and identification of a mental or psychological disorder. A clinical psychologist or psychiatrist may diagnose **depression** or **schizophrenia** in the same way a medical doctor may diagnose a heart murmur or a broken leg. Diagnosing symptoms within the mental health professions can prove more difficult than in general medicine, as presenting symptoms often cannot be defined within clear diagnostic categories, as can be done in medicine. Mental health practitioners therefore do not attempt to categorize symptoms into one specific, distinct disorder, but rather look for patterns of symptoms displayed and experienced by the client.

See **depression, schizophrenia.**

Diagnostic and Statistical Manual of Mental Disorders

See **DSM IV.**

Diathesis-stress model

The diathesis-stress model adopts a psychosocial approach to understanding and explaining human behaviour. This approach determines that some individuals may have a fixed predisposition (diathesis) that may make them more vulnerable to certain types of disorders, experiences and emotional states when exposed to particular life events or social stressors (stress).

An individual who possesses this predisposition towards a disorder, through genetic factors or psychological **traits**, would not necessarily develop the disorder. This would only happen if the individual experienced particular life stressors that triggered the stress **response** (such as mental abuse or physical trauma).

Research has indicated that disorders such as **schizophrenia**, **depression**, alcoholism and general **addictions** may involve an inherited disposition that makes some individuals more susceptible to those behaviours when they face difficulties in their social lives.

See **addiction, depression, research, response, schizophrenia, trait theories of personality.**

Abela, J. (2001) The hopelessness theory of depression: a test of the diathesis–stress and causal mediation components in third and seventh grade children, *Journal of Abnormal Psychology*, 29, 241–55.
Nolen-Hoeksema, S. (1990) *Sex Differences in Depression.* Stanford, CA: Stanford University Press.

D

Discourse analysis

Discourse analysis is a method of interpreting **data** that includes (but is not restricted to) **qualitative research** and is a field of study that focuses upon understanding all forms of spoken and written language. It attempts to understand the meanings hidden within language, the interrelationships between language and society, and the interactive properties of everyday communication. It views the reality of the world as being actively constructed through the use of language and human behaviour as being powerfully negotiated and influenced by – and originating through – the communication of dominant discourses. A discourse may be seen as a particular view of the world, such as that childhood is a time of fun and innocence, a romantic discourse prevalent in modern Westernized cultures.

Discourse analysis involves searching through **data** that has usually been gathered through methods such as interviews, **questionnaires** or in written material, literature and/or documents. The **data** and language are then analysed for the use of discourses and discursive themes that are related to the aims and focus of the **research**. There are many forms of discourse analysis, varying according to the **research** approach and focus. They include:

- Foucauldian discourse analysis: this form of discourse analysis is derived from the work and writings of Foucault. Such analysis focuses on exploring relationships between the subject, power and knowledge as represented within the text.
- Critical discourse analysis: this form of discourse analysis views language as a form of social practice. It attempts to examine the use and effects of discourse within social systems and institutions in **shaping** social practices and individual behaviours.

See **critical social psychology, data, qualitative research, questionnaires, research, shaping, social constructionism.**

Banister, P., Burman, E., Parker, I., Taylor, M. and Tindall, C. (1994) *Qualitative Methods in Psychology: A Research Guide*. Buckingham: Open University Press.
Fairclough, N. (1995) *Critical Discourse Analysis*. Harlow: Longman.
Wetherall, M., Taylor, S. and Yates, S. (2001) *Discourse as Data: A Guide For Analysis*. London: Sage.

Disengagement theory

See **Gould's theory of adult development.**

D

Disorder

A disorder is defined as a factor that prevents, prohibits or restricts the natural and regular functioning (of body or mind) of an individual. The **DSM IV** classification system has classified over 200 mental health disorders, such as **schizophrenia** and **depression**, that are considered to reduce normal psychological and physical functioning.

See **DSM IV, depression, schizophrenia.**

Dispositional attribution

A dispositional attribution is a way of understanding another individual's (or our own) behaviour, through attributing the cause of that behaviour to factors innate and inherent within that individual. For example, if a person slips on the pavement, using a dispositional attribution we are more likely to explain the cause of that behaviour as clumsiness or ignorance. We are less likely to look towards external influences (**situational attributions**), such as a broken paving stone, or the person having lost his or her glasses and so not being able to see very well.

Individuals have a tendency to overuse dispositional attributions when judging other people's behaviours as opposed to their own, this is known as **actor/observer bias.** Individuals tend to judge their own behaviour in terms of **situational attributions**: for example, 'Sorry I'm late, my alarm didn't go off'.

See **actor/observer bias, attribution, causal schemata model, co-variation theory, situational attribution.**

Dissociation

Dissociation can be regarded as a mental process that produces a lack of connection in a person's thoughts, actions, **memories**, feelings or sense of identity. When a person is dissociating, certain information is not linked with other information as it normally would be. For example, following a traumatic experience, people may dissociate the place and circumstances of the trauma from their **memory**, resulting in a temporary mental escape from the fear and pain resulting from the trauma. As the process of dissociation can produce changes in **memory**, individuals can often find their senses of personal history and identity are affected.

See **defence mechanism, memory, psychoanalysis, repression.**

D

Distribution dependent tests

See **parametric tests.**

Dizygotic twins

'Dizygotic twins' is another term for fraternal or non-identical twins. They are no more genetically alike than any other pair of siblings.

See **twin studies.**

Double-blind procedure

This is a **research** design that is used in an attempt to reduce the possibility of the experimenter affecting the **research** findings. In a double-blind procedure, neither the experimenter nor the **research** participants knows the particular aims of the study. When possible neither knows whether participants have been assigned to the **experimental** or **control condition**.

See **control condition, experimental condition, research.**

Dream analysis

Dream analysis is a technique originating and used within **psychoanalysis**, in which the process of **free association** enables the content and underlying meanings of dreams to be examined. **Free association** involves the client relating all thoughts, feelings, memories and whatever springs to mind to the analyst, no matter how trivial or embarrassing. According to **psychoanalytic** theory, dreams are wish-fulfilments, symbolic representations of an individual's unconscious desires.

See **free association, Freud, psychoanalysis, wish-fulfilment.**

DSM IV (Diagnostic and Statistical Manual of Mental Disorders)

This is a manual that contains the description, classification and definitions of over 200 mental health disorders. DSM IV (1994), the current updated version, contains a list of classified disorders and their associated symptoms, rather than providing/determining the **etiology** or treatment of the disorder. This is to avoid the potential pitfalls of subscribing to a particular approach to **abnormal behaviour.**

DSM IV uses a system of classification of axis and category groups to classify disorders in relation to common features. **Diagnosis** of any disorder involves taking all five axes into consideration, as individuals may have multiple and diverse disorders. The five axes of classification are shown in Table 1.

Some suggested advantages of using the DSM IV classification system are:

- It can provide a guide for mental health professionals of agreed terms and categories of disorders, by which they can determine relevant treatments and discuss these with their clients.

D

* It can provide an insight into the 'possible' causes or origins of a disorder.
* It can offer direction as to how to provide the most appropriate plan of treatment for the range of symptoms experienced.

Table 1 The five axes of DSM IV

Axis	Classification of information	Description
I	Clinical disorders	This axis contains mental disorders that present symptoms or patterns of behaviour that are painful or impair an area of functioning (such as anxiety or schizophrenia).
II	a) Personality disorders	This axis contains dysfunctional ways of responding and viewing the world. (e.g. paranoid personality disorder).
	b) Mental retardation	This axis contains disorders that affect specific skills, such as reading and language skills.
III	General medical conditions	This axis involves gaining information about physical problems that may help understand, manage or treat the individual's mental health disorder.
IV	Psychosocial and environmental problems	This axis involves rating (from none to extreme) the psychosocial factors (environmental and social factors) that might contribute to the disorder.
V	Global assessment of functioning	This involves assessing the highest level of adaptive functioning during the previous year. By examining the individual's general abilities, a prediction can be made about the likely outcome of the disorder.

Reprinted with permission from the Diagnostic and Statistical Manual of Mental Disorders, Fourth Edition, Text Revision. Copyright 2000, American Psychiatric Association.

Some suggested disadvantages of using the DSM IV classification system:

* There may be a lack of **reliability** and consistency between health practitioners in determining and treating disorders, as not all practitioners will arrive at the same outcome when presented with an individual's symptoms and information about those symptoms.
* The DSM IV cannot provide information about the 'actual' causes of disorders or behaviours, so treatment could be argued to treat the symptom but not the cause.
* **Humanists** and **feminists** (Stoppard 2000; Nicolson 1998) have argued that such a set of medical diagnostics only serve to de-personalize and separate individuals from their experience, and do not acknowledge the capacity of human knowledge and autonomy in addressing disorders.

See **abnormal behaviour, abnormal psychology, depression, diagnosis, etiology, feminist psychology, humanistic psychology, reliability.**

American Psychiatric Association (1994*). Diagnostic and Statistical Manual for Mental Disorders*, (4th edn.), Washington: APA Press.

Nicolson, P. (1998) *Postnatal Depression: Psychology, Science and the Transition to Motherhood*. London: Routledge.

Stoppard, J. M. (2000) *Understanding Depression: Feminist Social Constructionist Approaches*. London: Routledge.

www.psychiatryonline.com (information from Psychiatry Online).

Dual process theories

See **attention, automatic processing, attenuator model of attention, Broadbent.**

D

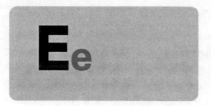

Ee

Echoic memory

See **memory.**

Ecological validity

See **validity.**

Educational psychology

Educational psychology is a branch of **applied psychology** that focuses on education. Educational psychologists predominantly work in school psychological services, child guidance clinics or private practices. Their work involves the treatment and **diagnosis** of any educational, emotional and behavioural concerns that may affect educational ability in children of all ages up to their late teens. In the United Kingdom, a candidate wishing to undertake training as an educational psychologist requires the Graduate Basis for Recognition (GBR) with the British Psychological Society (BPS). It will also be expected that the candidate has relevant work experience, such as working as a learning support assistant, learning mentor, educational social worker or teacher, or working in an early-years or school setting.

A recent change to the training of educational psychologists has brought training more in line with the training of clinical psychologists. This means that from 2006, applicants with a BPS-recognized psychology degree will be able to apply to undertake a three-year doctorate training course to work towards chartering as an educational psychologist. Applications for courses are dealt with by the Employers Organization for Local government, which acts as a clearing house for postgraduate courses in educational psychology.

See **applied psychology, diagnosis.**

www.lg-employers.gov.uk/skills/ed_psych/ (Employers Organization for Local government).

www.bps.org.uk (British Psychological Society website with further details on educational psychology training).

Efferent neurons

An efferent neuron (or motor neuron) transmits information in the form of nerve impulses, away from the **central nervous system** and towards the muscles and glands.

See **afferent neurons, central nervous system, neuron.**

Ego

In **psychoanalysis** the ego is one of three parts that constitute the human mind or psyche. The ego is the part in touch with reality; it acts as the mediator between the innate, **instinctual** urges and desires of the **id**, and the moral, puritanical disapproval of the **superego**. The ego in mediating can repress conscious awareness of the wayward desires of the **id**, but is seen to allow these to surface and to be released within dreams and slips of the tongue, the proverbial **Freudian slip**.

See **defence mechanism, Freud, Freudian slip, id, instinct, psychoanalysis, superego.**

Egocentrism

Egocentrism is a term theorized within **Piaget's theory of cognitive development.** Piaget suggested that a child who is in the **preoperational stage** of cognitive development (before the age of seven) is only able to understand the world from his or her own point of view, and is unable to comprehend other people's points of view. Piaget argued that in this stage a child could not differentiate between **subjective** and **objective** features of experience. Piaget developed and used the **conservation** task and the **three-mountain task** to support his claims.

See **conservation, concrete operational stage, formal operational stage, Piaget's theory of cognitive development, preoperational stage, sensorimotor stage, three-mountain task.**

E

Ego control

Ego control refers to an individual's ability to control his or her impulses, such as to refrain from voicing an opinion, withold aggressive action or delay gratification and reward.

Ego defence

See **defence mechanism.**

Ego psychology

This is a particular school of **psychoanalysis**, which suggests that the **ego** can act and develop autonomously and independently and is not governed solely by the internal conflicts of the **id** and **super-ego**. Ego psychologists do not accept the traditional **psychoanalytical** notions that view all **motivation** for an individual's behaviour as occurring solely through attempts to resolve mental conflict.

See **ego, id, motivation, psychoanalysis, superego.**

Electra complex

The Electra complex is theorized within **psychoanalytic** theory to define the inner mental conflict that females experience as they journey through the **psychosexual stages** of development. This suggests that a daughter will experience a desire to sleep with her father and that accompanying this there will be a jealousy and hatred for her mother for removing her (the daughter's) penis. This is the female equivalent of the **Oedipus complex**.

See **Oedipus complex, psychoanalysis, psychosexual stage, superego.**

Embedded figure

See **ambiguous figures, field dependence, field independence.**

Empiricism

This is a doctrine that claims that all knowledge is, or should be, gained from logically derived inferences, **observations** and experience. It is a major theoretical psychological approach that defines that all human behaviour should be a product of learning and experience, as opposed to **genetic determinism** or predisposition. Empiricists view the experimental approach to collecting, analysing and evaluating **data** as the most appropriate way to acquire knowledge.

See **data, experimental psychology, genetic determinism, observation, qualitative research.**

Heft. H. (2001) *Ecological Psychology in Context: James Gibson, Roger Barker, and the Legacy of William James's Radical Empiricism.* Mahwah, NJ: Lawrence Erlbaum,

E

Epidemiology

Epidemiology is concerned with the study of the occurrence, prevalence, incidence, distribution and control of disorders, in fact, the study of all factors associated with the origins and presence of disorders.

Episodic memory

See **memory.**

Epistemology

Epistemology is a branch of philosophy that is concerned with the theory of knowledge. It attempts to ask and answer questions about how and what we can know and what methods are most appropriate to generate knowledge. Epistemology involves considering the nature of knowledge, the **validity** and **reliability** of knowledge claims, and how we can successfully distinguish mere belief from knowledge.

There are many epistemological positions that favour particular beliefs and assumptions about the nature of knowledge and about how it can be produced. These include, **empiricism**, positivism, **social constructionism**, postmodernism, feminism, relativism and **phenomenology**, to name just a few.

See **empiricism, phenomenology, reliability, social constructionism, validity.**

Equity theory

The equity theory is a social justice theory, arguing that people perceive a given situation as fair when they feel that they have given and taken out of that situation as much as any other person taking part. In some cases people feel they are giving too much or gaining too little. For example, in relationships, women may find they are investing much of their time outside work in cleaning and cooking, in contrast to their partners who instead invest their spare time simply watching TV. The female identifies herself as the giver, providing much more than her partner, and her partner as the receiver, gaining much more than she does.

The equity theory suggests that in such situations individuals strive to maintain a balance between what they put into any situation or relationship and what they get out of it. Most individuals, the theory claims, expect to receive rewards from any situation that are at least proportional to what they put into it.

When imbalance in giving and receiving are experienced, inequity is experienced as an uncomfortable feeling, and this theory suggests that individuals will attempt to restore balance or equity. Equity can be restored by a number of methods: by altering gains and losses, by cognitively distorting them (fooling ourselves), or by members ending the relationships or leaving the situation.

Research (Hatfield et al. 1979) has shown in studies of married couples that those couples that perceived the investments and gains as being equal stated that they were happy in their marriages. In contrast those who felt there were discrepancies in the amount each put into the relationship and the amount each gained reported feeling unhappy with the relationship.

See **exchange theory, relationship theories, research.**

Allen, R. and White, C. (2002) Equity sensitivity theory: a test of responses to two types of under-reward situations, *Journal of Managerial Issues*, 14, 435–51.
Hatfield, E., Utne, M. K. and Traupman, J. (1979) Equity theory and intimate relationships. In R. L. Burgess and T. L. Huston (eds) *Exchange Theory in Developing Relationships.* New York: New York Academic Press.

Erikson's psychosocial development stages ('Eight stages of man')

Erikson (1959) built upon **Freud**'s psychodynamic theories of **personality** that depicted it as developing in stages and stated that the human psyche was made up of the **id**, **ego** and **superego**. Erikson in contrast, viewed **personality** as being developed not just through childhood but in **adulthood** also. **Erikson** also disagreed with **Freud** as to the nature of the development stages, focusing on psychosocial rather than **psychosexual stages**.

Erikson theorized that it was an individual's interaction with social forces, rather than sexual forces, that were more important in **shaping** an individual's **personality**. Erikson viewed **personality** as developing through eight stages: 'the eight stages of man' shown in Table 2.

Erikson suggests that each stage represents a psychosocial crisis or conflict, related to an approximate developmental age, that an individual needs to work through and resolve. Each stage represents a psychological conflict relating to an individual's interaction with others in increasingly wider social settings. The psychological conflict takes place in a particular social setting and if resolved the

Table 2 Erikson's eight stages of development

Stage	Approx. age	Psychosocial crisis	Optimal outcome
I Oral-sensory	1	Trust vs mistrust	Trust and optimism
II Musculur anal	2	Autonomy vs shame and doubt	Sense of control over oneself and environment
III Locomotor-genital	3–5	Initiative vs guilt	Goal directedness and purpose
IV Latency	5–12	Industry vs inferiority	Competence
V Puberty and adolescence	13–18	Identity vs role confusion	Reintegration of past with present and future goals' fidelity
VI Early adulthood	19–22	Intimacy vs isolation	Commitment, sharing, closeness, and love
VII Young and middle age	23-45	Generativity vs self absorption	Productivity and concern about larger issues
VIII Mature adult	46+	Integrity vs despair	Wisdom, satisfaction with one's past life

Adapted from Erikson, E.H. (1959) *Identity and life styles: selected papers*. New York: International Universities Press.

E

individual will develop a particular psychological strength and a certain virtue. **Erikson** did not view the stages as being categorically fixed to age, as he suggested that it was possible to return to unresolved conflicts later in life where they can be successfully resolved.

See **adulthood, ego, Freud, id, personality, psychosexual stages, shaping, superego.**

Erikson, E. H. (1959) *Identity and Life Styles: Selected Papers*. New York: International Universities Press.

Errors

- *Type I*
  This is a type of error made after statistical analysis, when the null **hypothesis** is rejected but the probability is that it may be supported. This type of error most commonly occurs when the **significance level** is not rigorous enough. An example would be rejecting the null **hypothesis** at the $p = 0.10$ level rather than the more commonly adopted $p = 0.05$ level. At a 0.10 level, the probability of chance causing the findings (or some other cause) are 1 in 10, which is insufficiently high. Rejecting the null **hypothesis** at this level can be seen as an optimistic calculation or being unnecessarily lenient.

- *Type II*
  This is a type of error made after statistical analysis, when the null **hypothesis** is retained even when the probability is that it is unsupported. The most predominant reason for this occurring is that the **significance level** is too rigorous. For example, not rejecting the null **hypothesis** at the commonly adopted $p = 0.05$ level and using the $p = 0.01$ level instead. At a 0.05 level the probability of the findings being caused by chance would be seen as being low enough; insisting on a level of 0.01 may be thought of as being unnecessarily harsh, or a pessimistic calculation.

Type I and II errors can be made at any **significance level**.

See **hypothesis, significance level.**

E

Ethics

When undertaking **research**, ethics is the consideration of what is morally appropriate and acceptable in meeting the **research** aims. The study of ethics has in the past been a concern of philosophy, but as there is increasing focus on accountability in science and medicine, the moral issues of conducting **research** are just as important as the practical aspects. Organizations such as The British Psychological Society publish clear ethical guidelines to ensure that psychologists conduct **research** in a manner that is in the best interests of the participants, and can be morally substantiated by those undertaking the **research**. **Informed consent** is an important aspect of ethical practice.

See **informed consent, research.**

Parahoo, K. (1997) *Nursing Research: Principles, Process and Issues*. Hampshire: Palgrave.

Stanley, B., Sieber, J. and Melton, G. (1996) *Research Ethics: A Psychological Approach*. Lincoln, NE: University of Nebraska Press.

www.bps.org.uk/the-society/ethics-rules-charter-code-of-conduct/code-of-conduct/ethical-principles-for-conducting-research-with-human-participants.cfm (British Psychological Society webpage for ethics).

Ethnocentrism

This refers to the tendency or disposition to judge other ethnic cultures', societies' and nations' customs, beliefs and behaviours by the standards and **social norms** of one's own social group. Ethnocentric views are also sometimes underpinned by a belief in the superiority of one's own ethnic group over others and a dislike and mistrust of other 'ways' of life.

See **gender bias, individualism, social norms, social psychology.**

Ethnography

This is a branch of anthropology that is concerned with the study of individual human societies, usually by a researcher who becomes actively involved as a member of that society for a number of years.

Etiology

Etiology is the cause or causes of a particular behaviour, mental disorder or illness. The term can also refer to the study of such causes.

E

Exchange theory

Exchange theory suggests that the exchange of social and material resources is a fundamental form of human interaction. It explores and examines how people arrive at the decisions they undertake within relationships, by measuring the outcomes, taking into account the actions of others, the rewards and costs (affection and

attention), minimizing and **maximizing** costs (devoting time and effort) and rewards, and comparing results. It suggests that people strive to minimize costs and **maximize** rewards and assess the desirability of developing a relationship with any individual on the perceived possible outcomes or consequences. When the positive outcomes are perceived to be greater than the possible losses, we disclose more and develop a closer relationship with that individual.

See **attention, equity theory, maximizing (game theory), relationship theories, social psychology.**

Lawler, E. J. and Thye, S. R. (1999) Bringing emotions into social exchange theory. *Journal of the Annual Review of Sociology*, 25, 217–44.

Thibaut, J. W. and Kelley, H. H. (1959) *The Social Psychology of Groups*. New York: John Wiley.

Komarita, S. S. and Parks, C. D. (1996) *Social Dilemmas*, Houston: Westview.

Existentialism

Existentialism can be viewed as a philosophical movement or doctrine that emphasizes an individual's existence, freedom and choice. There are many diverse positions associated with existentialism, and as such it is impossible to precisely define. There are however, common themes within such contrasting positions, these being:

- the importance of actual individual existence and of **subjectivity**, individual freedom and choice
- a stress on the importance of intense individual action in deciding questions of both morality and truth
- the freedom of individuals to act independently of determination by outside influences
- that personal experience and acting on one's own beliefs are essential in arriving at the truth
- a view that human beings do not have a fixed nature or essence, but rather that each human being actively makes choices that create his or her own nature or existence
- thus, a view that places **subjective** knowledge above **objective** knowledge claims, the knowledge of a situation by an individual involved in that situation being more important than that of a detached, **objective** observer.

It is difficult to state clearly who are regarded as existentialists, since nineteenth-century philosophers such as Kierkegaard and Nietzsche are sometimes considered too early to be called existentialists.

Twentieth-century philosophers such as Heidegger, Sartre and Camus are often quoted as being central to existentialism.

See **objectivity, Rogers, subjectivity, unconditional positive regard.**

Collins, J. and Howard, S. (2001) *Introducing Heidegger*. London: Icon books.
Mairowitz, D. Z. and Korkas, A. (1999) *Introducing Camus*. London: Icon books.
Jones, G., Hayward, J. and Cardinal, D. (2003) *Existentialism and Humanism: Jean-Paul Sartre*. London: Hodder Murray.

Experimental condition

In undertaking an experimental **research** study, participants allocated to the experimental condition are given the actual treatment or **variable** under study. Participants in the **control condition** are given a **placebo** (non-responsive) treatment or **variable** in contrast. The experimental participants' behaviour/s to the **variable** can thus be compared to the **responses** of participants in the **control condition**. Any differences in participants' behaviours between the **experimental condition** and **control condition** can therefore be attributed to the **variable** under study.

See **control condition, placebo, research, response, variables.**

Experimental psychology

Experimental psychology is usually referred to as a branch of psychology that focuses on the psychological processes within an individual that can be examined through rigorous scientific methods of enquiry. Such processes include exploring **perception**, **memory**, cognition, **motor skills**, language and learning.

See **memory, motor skills, perception.**

www.eaesp.org/ (The European Association of Experimental Psychology).

E

Explicit memory

See **memory.**

Externalization

In psychology there are many different uses of the term externalization.

* In **attribution** theories, externalization refers to the **attribution** of the cause of an action to external factors (**situational**

attributions) rather than factors inherent in a person (**dispositional attributions**).

- In **psychoanalysis**, the term externalization is related to the process of projection. Projection is a **defence mechanism** in which individuals unfairly project onto another individual their own **traits** or characteristics, which they are unconsciously ashamed of.
- In **developmental psychology**, externalization refers to the understanding of a difference in childhood between the self and the external world.

See attribution, defence mechanism, developmental psychology, dispositional attribution, internalization, psychoanalysis, situational attribution, trait theories of personality.

Eysenck personality questionnaire (EPQ)

The Eysenck personality questionnaire (1978) is designed to measure three **personality** dimensions, these being neuroticism, extroversion–introversion and psychoticism.

See Cattell, five-factor model of personality, Freud, personality.

Eysenck, H. J. (1978) Superfactors, P, E and N in a comprehensive factor space. *Multivariate Behavioral Research*, 13, 475–82.

E

Ff

Face recognition

Studies in **social psychology** have particularly explored the area of eyewitness testimonies, examining the accuracy of individuals' memories when they describe people involved in particular events, such as crimes. Studies found that individuals often paid too much **attention** to external factors, which are subject to change, rather than stable characteristics like facial features. Young and Bruce (1991) named this the Red-Ridinghood effect, as like Red Riding-hood (who mistook the wolf for grandma), individuals would be less likely to recognize people outside the contexts in which they would most frequently encounter them. For example, they would be less likely to recognize the dentist at the library or the doctor at the swimming pool. Factors that have been shown to improve facial recognition are familiarity and distinctiveness. Particular branches of psychology have explored different factors. For example:

- Studies in **cognitive psychology** have particularly focused on how face recognition occurs via **pattern recognition** and the **perception** of faces.
- Studies (Fantz 1961) in **developmental psychology** have revealed that infants appear to be innately pre-determined to exert a preference for viewing a human face, rather than abstract images.

See **attention, cognitive psychology, developmental psychology, Gestalt psychology, pattern recognition, perception, social psychology.**

BenAbdelkader, C and Griffin, P. A (2005) Comparing and combining depth and texture cues for face recognition. *Image and Vision Computing*, **23** (3), 339–52.

Fantz, R. L. (1961) The origin of form perception. *Scientific American*, 204, 66–72.

Rozin, P., Lowery, L., and Ebert, R. (1994) Varieties of disgust faces and the structure of disgust. *Journal of Personality and Social Psychology*, **66** (5), 870–81.

Young, A. W. and Bruce, V. (1991) Perceptual categories and the computation of 'grandmother'. *European Journal of Cognitive Psychology*, 3, 5–49.

Face validity

See **validity.**

Factor analysis

Factor analysis, which is used predominantly by **trait personality** theorists, such as **Cattell** and **Eysenck**, uses information about the intercorrelations of items gained from **questionnaires**, rating scales and other **personality** measures. They can be seen to measure the same factor or aspect of **personality** if the two items strongly correlate (have a relationship) with each other. If the two items do not correlate then they are probably measuring different factors. For example, items such as aggression and coldness would correlate highly under the factor of psychoticism.

> *See* **Cattell, Eysenck, five-factor model of personality, personality, questionnaires, trait theories of personality.**

> Eysenck, M. W. (1982) *Attention and Arousal: Cognition and Performance.* Berlin: Springer.

Feminist psychology

Feminist psychology is concerned with valuing and examining women's lived experiences in their own right. It challenges **epistemological** claims, the assumptions that what constitutes knowledge is derived through traditional, empirical, scientific enquiry. It attempts to use and develop alternative modes of enquiry that can reflect the commitment it has to addressing the exclusion, **prejudice** and oppression that women experience within positivist and patriarchal systems.

> *See* **critical social psychology, epistemology, prejudice, social psychology, qualitative research.**

> bell hooks (2000) *Feminist theory, from margin to centre*, 2nd edn, London: Pluto.
> Gilligan, C. (2003) *In a Different Voice: Psychological Theory and Women's Development*, Harvard: Harvard Press.
> Unger, R. and Crawford, M. (2003) *Women and Gender: A Feminist Psychology*, New York: McGraw-Hill Education.

F

Field dependence

Field dependence refers to the extent to which any individual's **perceptions** are influenced by the background environment (field) and environmental cues. One particular field dependence test involves asking a participant to place a rod vertically within a tilted frame. Field-dependent individuals display a tendency to place the rod towards the tilting orientation of the frame, more so than non-field-dependent (**field independent**) individuals.

See **ambiguous figures, field independence, perception.**

Field independence

Field-independent individuals have the capacity to make correct judgements even when background or environmental cues may mislead. Field-independent individuals are more likely than field-dependent individuals to find embedded figures, as in the Schroder staircase.

See **ambiguous figures.**

www.cs.brown.edu/~deus/courses/optical/Reversible2.htm (information about the Schroder staircase from Brown University, Providence, United States).

Fieldwork

Fieldwork is **research** that is undertaken in natural settings, such as in school, in the streets or in a particular culture or society. While experimental designs can be applied to fieldwork, it is traditionally associated with **ethnographic** research methods that focus on collecting **data** by the use of **observational** methods. However, many methods can be used in fieldwork, including participant **observation**, unstructured interviews and documentary methods to build up a **case study**.

See **case study, data, ethnography, observation, research.**

De Laine, M. (2000) *Fieldwork, Participation and Practice: Ethics and Dilemmas in Qualitative Research*, London: Sage.
Lynd, H. M. (1945) *Field work in College Education*. Morningside: Columbia University Press.

F

Fight–flight response

The flight or fight response refers to the ways in which individuals or organisms respond when preparing to meet a perceived threat or danger. Any situation that creates fear, anger or pain or evokes the release of stress hormones such as catecholomines and adrenalin, that diverts blood to all the major organs of the body. This creates a range of physiological **responses**, such as increased blood pressure, quickened pulse and heart rate, increased sweating and dilated pupils. Such physiological changes are seen to prepare the body to be able to fight (address the threat or danger) or take flight (flee from the threat or danger). The flight or fight response can therefore be seen as an innate self-protection mechanism that enables individuals to address perceived threat or danger.

See anxiety, defence mechanism, response.

Figure-ground illusion

Another term for **ambiguous figures**.

See ambiguous figures, Muller–Lyer illusion, field dependence, field independence, object recognition, pattern recognition, perception.

Filter model of selective attention

See Broadbent.

Five-factor model of personality

Over the last several years, many theorists have suggested that there are five major **personality traits**, although their opinions of what these five factors are have differed. Following on from **Cattell's** 16PF rating scales in determining an individual's **personality traits**, Norman (1963) used small groups of students to rate each other according to **Cattell's** rating scale. Norman found that individuals have a tendency to rate each other according to five major factors, these being:

* extroversion
* agreeableness
* conscientiousness
* emotional stability
* culture.

Further studies, such as Digman (1990), Costa and Macrae (1980) have corroborated Norman's findings.

See Cattell, Erikson's psychosocial development stages, Eysenck personality questionnaire, Freud, personality, trait theories of personality.

Costa, P. T. and Macrae, R. R. (1980) Influence of extraversion and neuroticism on subjective wellbeing: happy and unhappy people. *Journal of Personality and Social Psychology*, 38, 668–78.

F

Digman, J. M. (1990) Personality structure: emergence of the five-factor model. *Annual Review of Psychology*, 41, 417–40.
Norman, W. T. (1963) Toward an adequate taxonomy of personality attributes: replicated factor structure in peer nomination personality ratings. *Journal of Abnormal and Social Psychology*, 66, 574–83.

Fixation

There are two main uses of the term fixation in psychology. These are:

- Visual fixation: this refers to the act or process of focusing the eye upon an object.
- **Psychoanalytical** fixation: when an individual remains fixed within a particular earlier **psychosexual stage** of development. The individual continues to gain pleasure from fixating upon a particular object or organ, specifically related to a stage that precedes the **genital stage**, such as the **oral, anal** or **phallic stage**.

  See **anal stage, Freud, genital stage, oral stage, phallic stage, psychoanalysis, psychosexual stages, perception.**

Flashbulb memory

See **memory.**

Flooding

Flooding is a therapy technique used in behaviour therapies. It can be used to treat disorders such as **phobias**, post-traumatic stress disorders and other **anxiety** disorders by exposing an individual excessively to the **anxiety** provoking **stimulus** or situation. It is based on **desensitization**: the more contact the individual has with the **anxiety**-provoking **stimulus**, the greater the reduction in the **anxiety** and stress **response**.

> *See* **anxiety, aversion therapy, behaviourism, classical conditioning, desensitisation, operant conditioning, phobia, reinforcement, response, stimulus.**

F

Forensic psychology

Forensic psychology is a branch of psychology that focuses upon the psychological aspects of legal processes in courts. The term can also refer to investigative and criminological psychology that applies psychological theory to enhance criminal investigation and understand psychological problems relating to criminal behaviour. Forensic psychologists' work can be diverse and can involve the design of treatment programmes, the modifying of offender behaviour, identifying the needs of staff and prisoners, undertaking research studies to support practice, offering evidence in court and advising parole boards and mental health tribunals.

The largest group of forensic psychologists in the United Kingdom work within HM Prison Service. Forensic psychologists can also be employed however, within health services such as rehabilitation units and secure hospitals, the social services, the police service, young offenders units and the probation service, and in university departments or in private consultancy (adapted from British Psychological Society career guidelines, 2004, www.bps.org.uk).

To become accredited as a forensic psychologist you would need to have an undergraduate degree in psychology, or to have taken a postgraduate conversion course if your first degree is in another area. It is usual also to have gained some work experience in a relevant setting, such as healthcare or social services. You would then need to undertake an accredited course for an MSc in forensic psychology. Following two years practice, under the supervision of a forensic psychologist you can then become accredited as a chartered forensic psychologist.

Adler, J. (2004) *Forensic Psychology: Concepts, Debates and Practice*. Cullompton, Devon: Willan Publishing.

http://www.bps.org.uk/bps/careers/accredited-courses/accredited-courses_home.cfm? (details of courses in forensic psychology).

Formal operational stage

In **Piaget's theory of cognitive development**, children are viewed as undergoing the formal operational stage at approximately 11 years of age. In this stage, cognitive changes in thought processing enable children to progress to being able to undertake abstract, systematic cognitive functioning, such as solving complex mathematical equations and other problems. Children's cognitive abilities are now so developed that they can now manipulate ideas in their heads; they can now explore hypothetical problems that they have never encountered before.

See **accommodation, assimilation, conservation, egocentrism, Piaget's theory of cognitive development**.

Free association

Free association is a technique used within **psychoanalysis** that involves clients relaying any thoughts, feelings, experiences, wishes, images and memories that spring to mind, no matter how trivial or embarrassing they may be. Free association is designed to reflect the internal dynamic conflicts that arise within an individual's unconscious mind between the innate **instinctual** urges of the **id** and the punitive moral restrictions of the **superego**. **Psychoanalysis**, as **Freud** (1924) suggests, enables an individual to bring unconscious conflict into a client's conscious thoughts so that conflict can be resolved.

> See **defence mechanism, ego, Freud, id, instinct, psychoanalysis, psychosexual stages, superego.**

> Appignanesi, R. and Zarate, O. (2003) *Freud For Beginners*, New York: Pantheon.
> Freud, S. (1924) *A General Introduction to Psychoanalysis.* New York: Washington Square Press.

Free will versus determinism

Free will perspectives within psychology assume that human beings are able to make autonomous and active choices about how they wish to behave. The concept of free will suggests that it is an individual's intention that is the underlying **motivation** in undertaking actions and behaviours. Behaviours are therefore not seen as mere **responses** to causes and external or internal **stimuli**. This notion of free will, which is categorized in psychological perspectives such as **humanism** and **existentialism**, sits in direct contrast to the idea of **determinism**. The latter views human behaviour as being beyond an individual's control and is supported in traditional scientific, behaviourist approaches as well as in psychodynamic theories. Depending on the perspective, deterministic approaches view behaviour as being 'caused' and elicited by:

F

- Environmental **determinism**: behaviourist approaches particularly view behaviour as being a product of social environmental learning that occurs through **reinforcement** and **conditioning**.
- Biological or genetic determinism: approaches such as psychodynamic theory and **nativism** view behaviour as being 'caused' by internal and genetic **traits** and factors. In these approaches, theorists view behaviour as a product of **instinctual** needs and unconscious processes.

In contrast the humanist school adopts a free will approach which views human beings as being free to design and develop their own futures and destinies. Individuals are represented as growing and developing throughout life, with each individual being uniquely responsible for his or her own behaviour.

> *See* **classical conditioning, determinism, existentialism, humanistic psychology, humanistic psychology, instinct, motivation, nativism, reinforcement, response, Rogers, self-actualization theory, stimulus, trait theories of personality.**

> Honderich, T. (2002) *How Free Are You? The Determinism Problem*. Oxford: Oxford University Press.
> Watson, G. (2003) *Free Will (Oxford Readings in Philosophy)*. Oxford: Oxford University Press.

Freud

Freud, Sigmund (1856–1939), developed the psychodynamic model of explaining the underlying causes and **motivating** factors of human behaviour. He developed his theory in the later part of the nineteenth century through his clinical work with mentally disordered patients. In his 'introductory lectures on **psychoanalysis**' (1915–1918), Freud suggested that individuals developed mental problems arising from the dynamics and conflicts engaged within the psyche, as opposed to physical, biological malfunctioning. He suggested that individuals are born with innate, **instinctual** urges and desires; this he claimed formed the **id** part of human **personality**. He viewed individuals as being socialized according to the moral codes of the culture that they existed within, which formed the punitive **superego** of an individual's psyche. Freud viewed these two parts of the human psyche as being in direct conflict, which he suggested needed constant regulation, monitoring and resolution by the **ego**. He suggested that a well-adjusted individual would have a well-adjusted **ego** that would be able to resolve any conflict that arose between the **id** and **superego**. Freud argued that psychological disturbance and disorders would occur through the inability of the **ego** to resolve conflicts arising between the **id** and the **superego**.

F

> *See* **dream analysis, ego, free association, id, instinct, motivation, psychoanalysis, psychosexual stages, superego.**

> Freud, S. (1917) Introductory lectures on psychoanalysis. In J. Strachey (ed.), *The Complete Psychological Works*, vol. 16. New York: Norton.
> www.freud.org.uk/ (Freud Museum).

Freudian slip

A Freudian slip can be defined within **psychoanalytic** theory as a verbal utterance that an individual is not consciously aware of until it has been spoken. It is also known as a slip of the tongue, something the individual had not consciously intended to say. It is suggested that such 'slips' represent the unconscious desires, urges, wishes and wants of the **id**. These desires and wants are usually repressed by the **ego**, which attempts to resolve the conflict that arises as it negotiates between the wants of the **id** and the moral disapproval of the **superego**.

See **ego, id, psychoanalysis, superego**.

Friedman test

A Friedman test is a multi-level, **non-parametric test** that is used when researchers are testing for differences in more than two **sample** designs and the **data** is **ordinal**. The test is used when the **data** are related, for example, coming from the **sample** of six participants but taken in three conditions.

See **data, non-parametric tests, ordinal measurements, sample**.

Coolican, H. (2004) *Research Methods and Statistics*, 4th edn. Bristol: Hodder and Stoughton.

Frustration–aggression hypothesis

The frustration–aggression hypothesis was suggested by Dollard et al. in 1939. Aggression was explained as the consequence of an individual's goals, needs or wants being 'unfulfilled', or restricted in some way. This they suggested creates and leads to frustration, which in turn produces aggression. This determines that an act of aggression is always seen to be a product of frustration.

Dollard et al. (1939) suggested that the resulting aggression is not always directed at the event or object creating or causing the frustration, as sometimes frustration can be displaced on to something else. The 'cue arousal theory' suggests that the expression of aggression, as a consequence of a frustrating event, depends upon the situation and environmental conditions (cues the individuals is situated within).

In explaining aggression, the cue arousal theory determines that aggression will only be experienced in response to a frustrating event if the individual feels the anger is appropriate or justified in some way, or that there are environmental conditions in which the individual has been **classically conditioned** to experience anger.

F

For example, an individual misses an important interview when the flight to Birmingham is delayed because of safety precautions. The frustrating events create aggression, but the individual (feeling aggression towards the event is inappropriate within the situation) directs and expresses the aggression towards him or herself, for not getting an earlier flight. The aggression is therefore not a product of the frustrating event; rather it is self directed. The individual feels that under the circumstances expressing aggression towards the people who created the frustrating event is not justified, as they were taking actions to protect his or her safety.

See **classical conditioning, social learning theory, social psychology.**

Dollard, J., Doob, LW., Miller, N. E., Mowrer, O. H. and Seers. R. R. (1939) *Frustration and Aggression.* New Haven, CT: Yale University Press.

Functional analysis of behaviour

This refers to the application of the laws of learning theories, usually Skinnerian **operant conditioning**, to analyse and establish the relationships between **stimulus** and **reinforcement** in determining and eliciting behaviour. This particular method is used within behaviour therapy to examine the **variables** that determine an individual's behaviour patterns, so that change can be promoted.

See **classical conditioning, operant conditioning, reinforcement, stimulus, variables.**

Fundamental attribution error (FAE)

The FAE, a concept within **attribution** theories explains how individuals have the tendency to overestimate the effect of **situational attributions** (time, weather) on their own behaviour, yet overestimate the effects of **dispositional attributions** (**personality**, characteristics, **traits**) on the behaviour of other individuals or groups. The reasons for this has been explained by the cognitive miser effect, in that individuals, unless alerted to **situational** factors, will emphasize an individual's **dispositional** factors when accounting for a particular behaviour, if they are satisfied that such factors offer adequate explanation. An individual, in acting as a cognitive miser, has no need to make things more complex by considering other possible information or explanations.

See **attribution, attributional biases, balance theory, cognitive dissonance, dispositional attribution, personality, situational attribution, trait theories of personality.**

Gg

Gain and loss theory of attraction

The gain and loss theory of attraction suggested by Aronson and Linder (1965) argues that individuals will become more attracted to other people when the latter's liking for them appears to have increased. Similarly an individual's attraction to another will decrease if he or she believes the other has come to like him or her less. Aronson and Linder conducted an experiment in which students overheard a fellow student discussing them, either entirely positively or entirely negatively. The conversation might either begin with negative comments and become more positive (gain) or conversely begin with positive comments and become more negative (loss). Later the students who had been talked about were asked how much they liked the fellow student; the findings revealed that students liked their fellow student more in the gain situation than the loss situation.

See **attraction theories, equity theory, exchange theory, relationship theories.**

Aronson, E. and Linder, D. (1965). Gain and loss of esteem as determinants of interpersonal attractiveness. *Journal of Experimental Social Psychology*, 1, 156–71.

Game theory

Game theory is concerned with the mathematical study of formal games that involve interactive decision making. Such games can take place in any social interaction where there are two or more players and where the outcomes depend on the strategies of the players, with each strategy having alternative payoffs and costs for each of the players. Game theory has been used within **experimental psychology** to study human behaviour such as individual and collective decision making, co-operation, conflict and competition, trust and suspicion, threats and commitment.

The prisoner's dilemma (Axelrod 1984) is a prime example of an interactive decision-making game, in which participants collectively and individually need to achieve a decision that is based on perceived costs and payoffs. It represents a social dilemma through which participants must reach a strategic decision.

> See **Asch, balance theory, conformity, experimental psychology, maximizing (game theory), social psychology.**

> Axelrod, R. (1984) *The Evolution of Cooperation*. New York: Basic books.
> Rapoport, A. and Chammah, A. M. (1965). *Prisoner's Dilemma*. Ann Arbor, MI: University of Michigan Press (an account of many experiments in which the psychological game Prisoner's Dilemma was played).

Gender bias

Gender bias refers to the assumptions that are made about the differences between the sexes. There are many different views of gender and forms of gender bias. For example:

* Alpha bias theories infer that there are actual and real differences between men and women. Studies such as Chodorow's (1978) use such theories to emphasize the value of women in terms of being more relational and caring. However, such theories can also be used to devalue women. Within psychodynamic theories, differences between men and women can be attributed to **genetic determinism** and so male dominance and sexual promiscuity may be viewed as a product of evolutionary adaptation.
* **Beta bias** theories ignore or deny any differences between men and women. Studies based on such views have failed to raise questions about the lives of women, or have assumed that findings from studies of men can apply just as validly to the lives and behaviour of women. Such studies, which **generalize** findings based on the views of what is only one half of the human race to the whole of the population, can be viewed as leading to an androcentric view of the world and individual behaviour.
* Androcentric theories, like **beta bias** theories, offer an understanding of women's lives and behaviour that stems from an understanding of men's lives and behaviour. Such a view leads to ideals of feminine norms of behaviour that are based on male behavioural norms, this can lead to many feminine behaviours being viewed as 'abnormal' or deficient.
* Gendocentric views assume that men and women's development will take entirely different paths. Such theories can be

G

seen as assuming an alpha bias, as they depict real differences between men and women.

• **Ethnocentric** theories view human development as being the same throughout different cultures and races. Such theories are usually dominated by Westernized, Anglo-European viewpoints, which specify and lead to 'normal' patterns of family structures and functioning and define 'appropriate' social roles for men and women. Such a theory does not take into account different social practices, cultural beliefs and sociocultural influences on human development. **Ethnocentric** theories can be regarded as adopting an **individualistic**, Westernized view of the world on understanding human development, whereas many non-Western countries such as China and Africa adopt collectivist social practices.

• Heterosexist theories of human development have a tendency to view heterosexual orientation as being 'normal', therefore representing orientation to same sex partners as being abnormal.

See **androgynous, beta bias, ethnocentrism, generalization, genetic determinism, individualism.**

Chodorow, N. (1978) *The Reproduction of Mothering*. Berkeley, CA: University of California Press.

Gender development

Gender development refers to the ways in which an individual acquires an understanding of what it is to be male or female. There are many theories of how gender is acquired, with quite contrasting viewpoints as to the 'fixed' or 'free' nature of gender. The acquisition of 'gender' is often debated within the **nature–nurture debate**. Theorists from a **biopsychological** viewpoint argue that gender is something we 'are' (male or female determined by our physical/genetic attributes), which contrasts with **social construc-tionists'** claims that 'gender' is something we 'do' (masculine and feminine **traits** are something we learn via social interaction and processes). Theories of gender development include:

• *Social learning theories*
  This approach views children's acquisition of gendered behaviour as being learnt through:
  * Modelling, in which children imitate the behaviour of other individuals of the same sex. Boys may imitate dad doing DIY

or playing football, and girls may imitate mum putting on cosmetics or dressing up. As Buckingham (2003) discusses, children are also subject to the numerous images in the media – TV, books, comics and so on – which can also shape the way in which girls and boys expect to behave. Girls who like a particular popular brand of doll may love the colour pink and want to wear pink clothes. Boys who like action characters may be interested in 'action and combat' games. As such children can be seen as acquiring gender-appropriate behaviours through imitation.

- Direct **reinforcement**: through the use of reward and punishment children can come to understand gender-appropriate and inappropriate behaviour. Parents may comment on how pretty their daughter looks in a new dress, and in doing so encourage feminine behaviours. Similarly parents may discourage their son from wearing pink clothing, saying he looks 'girly' and so discourage feminine behaviour while encouraging masculine behaviour. Gender-appropriate behaviour can therefore be encouraged or discouraged by teasing and praising.

- Indirect **reinforcement**: gender-appropriate behaviour can also be reinforced through observing how other individuals are treated and praised. The media is a very powerful agent in reinforcing how children's behaviour is shaped. TV programmes that feed into **stereotypical** gendered behaviour, in which praise is elicited to 'pretty girls' or 'strong boys', only serve to perpetuate gender specific behaviour expectations and reinforce traditional gender roles.

- *Cognitive development theories*
  Cognitive theories focus upon gender development and how children's thinking capabilities change as they get older:
  - **Kohlberg's** stage theory of gender identity (1966) proposed that a child's understanding of gender changes as the child's thinking capabilities mature. **Kohlberg** viewed children as acquiring gender concepts and understandings (of what it means to be male/female) only when they have reached a particular age and are ready to acquire the knowledge. He suggested that when children are ready they will seek out members of the same sex and gather information that will help them to make decisions about gender-appropriate behaviour.
  - The gender **schema** theory, proposed by Martin and

Halverson (1983), takes a slightly different view from **Kohlberg**. Martin and Halverson suggest that gender **schemas** (knowledge of what it is to be male/female) begin to form as soon as children notice a difference between men and women, not as **Kohlberg** suggests, when a child reaches a particular stage or age. Children, according to this theory acquire **schemas** – clusters of conceptual knowledge about gender-appropriate behaviour – and this helps them to organize and interpret their own gender role and behaviour.

- *Biological theories*
  These theories view gender as being determined by biological, innate, fixed factors and not influenced or acquired via social, cultural, environmental or any external causes:
  - **Freud**'s psychodynamic theory, which focuses upon the **psychosexual stages** of gender development, suggests that gender as the whole of an individual's **personality** is related to innate, biological drives, which interact with the environment. **Freud** viewed gender identity as occurring through an individual's **identification** with his or her same-sex parent during the **phallic stage**. **Freud's** theory is often criticized as it is based upon the traditional nuclear family of a child living with two different-sex parents and purports to enable children to resolve the conflicts experienced within the **Oedipus** and **Electra complexes**, to associate with the same sex parent and allow gender **identification** to occur. **Freud**'s theory does not consider how children in single-parent or same-sex-parent families resolve such conflicts and undergo gender **identification**.

- *The evolutionary account*
  This theory proposes that any individual's gendered behaviour is determined through the degree of successful **adaptation** it makes to the environment. Any gender behaviour that promotes survival and reproduction will be retained and such behaviours passed down to the next generation. Such accounts attempt to explain the gender behaviours of females who wish to stay at home to care for children, and men who go to work, by explaining this in terms of acquiring gender roles that serve to promote the survival of their offspring.

G

See **adaptation, biopsychology, Electra complex, Freud, identification, Kohlberg, nature–nurture debate, Oedipus complex, personality, phallic stage,** psychosexual stages, reinforcement, schemas, social constructionism, stereotyping, trait theories of personality

Buckingham, D. (2003) Multimedia childhoods. In M. J. Kehily and J. Swann (eds), *Children's Cultural Worlds*. Milton Keynes: Open University Press and John Wiley.

Kohlberg, L. (1966) A cognitive development analysis of children's sex role concepts and attitudes. In E. E. Macoby (ed.), *The Development of Sex Differences*. Stanford, CA: Stanford University Press.

Martin, C. and Halverson, C. (1983) Gender constancy: a methodological and theoretical analysis. *Sex roles*, 9, 775–90.

Stainton Rogers, W. and Stainton Rogers, R. (2001) *The Psychology of Gender and Sexuality*. Milton Keynes: Open University Press.

Gene

A gene is a part of a **chromosome** that codes for a particular protein, which in turn determines a particular trait, such as hair colour or sex.

See **chromosome, genotype, phenotype.**

Generalization

A generalization is a statement about 'something' that can usually be universally applied to all members of society or members of a group. A faulty generalization is said to occur when we universally apply that statement to all members of the group after speaking to or observing only a few members of that population. For example, a researcher conducts a study to determine whether the UK population 'generally' watches a particular TV show. The study's findings suggest that the population, based on the participants' answers, 'generally' do watch the show. However only four people were interviewed; it would be impossible to generalize on the basis of such a limited **sample**.

See **attribution, fundamental attribution error, sampling.**

G

Genetic determinism

This refers to the belief that genetic factors are responsible for an organism's development. This theory is often critiqued when attempting to explain human behaviour, as it fails to acknowledge human agency, autonomy, action, **free will** and the impact of social, cultural and environmental factors upon human behaviour. The suggestion that human development is determined and regulated solely by genetic influences is also a major element that underpins evolutionary explanations of human behaviour.

See **free will versus determinism, theory of evolution, Darwinism, nativism, biological model of abnormality, biopsychology, biopsychosocial model.**

Genital stage

In **Freud**'s stage theory of **psychosexual development, Freud** suggested that individuals undergo development through childhood, in which particular **psychosexual** conflicts must be resolved, to ensure a well-adjusted individual. Within the genital stage, conflicts arise through the interaction of the driving, **instinctual** force (pleasure), **personality** structure (**id**) and the organ focus (genitals). The source of pleasure in this genital stage (as you may have guessed) is focused upon the genital organs, and the focus is on the development of human independence. If conflicts are not resolved at this stage, **Freud** suggested that individuals would be unable to transfer focus from their immediate needs to their larger responsibilities towards others.

See **Freud, id, instinct, personality, psychosexual stages.**

Genotype

A genotype is an organism's genetic composition, the genetically coded, inheritable information carried by all living organisms. This information is copied at the time of reproduction and is passed down from one generation to the next. The genotype is used as a blueprint, a set of instructions for developing and maintaining a living organism.

See **phenotype.**

G

Gestalt psychology

Gestalt psychology is a school of psychology that is concerned predominantly with the Gestalt phenomena of **perceptions**. Gestalt refers to how perceptual structures or configurations cannot be perceived on the basis on their parts or elements alone, but in relation to how an individual subjectively experiences those parts. For example, a sequence of notes, C, D, E, C, C, D, E played on a piano will be quickly recognized as *Frère Jacques*, yet when the notes are changed to F, G, A, F, F, G, A, it is still recognizable as the same tune.

The parts are different but the **subjective perception** is still the same. Gestalt psychology was founded by Wolfgang von Goethe (1749–1832), Mach (1838–1916) and von Ehrenfels (1859–1932), but the dominance of the school emerged in 1912 with the psychologist Wertheimer (1880–1943). The main assumptions of Gestalt psychology are the absolute importance of **subjective** experience within psychology, and the rejection of elementalism.

See **grouping, perception, subjectivity.**

Albertazzi, L. (1999) *Shapes of Forms: From Gestalt Psychology and Phemenonology to Ontology and Mathematics.* Boston, MA: Kluwer Academic Publishers.

Goodness of fit

This refers to the degree of agreement between actual observed **data** points, and the expected hypothesized frequencies, as measured by such tests such as the **chi-square.**

See **data, chi-square.**

Gould's theory of adult development

There are numerous stage theories of human development. Many, such as **Piaget**'s and **Freud**'s, focus on stages that begin and end in childhood. Gould (1978) suggested that humans develop and move from childhood into adult **consciousness** through resolving and confronting four major false emotional assumptions (Table 3). These assumptions provide illusions of security and safety from **anxiety** in an individual, but facing up to such assumptions can be painful and difficult.

By the time individuals reach the age of 50, Gould suggested, they should have rejected such illusions and attained autonomy: a sense of 'me', that an individual finally owns 'myself'. Gould ultimately viewed adult development as finally realizing that we are alone, are the creators of our lives, and are not constrained by the false assumptions held in earlier life. In contrast, theorists such as Cumming and Henry (1961) have suggested a 'disengagement theory' in which, as individuals grow old, changes in social roles and lifestyle factors (such as mobility issues or lack of money) lead to decreased social interaction, causing them to become more isolated and to 'disengage'. In this theory social factors are seen as a major factor in how individuals behave as they go through **adulthood** and enter old age.

G

Table 3 False assumptions to be dealt with through adulthood

Age: Late teens to early 20s
I will always belong to my parents and believe in their world.
It will be a disaster if I become any more independent.
I can only view the world through my parents' assumptions.
Only my parents can guarantee safety.
They must be my only family.
I don't own my body.

Age: 20s
Doing it my parents' way with willpower and perseverance will probably bring results. But when I am too frustrated, confused or unable to cope, my parents will step in and help me.
Rewards will come automatically if we do what we are supposed to do.
There is only one right way to do things.
My loved ones will do for me what I am unable to do.
Rationality, commitment and effort will always prevail over other forces.

Age: late 20s to early 30s
Life is simple and controllable. There are no significant co-existing contradictory forces within me.
What I know intellectually, I know emotionally.
I am not like my parents in ways I don't want to be. I can see the reality of those close to me.
Threats to my security aren't real.

Age: mid-30s to 50s
There is no evil in me or death in the world. The sinister has been expelled.
My work (for men) or my relationship (for women) grants me immunity from death and danger.
There is no life beyond this family.
I am innocent.

Source: Gould, R. L. (1978) *Transformations: Growth and change in adult life*, New York: Simon and Schuster.

> See **adulthood, anxiety, consciousness, Erikson's psychosocial development stages, Freud, Levinson's seasons of a man's life, Piaget's theory of cognitive development.**
>
> Cumming, E. and Henry, W. H. (1961) *Growing Old.* New York: Basic Books.

G

Grouping

Grouping refers to any of the four laws developed by **Gestalt** psychologist Wertheimer (1880–1943) to attempt to explain how parts or elements of a structure are organized into whole structures by the visual system. This is also known as a **Gestalt** principle of organization.

See **Gestalt psychology.**

Group dynamics

Group dynamics are concerned with the interactions and relationships that are experienced within groups and between individuals. These include interactions such as **in-group** and out-group behaviour, hostility, leader–follower relations, relationship formation and group decision making. Social psychologists studying group dynamics have particularly focused upon group belonging: how people get on together, how people interact and how individuals and teams can work together.

See **in-group.**

G

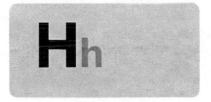

Habit

A habit is a persistent behavioural pattern that is learnt through repeated performance and experience. A habit becomes an almost automatic **response** to an object or situation. Examples of habits are the desire to indulge in particular drugs, such as alcohol, nicotine or cannabis, which satisfy a psychological craving through binge drinking or chain smoking. There are many theories that attempt to explain why individuals acquire habits:

- **Behaviourist** and learning theorists perceive habits as a type of conditioned behavioural **response**, in which **behavioural responses** are elicited via **reinforcement** (the reward or experiences that follow the habit). Once the habit is firmly learnt, it can become difficult to eradicate and change, as it is associated with self-rewarding. An example is having a few glasses of wine after a hard day's work.
- Psychodynamic theorists suggest that habits are expressions of repressed impulses or desires. For example a person who lacks confidence may develop a habit for drug use, using it to compensate for his or her low **self-esteem** and confidence.

See **addiction, behaviourism, reinforcement, response, self-esteem.**

Habituation

Habituation refers to the process of becoming used to something, in particular developing a mild form of tolerance for a particular object, event or action, for example, the effects of alcohol or drugs. Habituation is seen to occur through the reduction in the experienced strength or frequency of an **unconditioned response** (feeling drunk, inhibited, relaxed) by repeated exposure to a specific **stimulus** (alcohol).

See **addiction, stimulus, unconditioned response.**

Hallucination

Hallucination is the **perception** of objects, events or 'things' that do not exist in reality. There are many types of hallucinations that can involve the individual perceiving non-existent objects, people, events and colours. These include:

- Tactile hallucinations: these involve experiencing feelings or sensations such as a tingling on the skin, or even feeling as if something is tickling or crawling over you.
- Somatic hallucinations: these involve an individual experiencing internal sensations, as if something were happening within his or her body. The person may feel, for example, that something is moving or wriggling within his or her stomach.
- Auditory hallucinations: these involve an individual hearing 'things', as in **schizophrenia** an individual may hear voices.
- Olfactory hallucinations: these involve an individual smelling particular odours that nobody else can smell, such as burning.

See **abnormal psychology, depression, perception, schizophrenia.**

Hassles and uplifts

Psychologists such as Kanner et al. (1981) suggest that factors such as financial worries, relationship issues, housing concerns and the daily 'hassles' of an individual's life can cause stress. Studies have attempted to examine the impact of such 'hassles' on an individual's well-being by asking participants to complete a 'hassles scale' that attempts to reflect the extent to which they have experienced 'hassles' in the last month.

Findings revealed that the more daily hassles an individual experienced, the greater the stress and the less psychological well-being they experienced. The positive things that happened to individuals, the 'uplifts', did appear to exert a greater effect upon women's well-being, but research on the effect on men's well-being has been inconclusive.

- Common hassles include:
  - weight concerns
  - concerns about the health of a family member
  - home maintenance
  - taxes, savings and property
  - crime.
- Common uplifts include:
  - having a good relationship with a partner

- having good relationships with friends
- finishing work tasks
- feeling fit and healthy
- sleeping well.

Kanner, A. D. (1981) Comparison of two modes of stress measurement: daily hassles and uplift versus major life events, *Journal of Behavioural Measurement*, 4, 1–39.

Hawthorne effect

The Hawthorne effect refers to the improvement in performance of workers when any new method of working is introduced. It is named after the Hawthorne Western electrical plant in which the effect was first observed and studies carried out. The improvement in performance is not caused by the actual changes implemented in the method or approach, but is due to the individuals responding to change with an initial, enthusiastic reaction. The workers simply feel more positive about their work as they feel their employers are interested in them and so respond positively.

In Roethlisberger and Dickson's (1939) study, changes in factory lighting were made as women workers inspected parts, wound coils and undertook various other tasks. Findings revealed that introducing lighting conditions that were considered likely to impede work progress was in fact found to improve productivity. The reason was regarded to be the Hawthorne effect.

In **research** nowadays, the Hawthorne effect is referred to when the behaviour of a participant in a study could be interpreted as being affected or altered in some way by simply knowing that they are being observed.

See **primacy effect, recency effect, research.**

Roethlisberger, F. J. and Dickson, W. J. (1939) *Management and the Worker*. Cambridge, MA: Harvard University Press.

H

Health belief model

The health belief model refers to an individual's willingness to change any behaviour (such as smoking or overeating) that could potentially create a health risk or a need to seek medical guidance. An individual's willingness is seen to depend upon two conditions:

- the degree to which the individual believes that changing such behaviour or seeking medical help will reduce the health risk

- the degree to which the individual believes the behaviour is actually posing a threat to his or her health.

This model provides an explanation of why certain groups of people frequently indulge in certain health-risk behaviours, for example why younger people are more likely to engage in more risk-taking behaviours such as extreme sports and taking drugs. The model suggests it is because they do not believe that avoiding these actions will lower their susceptibility to illness, as they do not perceive danger and do not feel a need to change their behaviour.

Older people often do not feel the need to change behaviours such as smoking because at their stage in life they do not believe that changing this behaviour will significantly reduce their susceptibility to illness or noticeably improve their well-being and health.

Health psychology

Health psychology is a branch of **applied psychology** that uses psychological principles to promote change in people's **attitudes**, behaviour, thinking about health and illness and health care provisions. Health psychologists apply the use of psychological theories and interventions to:

- prevent damaging behaviours such as smoking and drug abuse
- promote and protect health by encouraging behaviours such as exercise, healthy dietary choice, brushing teeth and having regular health checks
- understand health-related cognitions by investigating the processes that can explain, predict and change health and illness behaviours.
- understand the processes that underpin and influence health care delivery
- examine the psychological aspects of illness and how psychological interventions may be used to promote self-management, facilitate coping with pain or illness, and to improve people's quality of life.

Health psychologists are employed in a number of settings, such as hospitals, academic health research units, health authorities and university departments (adapted from the British Psychological Society, 2004 career pages, www.bps.org.uk).

To become accredited as a health psychologist requires an undergraduate degree in psychology or a psychology conversion course that confers Graduate Basis for Registration (GBR) with the British

Psychological Society (BPS). To become a qualified health psycholo gist requires completion of two stages. Stage one is usually the completion of a BPS-recognized MSc in health psychology. It is also usual to have gained relevant work experience in a healthcare setting. Stage two consists of two years of supervised practice in an area relevant to health psychology under the guidance of a chartered health psychologist; this will lead to eligibility for chartered health psychology status.

See **applied psychology, attitude.**

www.bps.org.uk/careers/areas/health.cfm#01 (a list of accredited courses).

Heritability

Heritability refers to the proportion of any observed individual's phenotypic behaviours or characteristic variation that can be attributed to genetic variation. For example, when studying a group of weaning pups, one would expect a variation in weaning weights, due to environmental factors such as the amount of milk available, the number of pups produced and placement to the mother. However a proportion of the observed variation would be due to genotypic variation (genetic characteristics) inherited from their parents' **genes**. These characteristics would enhance or impede the pups' 'natural', innate ability to feed or gain/lose weight through their innate metabolic rates. Studies have shown that **traits** with low heritability are influenced more by environmental factors than genetic influence, and conversely, high heritability is influenced more by genetic, innate factors. Hence, the level of heritability will depend on both the **variance** of the environment and the **variance** of the **genes**; both can differ from one generation to the next, within the same species.

See **gene, variance, trait theories of personality.**

H

Heuristics

This is a method of solving a problem or making a decision or judgement without being sure that a correct answer or decision will be achieved. Individuals use heuristics when they are unable to explore all available information and options, and need to use alternative procedures to reach a rational decision. Heuristics are 'rules of thumb' that simplify thinking and make judgements and inferences easier by stripping away the complexity from persons, objects and events. We abstract from diverse instances a heuristic for deal-ing with similar situations and persons, for example to know what to do at a funeral or how to react when a car salesman tells us the price of a car. Using heuristics means that we do not have to start from scratch!

Kahneman and Tversky (1973) introduced heuristics into psychol-ogy, identifying heuristics such as **anchoring**, availability, similarity and representiveness heuristics.

- *Simulation heuristics:* when making predictions, we often use the simulation heuristic; we make judgments about what might happen in a situation by playing out a simulation in our heads. For example, suppose you have never thought that your partner might cheat on you, but now your best friend's partner has been found to be cheating. Now you may find yourself imagining how you would react in a similar situation. Simply imagining this event leads you to be more likely to believe that your partner could be unfaithful.

- *Availability heuristics:* this is another kind of inference, an esti-mate of probability. How often does a particular type of event happen? When making judgments of this type we often use the availability heuristic. How likely is it that the no. 10 bus will be on time? A common way people answer these questions about probability is to use examples that come to mind. People often use this shortcut when making judgments if they can think of an example easily. If the no. 10 bus is often late, then you are likely to judge it will not be on time.

- *Representativeness heuristics:* we use another kind of proba-bility estimate or judgment when inferring whether an indi-vidual belongs to a particular social group. We do this is by using a cognitive shortcut called the representativeness heuristic. For example, the person on your doorstep is wear-ing overalls, has a bucket and chamois leathers in hand and has a pair of ladders against the wall. What are you likely to guess? Window cleaner. How have you done this? Probably, by comparing him against typical members of a given group, a prototype. He simply fitted into the category or prototype of information we hold (based on existing knowledge) of what represents a window cleaner.

See **anchoring, social representations, Towers of Hanoi.**

Kahneman, D. and Tversky, A. (1973) On the psychology of prediction, *Psychological Review*, 80, 237–51.

Hippocampus

The hippocampus is located in the temporal lobe of the **brain** (under the temples). It forms part of the limbic system, the emotion system of the **brain**, and it is responsible for transferring information into **memory**. The hippocampus has been identified as being important in the production of new memories in the onset of mental illnesses, such as **schizophrenia** and severe **depression**.

See **brain, depression, schizophrenia.**

faculty.washington.edu/chudler/bipolar.html (information on the hippocampus and bipolar disorder).

Homeostasis

Cannon (1891–1945) first used the term homeostasis to refer to the maintenance of a state of balance within any physiological or psychological system or social process. All organisms contain a range of homeostatic mechanisms that serve to regulate and maintain balance within the bodily systems. They serve, for example to maintain blood sugar levels and oxygen levels, and to regulate toxins in the system. Homeostasis also initiates processes that can trigger or initiate behavioural drives, such as the desire to drink when thirsty, that re-establish the body's initial optimum condition.

Society also contains numerous homeostatic mechanisms, such as law, justice and welfare systems that attempt to regulate and establish optimal conditions for social justice and order.

Homogeneity of variance

This refers to the degree of similarity in **variance** between two or more **variables**; that is, the **variances** of the scores in each condition are roughly the same.

See **variables, variance.**

H

Humanistic psychology

Humanistic psychology is concerned with the subjective experience of human beings, and positions itself against the use of traditional scientific, objective, **quantitative** methods of investigation in understanding human behaviour and experience. Instead, the discipline stresses a view that is based on **phenomenology** and seeks to understand human beings and their behaviour by using **qualitative** research methods that can incorporate the **subjective** accounts and experience of individuals.

Among the founding theorists behind this school of thought are Maslow, who presented a **self-actualization theory**, and Rogers, who created and developed a client-centred therapy known as **Rogerian psychotherapy.**

See **existentialism, objectivity, phenomenology, qualitative measurements, quantitative measurements, Rogers, self-actualization theory, subjectivity.**

Schneider, K. (2003) *Handbook of Humanistic Psychology*. London: Sage. www.americanhumanist.org/index.html (American Humanist Association).

Hypno-analysis

This is a form of psychotherapy that is based on psychodynamic principles. It uses **hypnosis** to facilitate an individual in relaxing and gaining access to repressed thoughts, desires and experiences. This then enables repressed or blocked emotion to be released and psychodynamic conflict to be resolved.

See **hypnosis, hypnotherapy, therapy, psychoanalysis.**

www.hypnoanalysis.com/ (International Association of Hypno-analysts).

Hypnosis

Hypnosis is a facilitated or self-induced state of relaxation or meditation in which an individual experiences an altered state of awareness and **consciousness**. Individuals within hypnosis can experience alterations in **perceptions**, feelings or behaviours brought about by suggestion (statements about how they will feel during and following hypnosis).

See **consciousness, hypno-analysis, hypnotherapy, perception.**

Lambrou, P. T. and Alman, B. (2004) *Self-Hypnosis: The Complete Manual for Health and Self-Change*. London: Souvenir Press.

Hypnotherapy

Hypnotherapy is a form of **hypnosis** in which individuals are facilitated into a relaxed state of awareness. Techniques such as visualization, suggestion or/and **hypno-analysis** are used to help a client to resolve and address a number of specific concerns. Hypnotherapy attempts to achieve a therapeutic outcome by alleviating issues such as fears, **phobias**, **anxiety**, weight loss, stopping smoking and stress.

See **anxiety, hypno-analysis, hypnosis, phobia.**

Hypothesis

A hypothesis is a statement about what you believe is true, which can be tested, refuted or supported through empirical **research**. There are many different types of hypotheses:

- *One-tailed hypothesis:* this predicts a difference between findings of observed **variables** or populations in a specific direction. For example, that men will run a marathon quicker than women.
- *Null hypothesis:* that there is no difference between findings of observed **variables** or populations in any direction. Findings have not supported the **research** hypothesis as there is no reported change.
- *Two-tailed hypothesis:* this predicts that there will be a difference between findings of observed **variables** or populations in two possible directions. For example, men will be faster or slower than women in completing a marathon run.

See **just world hypothesis, research, variables.**

Hysteria

The term hysteria is used to refer to a type of mental disorder or behavioural outburst characterized by fainting and emotional outbursts, and where an individual appears to seek **attention**.

Two particular forms of hysteria are:

- Conversion hysteria: an individual experiencing this particular **neurosis** will suffer physical symptoms and sensations, such as paralysis, deafness and loss of feeling in areas of the body, that cannot be linked to any physical or biological causes.
- Dissociative hysteria: this is a particular form of hysteria in which an individual displays dissociative symptoms, such as withdrawing from social interaction and situations.

See **attention, neurosis.**

H

Iconic memory

See **memory.**

Id

In psychodynamic theory, suggested by **Freud**, the mind or human psyche consists of three parts: the id, **ego** and **superego**. It is the way that these three parts interact and conflict that **Freud** identified as creating the **motivation** and origins of human behaviour.

The id, **Freud** suggested, is the unconscious part of the mind that contains all **instinctual** and innate urges, drives and desires. It contains all forbidden wishes, urges and thoughts that have been repressed by the punitive moral **superego**.

See **ego, Freud, instinct, motivation, psychoanalysis, superego.**

Identification

In psychology there are many particular uses of the term identification. For example:

- In **cognitive psychology,** identification refers to the act or process by which an individual recognizes, perceives or distinguishes an object, event or person.
- In **social psychology,** it is the integration or adoption of another individual's ideas or actions within a person's own behaviour, through perceiving that person as being similar in some way. It is a type of **conformity**.
- In **psychoanalysis**, **Freud** suggested that the process of identification is an unconscious **defence mechanism**, by which an individual integrates the characteristics of another person into his or her own **personality**. This process, **Freud** argues, enables individuals to achieve needs that they are afraid of achieving themselves, through identifying with someone who has already achieved those needs.

● Where people face external threat by a figure of authority, they seek strength by identifying with the person they are afraid of. The individual attempts to reduce the threat by identifying with or adopting the attributes of the aggressor. This was evidenced within Nazi concentration camps in the way prisoners came to identify with the SS guards.

See **cognitive psychology, conformity, defence mechanism, Freud, personality, psychoanalysis, social psychology.**

Identity

Identity can be viewed as an individual's sense and understanding of 'self'. A knowledge of what makes us unique and individual is seen in various theories as being developed and furthered according to an individual's various experiences, roles and learning, engaged in within childhood, **adolescence** and **adulthood**.

See **adolescence, adulthood, Erikson's psychosocial development stages, Gould's theory of adult development.**

Idiographic psychology

Idiographic is a term used to define the study of individuals, and to stress the unique nature, attributes and characteristics of individuals. Ideographic psychology particularly focuses on the study of **personality** that strives not to identify or create universal, general laws or **personality traits**. Contrast idiographic with **nomothetic**.

See **nomothetic psychology, personality, trait theories of personality.**

Implicit learning

Implicit learning is learning or knowing something without having any conscious awareness or understanding of how, or why it was learned. An example is being able to recognize a familiar face without knowing anything else about it, whom it belongs to, or why you know the face.

Implicit personality theory

Implicit personality theories suggest that individuals make a series of assumptions, often unconsciously derived from their own experiences, about what kind of **personality traits** or characteristics, other individuals possess. For example, we may believe that artistic individuals tend to be unconventional, writers to be romantic and withdrawn, and librarians bookish and dowdy.

Such theories are regarded as 'implicit' because, even though these assumptions do affect and certainly influence our judgements and understandings of other people, they are not based on substance or any conscious awareness that these **traits** or characteristics actually exist.

> *See* **attribution, personality, social representations, stereotypes, trait theories of personality.**
>
> Bruner, J. and Taguiri, R. (1954). Person perception. In G. Lindzey (ed.), *Handbook of Social Psychology* (vol. 2). Reading, MA: Addison Wesley.

Imprinting

Imprinting is a form of learning that occurs in the early stages of an animal's life, usually occurring soon after birth. It leads to a firm and stable **attachment** being developed towards another animal (usually the mother) following birth. This **attachment** is difficult to change or alter through subsequent development and experience. Imprinting usually occurs in what is termed the 'sensitive period' of early development when young animals adopt the 'following **response**': they follow the imprinted object, the mother, and the **response** is innately determined. Just think of baby ducklings all following the mother.

This form of imprinting is known as 'filial imprinting'; when young animals have imprinted specific characteristics of the mother, they will only approach her, as opposed to other adults that could have the desire or potential to harm or kill.

Another form of imprinting is sexual imprinting, in which young animals learn the characteristics, such as colours or plumage of members of the opposite sex within their own species, which is crucial if they are to successfully reproduce.

> *See* **attachment, response.**

Independent variables (IV)

> *See* **variables.**

Individualism

Individualistic cultures, such as those prevalent in the West, are those in which the dominant social arrangements and family structures are the nuclear family of for example, two parents and children. In such individualistic cultures, issues such as **identity**, behaviour and human development are viewed primarily in terms of an individual perspective. This contrasts with collectivist cultures, which are prevalent in countries such as China and India, in which more emphasis is placed upon people's actions in relation to communal groupings and kinship groups. In collectivist cultures, individual behaviour is seen as being greatly influenced by the community's needs and desires. In individualistic cultures, behaviour is perceived and understood as a product of the individual's own needs and desires.

See **identity**.

Halman, L. (1996) Individualism in individualized society? Results from the European Values Surveys. *International Journal of Comparative Sociology*, 37, 195–214.

Triandis, H. C. (1995) *Individualism and collectivism*. Houston: Westview.

Individuation

Individuation refers to the act or process by which an individual strives for individuality: a certain quality that sets him or her apart from other people, as opposed to being seen as feeling and acting in the same way as everyone else. While individuals do seem to require some aspects of similarity with other individuals in their lives, such as the sharing of hobbies, fashion, interests, people still strive for an individual sense of **identity**. Sometimes striving for individuality can create tensions and conflicts, and can cause people to behave bizarrely or unusually on occasions. Such actions can create a risk of social disapproval, but this in turn serves to confirm and support a person's sense of individuality.

Many argue that individuation is a form of **'self-actualization'**, as individuals are seen to grow into a higher self. People may however, seek **individualism** in an attempt to take greater control of their life, to counteract the sense of loss of personal freedom that may be experienced when **conforming** to a social or cultural group. For example:

- Rebellious teenagers may reject popular fashion and music to immerse themselves in what they perceive to be an alternative, **individualistic** 'goth' fashion and music style.
- Individuals who were raised as strict Roman Catholics may choose to become atheists as they enter **adulthood**.
- Retired police officers, after years of confirming to police dress

codes, might burn their uniforms and move to Spain to set up a nudist retreat!

See **adulthood, conformity, identity, individualism, self-actualization, social identity theory.**

Induction

There are many definitions of the term induction within psychology. For instance:

- Empirical induction: this involves drawing general conclusions and findings from specific events that have been observed. An example would be determining the different TV preferences of men and women by drawing findings from **observation** of a percentage of the population.

- Positive induction: this is a term theorized by **Pavlov** for the process by which the **response** to an excitory and **conditioned stimulus** is increased if it is immediately followed by an **inhibitory** one. Negative induction in contrast is when the **response** to an **inhibitory conditioned stimulus** is increased if it is immediately followed by an excitory one. In dog training, for example, the sitting **response** can be increased by positive induction and biting or barking can be decreased by negative induction.

- Neural induction: this is a process in which a neural plate in an embryo becomes committed to forming the **central nervous system**, when the release of particular substances is triggered.

- Induction: this is a type of child rearing method by which children are encouraged to behave appropriately and have a sense of responsibility for their actions by, for example, the use of a gold star and reward chart for 'good' behaviour.

See **central nervous system, conditioned stimulus, inhibitor, observation, Pavlov, response.**

Inferential statistics

These are statistical tests used to infer whether associations and differences between sets of **data** are significant. They serve to show whether the levels of **significance** are due to there being real differences or associations within the population. Inferential tests include **Chi-square, sign** and **Wilcoxon tests** and **Spearman rank order correlation**.

See **Chi-square data, significance level, sign test, Spearman rank order correlation, Wilcoxon test.**

Thorne, M. and Giesen, M. (2003) *Statistics for the Behavioral Sciences.* New York: McGraw Hill.

Informed consent

Informed consent is a voluntary agreement by a **research** participant, client or patient to undergo, or be involved in, a **research** study, therapy or medical procedure. Informed consent denotes that an individual agrees to undertake the procedure/study/therapy after receiving full information and details of the possible effects, risks and benefits of taking part. Informed consent usually also offers the participant the opportunity to withdraw from the study/therapy or procedure at any time without experiencing pressure to continue. Gaining informed consent is viewed as necessary to comply with **ethical** codes of conduct and practice.

See **ethics, research.**

In-group

The term 'in-group' refers to any type of group in which we regard ourselves as members. Membership may be based on the sharing of similar characteristics such as race, age, religion or class, or on possessing similar likes and dislikes, such as friendships or hobbies. In-groups are usually contrasted with out-groups, which comprise those who are not part of our own group. In-groups tend to possess an 'us and them' **attitude**, and this is manifest in many social encounters. Individuals have a tendency to be biased towards their own groups and this leads them to experience feelings of superiority and a sense of elitism with regard to the out-group.

See **Asch, attitude, conformity, social identity theory, social psychology.**

Inhibitor

In psychology, an inhibitor is a **stimulus** that inhibits or prevents a **response**. The **response** and the inhibitor can occur through a natural, innate reaction, or via learning. In biochemistry, an inhibitor is any substance or **gene** that restricts or prevents any process, such as the synthesis of biochemical substances.

See **gene, response, stimulus.**

Insecure attachment

An insecure attachment is a poorly developed form of **attachment** between infant and caregiver; it is seen to develop through the caregiver's lack of responsiveness to the infant's needs. **Bowlby** suggested that the development of insecure attachments might lead to poor cognitive and emotional development later in life. **Ainsworth** identified two particular types of insecure attachments:

* Insecure/avoidant: infants of this style have a tendency to avoid social interaction with others.
* Insecure/ambivalent: infants of this style have a tendency to both reject and seek social interaction with others.

See **Ainsworth, attachment, Bowlby.**

Instinct

Instincts are generally regarded as any **responses** or drives that are natural, innate and unlearnt and are characteristic of any given species. Behaviours and goals such as courtship, sex drive, mating and parenting styles are seen as originating from the **motivating** drives of instinctual urges. **Freud** referred to the 'instincts' as *thanatos* and *eros* (the death and life instincts), which he suggested underpinned many aspects of human behaviour, such as aggressive and sexual behaviours. He suggested that instincts do innately **motivate** individuals, but that they do not always lead to specific behavioural patterns.

See **Freud, motivation, nativism, response, theory of evolution.**

Internalization

In **social psychology**, internalization refers to the process by which an individual incorporates within him or herself the **attitudes**, views and standards of others. In **psychoanalysis**, it particularly refers to the way in which relationships such as those of children with parents can lead to the absorption of standards and views into an individual's mental structures, thus leading to the development of the **superego**: an individual's understanding of moral and social codes of behaviour.

See **attitude, externalisation, psychoanalysis, social psychology.**

International classification of diseases (ICD)

The ICD is a classification system published by the World Health Organization. It contains statistical information gathered from many countries about the variety of characteristics associated with particular disorders, which ensures practitioners can reach an understanding of the disorders that they are treating. The ICD, unlike the **DSM IV**, is not designed to be used as a clinical manual for **diagnosis** but rather to provide an insight into the patterns of symptoms and the likely course of the disorder. The ICD does not attempt to identify the **etiology** or causes of the disorder or provide details of possible treatment regimes.

See **diagnosis, DSM VI, etiology.**

World Health Organization (1981) *International Classification of Diseases and Related Health Problems*. Geneva: WHO.

Interval measurements

Interval measurements have meaningful differences between measurements but no 'true' starting point. An example would be differences in temperature, say −3 °C on Monday compared with 4 °C on Wednesday.

See **nominal measurements, ordinal measurements, levels of measurement.**

I

Jonckheere test

This is a multi-level trend analysis test that looks for specific differences in directional trends within **data**. It can used only in unrelated study designs that have **ordinal data**.

See **data, ordinal measurements.**

Coolican, H. (2004) *Research Methods and Statistics in Psychology*, 4th edn, Bristol: Hodder and Stoughton.

Jung

Jung, Carl Gustav (1875–1961), was a Swiss psychiatrist who founded the neopsychoanalytic school of psychology, which he termed analytical psychology. In the early days of **psychoanalysis** Jung and **Freud** were close colleagues, but their different views around the manifest and latent content of dreams, led to a break-up of the collaboration. Jung believed that dreams directly reflected the mind's current status and did not hold deliberately disguised meanings, as **Freud** suggested.

After the break with **Freud**, Jung questioned how such contrasting views as **Freud's** and his own could constructively move forward from **psychoanalysis**. He developed a framework within which psychological orientations could be identified, and the terms 'extrovert' and 'introvert' originate in this work. In contrast to the many meanings now placed on such terms, Jung's original use of the extrovert orientation placed meanings outside the self in the external environment and world, whereas the introvert focuses within. Jung also suggested four modes of experience or function which can be either extroverted or introverted: thought, feeling, sensation and intuition. He suggested that individuals work from their most developed function and that to enhance and build on their personalities they should develop the others.

Jung suggested that an individual's psychological health required a balance between the conscious and the unconscious mind, and that repressed material that needed to be resolved was expressed as imagery in dreams. He believed that dreams could offer possible areas for future individual development and direction. He highlighted the positive and constructive nature of dreams, whereas **Freud** focused upon the destructive forces of unconscious influences within dream imagery. Jung's approach to dream interpretation differed from **Freud's**, as he focused upon the identification of archetypal symbols.

Archetypal symbols, Jung suggested, were universal images found within and across all cultures, and further developed through human evolution. He viewed archetypes as an aspect of the collective unconscious, which is a dimension of the mind that is common to all individuals and that is located below personal unconsciousness and **consciousness**. Archetypes influence an individual's thoughts, actions and behaviours in the present.

Examples of Jungian archetypes are:

* *Persona:* a need or drive to present yourself in the best possible light. Individuals who possess a weak persona may dream of panic and **anxiety** in social situations.
* *Anima/animus:* the male aspect of the female and the female aspect of the male. Jung suggested that all individuals carry with them aspects of the opposite gender; the appearance of such features helps individuals to reconcile and balance their feminine and masculine sides.
* *Self:* an individual's drive towards self-wholeness. The expression of the perfect harmony and balance between an individual's unconscious and conscious world, which is rarely achieved. In dreams this is often symbolized by complex symmetrical patterns in the shape of circles or crosses, known as *mandala* symbols.

Jung would work on equal terms with clients to aid them in analysing dream symbolism, providing guidance on how to restore balance between the unconscious and conscious aspects of the mind.

See **anxiety, consciousness, Freud, dream analysis, psychoanalysis, social representations.**

Jung, C. G. and Hull, R. F. C. (1991) *The Archetypes and the Collective Unconscious*. London: Routledge.
www.cgjungpage.org/ (information on Carl Jung).

Just world hypothesis

A widespread belief that the world is ultimately fair, that the good will be rewarded and the bad will be punished. Such a belief can create misleading interpretations, such as believing that individuals who suffer misfortune deserve this in some way.

See **hypothesis.**

J

Kk

Kin selection

Kin selection is a type of **natural selection** in which altruistic behaviours (behaviours that may reduce the survival or reproductive abilities of the individual animal) are shown by animals towards siblings and family members. Such altruistic behaviour increases their inclusive fitness in relation to that family group, through helping to perpetuate the survival of the **genes** that they all share. Parental care is an example of kin selection, as parents who feed and care for their offspring are practising behaviours favoured by **natural selection**, as they invest and **maximize** the perpetuation of their **genes** in subsequent generations. Altruism can increase their inclusive fitness, as they can pass on more copies of their **genes** through helping others to survive and reproduce, as opposed to depending only on their direct offspring. Different types of fitness are:

- Direct fitness: the reproductive gain achieved through an animal's own offspring.
- Indirect fitness: the reproductive gain achieved through non-descendant genetic relatives.
- Inclusive fitness: the reproductive gain achieved through investing in both direct and indirect fitness.

See **gene, maximization, natural selection, theory of evolution.**

Kohlberg's theory of moral development

Kohlberg's (1981) theory of moral development shares similar characteristics to **Piaget's theory of cognitive development**, as both focus upon cognitive development and suggest that:

- Moral development proceeds through a number of innately determined stages. Each of these is cognitively qualitatively different to the last, but they follow a particular sequence.
- Each stage is characterized by the kind of thinking or cognition that is used to achieve and make moral judgements.

- The focus should be on examining and understanding how individuals think rather than what they think.
- The theories are underpinned by the assumption that moral principles are connected with moral behaviour.

Kohlberg's theory built upon **Piaget's** but extended the theory to cover **adolescence** and **adulthood**. Kohlberg based his theory upon a series of ten moral dilemmas, which were used to explore individuals' responses to resolve them. Kohlberg suggested that it was not the individuals' ultimate answer or decision that was important, but the process of reasoning behind the decisions that provides insights into moral development.

Kohlberg's findings revealed that individuals used three levels of moral reasoning, with each level split into two stages. He suggested that individuals experience and progress through these stages in a fixed sequence, which is applicable to all humans, regardless of race, culture, religion and background. Kohlberg believed that all humans would progress in the same direction of moral development, although some individuals would not attain the higher, more advanced stages. Gilligan (1982) has challenged Kohlberg's theory for having a sexist bias, as his theory was initially based upon interviews with male (not female) respondents.

There are two key factors that Kohlberg claimed affects an individual's development and progression from one stage to another. They are:

- Disequilibrium: when children face a moral issue and notice weaknesses or flaws in how they reason it, they may be more induced to listening and seeking the views of others.
- Gains in perspective taking: as children grow, they become less **egocentric** and are able to understand and view issues from the perspective of others. A child at a pre-conventional stage of development may focus on the likely personal consequences to themselves of the dilemma. A child in the conventional level, in contrast, may consider the dilemma from the perspective of others, reflecting on consequences to others and to themselves.

See **adolescence, adulthood, egocentrism, Piaget's theory of cognitive development**.

Kohlberg, L. (1981) *Essays on moral development, Vol, 1, The philosophy of moral development*. San Francisco: Harper and Row.

Gilligan, C. (1982) *In a Different Voice: Psychological Theory and Women's Development*. Cambridge, MA: Harvard University Press.

Box 1 Kohlberg's stages of moral development

Level 1: Preconventional morality
Stage 1: Punishment and obedience orientation
The child decides what is wrong on the basis of what is punished.
Stage 2: individualism, instrumental purpose and exchange
The child follows rules when it is in his or her immediate interest.
What is good will be rewarded.
Level 2: Conventional morality
Stage 3: Mutual interpersonal expectations, relationships and interpersonal conformity
The family or small group to whom the child belongs becomes important. Moral actions are those that live up to others' expectations.
Stage 4: Social system and conscience (law and order)
There is a shift in focus from family and close groups to the larger society. Good is behaving in ways that conform to society.
Level 3: Principled or postconventional morality
Stage 5: Social contract or utility and individual rights
The child is aware that there are different views and values, that values are relative. Laws and rules should be upheld in order to preserve the social order, but they can sometimes be broken.
Stage 6: Universal ethical principles
The person develops and adheres to self-chosen ethical principles in determining what is right. Since laws usually support those principles, laws should be obeyed, but when there is a difference between law and conscience, conscience dominates.

Kruskal-Wallace test

This is a test for **significance** when there are three or more, unrelated, **ranked samples** of **data**. This test tells us the probability of each of the **samples** originating from an identical population.

See **data, sample, significance levels, rank.**

K

Kurtosis

Kurtosis is a measure of the 'peakedness' of the probability distribution of a set of scores for a given **variable**. Higher kurtosis means that more of the **variance** is due to extreme, infrequent deviations rather than modest, frequent deviations. Two forms of kurtosis are leptokurtic, which has sharper peaks or fatter tails, and platykurtic, with smaller peaks or thin tails.

See **ceiling effect, normal distribution, skewed distribution, variables.**

Joanes, D. N. and Gill, C. A. (1998) Comparing measures of sample skewness and kurtosis. *Journal of the Royal Statistical Society (Series D): The Statistician* 47 (1), 183–189.

K

Labelling

Labelling refers to the way in which individuals have a tendency to perform particular styles of behaviour according to the types of labels that have been placed upon them. The apparently self-destructive actions of some individuals are thus explained by the notion of a **self-fulfilling prophecy**: if they are labelled negatively they are likely to respond and behave in a negative style. Labels such as 'remedial', 'stupid' and 'unintelligent' when used within the context of education may lead children into undertaking a range of behaviours that support and justify the labels given. Labelling is a tremendous cause for concern, not just in education but also healthcare settings. When **diagnostic** labels such as 'mentally ill' or 'special needs' are used, individuals to whom they are applied may undergo a series of unpleasant, negative experiences. Mental health practitioners and healthcare staff may **stereotype** such individuals accordingly, and individuals may experience social rejection and begin to view themselves in the negative manner that others may expect.

Alongside the negative effects of labelling, positive effects are also seen as being elicited. In terms of education, there is a suggestion that where positive labels such as 'top group' or 'star pupil' are projected onto individuals and groups, this will encourage children to adopt positive behaviours, respond more positively and reach higher levels of achievement. However, labelling can be seen to be built upon oppositions: an individual is only seen as positive, better in some way, in relation to an opposite, those who are not as good. This positive labelling of individuals and groups therefore may exert a detrimental labelling effect on those who are not selected to be in the 'top group' or to be the 'star pupil'.

See **diagnosis, self-fulfilling prophecy, stereotyping.**

Language acquisition device (LAD)

See **Chomsky.**

Language development

'Language development' relates to how children learn and develop their language skills. To master language, children are seen to progress through a series of four stages of language development:

* Phonology: developing the skill to understand and elicit speech sounds.
* Semantics: developing the skill to understand and attribute meaning to words and different combination of words.
* Grammar: developing the skill to understand the rules by which words can be arranged to produce meaning (into sentences), and by which words can indicate tense and gender.
* Pragmatics: developing the skills and learning the rules by which effective communication can be achieved, such as turn taking and strategies for beginning and ending conversations.

There are many widely varying language development theories, tending to differ on the degree to which they attribute language acquisition to natural (biological, innate and hereditary structures or processes) or experiential (social, environmental cue, social interaction and social learning) factors. Theories include:

* The **behaviourist** approach: this stresses the importance of social learning and a child's interaction with the environment of language development. Language is viewed as being developed through imitation, conditioning and **reinforcement**.
* **Nativist** theory: **Chomsky** viewed language as being acquired through a language acquisition device that enabled children to understand language and construct and reinvent their own grammatically appropriate language.
* **Cognitive** theories: **Piaget** suggested that children develop language ability according to the stage of cognitive development they are at, developing specific skills related to the stage they are within. He viewed children's language ability as developing only when their cognitive abilities and mental structures were suitably equipped and could allow it to occur.

See **behaviourism, Chomsky, cognitive psychology, reinforcement, Piaget's theory of cognitive development.**

Latency stage

According to **psychoanalysis** and **Freud**, the latency stage is the fourth libidinal stage, which occurs at the end of the **phallic stage** (after the resolution of the **Oedipus/Electra complex**) at around the age of five or six. It extends up until the onset of the **genital stage**, which is experienced at puberty. It therefore lasts from five to 11 years of age approximately. The latency stage is characterized by a lack of interest in sex and the onset of emotions such as shame and disgust.

See **Electra complex, Freud, genital stage, Oedipus complex, phallic stage, psychoanalysis, psychosexual stages.**

Law of effect

The psychologist Thorndike (1874–1949) put forward this law, in which he suggested that there are environmental contexts and situational factors that serve to offer rewards for some behaviours but not for others. Accordingly, the behaviours that are seen to elicit the reward effect are continued and repeated, while the behaviours that are 'punished' or viewed as eliciting negative effects are diminished. Such production and restriction of such behaviours can be compared with **natural selection** processes, as only adaptive, appropriate, positive behaviours are sustained and reproduced, while species with less appropriate behaviours become extinct.

See **behaviourism, natural selection.**

Levels of measurement

These are the different ways that **data** can be categorized into **nominal**, **ordinal**, **interval** and **ratio** types of measurements.

See **data, interval measurements, measures of central tendency, nominal measurements, ordinal measurements, ratio measurements.**

Levinson's seasons of a man's life

L

Levinson put forward a theory of human development in which he viewed development as possessing a 'life structure'. Levinson (1978) suggested that there was an underlying pattern or series of particular stages, which are relative to any individual's life at any given time. He suggested the life span stages change as individuals progress through life, and that people undertake and develop through life transitions according to the relationships and work they experience.

Levinson based his theory on a study (1969) in which he interviewed

40 men from a range of occupations, interviewing each man between five and ten times over a period of two or three months.

From **research** findings, Levinson suggested that the life structure of an individual's life evolves through a series of alternating, stable and transitional crisis stages. These stages he called the seasons of a man's life.

The human lifespan, he suggested, consisted of four stages, pre- and early **adulthood**, and middle and late **adulthood** (Box 2). He suggested that an individual needed to master each stage before being able to progress to the next. He also viewed the stages as overlapping: at certain points an individual would experience a life transition before moving on to the next stage and this would last approximately five years.

Box 2 Levinson's life stages and transitions

Pre-adulthood: 0–17 years
Individuals in this stage grow and develop from baby to early adult.
Early adult transition: 18–22 years
Individual move towards autonomy and independence as they separate themselves from pre-adulthood.
Early adulthood: 22–40 years
Individuals attempt to give life more structure, making links between themselves and the outside world. They make career and personal life choices that enable them to make their own place in the world.
Middle transition: 40--45 years
Physical signs of aging become more obvious as individuals experience a sense of their own mortality. Earlier goals and plans may not have been achieved and individuals may experience a midlife crisis.
Middle adulthood: 45–60 years
Illusions of external growth and mortality usually fade and attempts, are made to achieve goals and plans made in middle transitions. This usually involves a change of some description as adults become less inward and more self-focused.
Late adult transition: 60–65 years
Signs of physical aging are becoming more obvious, and the individual is aware of being perceived as 'old' by society and culture.
Late adulthood: 65–end of life
Final acceptance that life is finite and coming to accept the realistic possibilities of what the future holds. For some this can be a time of crisis, for some a time of calm acceptance.

Source: Levinson, D. J. (1978) *The Seasons of a Man's Life*, New York: Ballantine.

L

There have been criticisms of Levinson's theory, as **Eysenck** (2000) discusses. The interview method used in Levinson's (1978) study posed a variety of issues over the **validity** of the **research data**. These included the participants having difficulty in accurately remembering experiences that happened to them 20 years previously, and a failure to consider the effects of the researcher on **data** collection and production. As Levinson had a particular theory in mind, it could be argued (Eysenck 2000) that the questions asked and answers received in the interviews might have been influenced by Levinson's own expectations and **research** aims.

See **adulthood, data, Eysenck, research, validity.**

Eysenck, M. W. (2000) *Psychology: A Student's Handbook.* Hove: Psychology Press.
Levinson, D. J. (1978) *The Seasons of a Man's Life.* New York: Ballantine.
Levinson, D. J. (1986) A conception of adult development. *American Psychologist*, 41, 3 –13.

Lexical decision task

This is an experimental task in which individuals are asked to decide whether a string of letters is or is not a word. It is used to examine the lexicon (the entire vocabulary of a language or an individual) and the processes used to access it.

See **language development.**

Life-span development

Life-span development theories, such as **Levinson's seasons of a man's life** and **Erikson's psychosocial stages of development**, uphold the view that individuals develop throughout their life span. This contrasts with the explanations of stage theorists such as **Piaget** and **Kohlberg**, who view life development as being contingent on early childhood development. There is no single unifying life-span development theory, but theories are underpinned by particular assumptions. These include assumptions that:

- The potential for human development is not fixed to childhood but extends throughout the life cycle.
- Development does not occur by progression through a series of fixed stages; rather it occurs through a wide range and variety of individual development routes.

- Development occurs at the same time within many different areas, such as social, intellectual, emotional and physical fields. It is possible to progress and decline in different areas at different times, and declining or progressing in one area does not instantly mean decline or progression in the others.
- Life development is affected by both environmental and individual factors; thus development can be seen as an interactive process.

See **Erikson's psychosocial stages of development, Kohlberg, Levinson's seasons of a man's life, Piaget's theory of cognitive development.**

Likert scale

A Likert scale is a form of **attitude** scale, where various statements are gathered together and the participants are asked to indicate how much they agree with the statement on a five-point scale.

For example, a **research** study is exploring children's **attitudes** to school. The children are provided with the statements:

- School is exciting.
- School is boring.

The children are then asked to rate on a scale of 1–5 their level of agreement, with 1 being 'strongly disagree' and 5 being 'strongly agree', and values 2, 3 and 4 at equal levels between.

See **attitude, research.**

Trochim, W. (2000). *The Research Methods Knowledge Base*, 2nd edn. Cincinnati, OH: Atomic Dog Publishing, www.socialresearchmethods.net/kb/scallik.htm (information on a variety of measurement scales from W. Trochim).

Linear regression

See **regression.**

Linguistics

Linguistics refers to the study of language, usually focusing upon the major branches of phonetics, phonology, semantics, grammar/syntax and pragmatics.

See **language development.**

Little Albert

Little Albert, in a classic study by Watson and Raynor (1920), was a ten-month-old boy who was said to be conditioned into developing a **phobia** of a white rat. In the study, a loud noise was made each time the child played with the rat. Following repeated exposure to the rat and loud noise, the child apparently developed a fear of rats, which then extended to other furry animals. Such a study now would be considered highly unethical, due to the detrimental factors to the child's health and well-being and the risk issues of such a young child undertaking such a task. Studies such as Munjack (1984) have questioned such behaviourist explanation to the nature of **phobias**, as similar studies have failed to reveal concurrent evidence.

See **ethics, phobia.**

Munjack, D. J. (1984) The onset of driving phobias. *Journal of Behaviour Therapy and Experimental Psychiatry,* 15, 305–8.
Watson, J. B. and Raynor, R. (1920) Conditioned emotional reactions. *Journal of Experimental Psychology,* 3, 1–14.

Longitudinal study

A longitudinal study is a method of **research** in which participants are studied over a long period of time, often years. The benefits of such studies are that they can provide an insight into how behaviour changes or remains constant over time and can examine the impact of environmental factors and experiences in childhood on human development. As a result of the time involved in conducting such **research**, the costs involved can be very high and the drop-out rate of participants who in later years no longer wish to be involved can create difficulties.

See **research, ethnography.**

Ferri, E. and Smith, K. (1996). *Parenting in the 1990s,* London: Family Policy Studies Centre.
Paci, P. Joshi, H. and Makepeace, G. (1995). Pay gaps facing men and women born in 1958: Differences within the labour market. In: J. Humphries and J. Rubery (eds) *The Economics of Equal Opportunity,* Manchester: Equal Opportunities Commission, 87–112.
www.cls.ioe.ac.uk (Centre for Longitudinal Studies).

Long-term memory

See **memory.**

L

Looking-glass self

Cooley (1864–1929) suggested that an individual's understanding and knowledge of self develops through interaction with other individuals. He viewed social interaction as a mirror that allows us to see ourselves as others see us; other individuals act like a mirror into which we can look and so judge ourselves.

Cooley, C. H. (1902) *Human Nature and the Social Order*. New York: Scribner.

L

Majority influence (conformity)

This is a form of social influence that occurs when individuals are exposed to the views of a majority. There are two main reasons why individuals choose to conform to the majority group:

* Normative influences: individuals conform to the views of the group in order to belong, to be liked and to gain the approval of others.
* Informational influence: individuals who experience uncertainty conform through their need to be correct and right.

Asch conducted the most famous experiments around **conformity** in the 1950s, and the effect that any majority group is seen to exert on the views of an individual has come to be known as the **Asch** effect. He found that when individuals are faced with the opinion of a majority, they are likely to repress their own views and sensory information by agreeing with the majority.

Moscovici (1980) challenged **Asch**'s findings, claiming that it was also possible for a minority to influence the majority through the process of conversion. Conversion, he suggested, is a way in which the minority can influence the majority by convincing the majority that the minority's views are correct. This often takes place through private rather than public agreements with the minority.

See **Asch, conformity, Milgram, social psychology, social representations.**

Asch, S. E. (1951) Effects of group pressure on the modification and distortion of judgements. In H. Guetzkow (ed.), *Groups, Leadership and Men*. Pittsburgh, Carnegie.

Asch, S. E. (1956) Studies of independence and conformity: a minority of one against a unanimous majority. *Psychological Monographs,* **70** (416), whole issue.

Moscovici, S. (1980) Toward a theory of conversion behaviour. In L. Berkowitz (ed.), *Advances in Experimental Social Psychology*, Vol. 13. New York: Academic Press.

Moscovici, S. (2000) *Social Representations: Studies in Psychology*. London: Polity.

Maladaptiveness

In general psychology terms, maladaptive refers to particular **traits**, behaviours or characteristics that do not serve the best interest of the individual. These might include engaging in **antisocial behaviour** that may lead to social rejection and/or isolation. In terms of the **theory of evolution,** maladaptive refers to any inherited **traits** or characteristics that decrease the organism's ability to survive and reproduce.

See antisocial behaviour, theory of evolution, trait theories of personality.

Manic depression

See bipolar disorder.

Mann-Whitney U test

The Mann-Whitney U test is a **non-parametric test**. This **rank** test is used when testing for differences or correlations between two unrelated **sample** groups of **data**. It can be used with **data** of at least **interval** level, but if the **data** meet other **parametric** assumptions, (**homogeneity of variance** and normal population distribution) the related t-test would be more appropriate. It is more likely that this test would be used with **data** at an **ordinal** level.

See data, homogeneity of variance, interval measurements, non-parametric
    test, ordinal measurements, parametric tests, ordinal measurements.

Coolican, H. (2004) *Research Methods and Statistics*, 3rd edn. Bristol: Hodder
    and Stoughton.

M

Maslow

See self-actualization theory.

Matched groups

These are groups of participants that are assigned to different **experimental conditions,** but do not differ in any other way, such as IQ, age or gender that may impact upon the effect of the study. In matched groups, participants are matched for important **variables** (such as gender, age) that may influence the study outcome.

See experimental condition, sample, variables.

Maternal deprivation

Maternal deprivation can be viewed as a form of inadequate mothering or the unavailability of a caring, responsive, affectionate mothering figure. **Bowlby** suggested that when infants experienced maternal deprivation and a lack of maternal affection in early infancy, then as children they would experience emotional, social and intellectual effects that would lead to juvenile delinquency and psychological problems later in life. **Bowlby**'s early **research** focused on the experiences of evacuee children in the Second World War, which led him to suggest that it was the long-term separation from the maternal figure that led to maternal deprivation.

Harlow's **research** with rhesus monkeys in the 1950s strengthened this finding, as monkeys that were separated from their mothers at an early age and reared in isolation suffered irreversible detrimental effects in later life. Studies undertaken in the 1950s and 1960s of orphaned children have also revealed that children experience long-lasting adverse social, linguistic and psychological effects. **Bowlby** suggested that such effects are the result of **attachment** failure, the children being unable to develop an **attachment** with the maternal figure; the symptoms being a consequence of maternal privation. **Bowlby**'s work has been extremely influential in developing and fostering change within social welfare systems and the institutionalized care of children. His findings have been criticized however, for putting unnecessary added guilt on many working mothers who worry about the dangers of being separated from their children, and how this may be affecting their children's well-being.

See **attachment, Bowlby, research.**

Bowlby, J. (1946) *Forty-four juvenile thieves*. London: Balliere, Tindall and Cox.
Bowlby, J. (1951) *Maternal Care and Mental Health*. Geneva: World Health Organization.
Harlow, H. F. (1959) Love in infant monkeys. *Scientific American,* 200, 68–74.

M

Maturation

Maturation can be viewed as a development process that takes individuals through particular developmental stages, leading them to adult maturity. It can be viewed as occurring through the effect of genetic and/or environmental factors:

- Genetically and biologically, maturation may be regarded as the ripening and emerging of innate tendencies, with no influence from environmental factors. Walking and running can be perceived as matured abilities in this sense.

- Environmentally, maturation can be seen as being triggered and furthered by environmental influence. Eating can be seen as being determined by innate needs and urges, but maturation also involves learning the style in which an individual eats, which is determined and triggered by environmental factors such as etiquette and cultural social styles of eating. These factors decide for example, whether as we mature we are able to master chopsticks and/or a knife and fork.

Maximizing (game theory)

Maximizing refers to any strategy within **game theory** that maximizes or increases the expected pay off. This is calculated by subtracting the possible costs from the possible gains, and weighing the result up against the probability of occurrence. In evolutionary accounts, such costs and gains are calculated in evolutionary terms, whereby organisms are viewed as maximizing their evolutionary adaptability and inclusive fitness.

See **game theory, theory of evolution.**

Mead

Mead, George Herbert (1863–1931), developed the idea that an individual's self-concept originates as a result of interaction with other people. Mead suggested that a person's understanding of 'self' does not exist at birth, but develops through social interactions and in relation to other individuals within that process.

Mead, G. H. (1934) *Mind, Self and Society: From the Standpoint of a Social Behaviourist*. Chicago: University of Chicago Press.

M

Mean

The mean in **descriptive statistics** is a **measure of central tendency**, the average value of a set of numerical values or scores. You calculate the mean by adding all the values together and dividing by the actual number of values. For example, $2 + 3 + 4 + 5 + 6 = 20/5 = 4$ (the mean).

See **descriptive statistics, measure of central tendency, mode, median.**

Measures of central tendency

This is a term used in **descriptive statistics** to determine the middle or typical value of any set of scores; this is normally calculated as the **mean, mode** or **median.**

See **descriptive statistics, mean, median, mode.**

Measures of dispersion

This is a term used in **descriptive statistics** to measure the spread or degree of variability across a set of values or scores. The **measure of central tendency** can tell us the typical score in a set of values, but it cannot provide an insight into how the other scores vary, or spread from that typical score; measures of dispersion allow such an insight to be gained.

See **descriptive statistics, mean, measures of central tendency, median, mode.**

Median

The median in **descriptive statistics** is a **measure of central tendency**; it is the middle value of a **data** set, obtained by selecting the middle values. For example, in a set of 1, 2, 3, 4, 5, 6, 7, the middle value would 4.

See **data, descriptive statistics, mode, mean, measures of central tendency.**

Meiosis

Meiosis is a form of cell division occurring within the body, which produces gametes: sperm and (ova) egg haploid cells. Each gamete has half the **chromosomes** of the parent. As the gametes combine at fertilization, the new diploid cell is called a zygote and will have the normal number, two sets of **chromosomes**. Meiosis is a process that converts a diploid cell into a haploid gamete, and causes a change in the genetic information when creating a new diploid cell, to increase diversity in the offspring.

See **chromosomes.**

M

Memory

Memory can be viewed as a psychological, mental function through which individuals are able to retain and retrieve information about experiences and events that have occurred in the past. While being regarded as a function, it can also be seen as a mental structure, a storage system in which memories are held within the **brain**. A memory also refers to the information itself, the memory that we recall and remember. Different types of memory are:

- *Autobiographical*
  This is a part of the long-term memory system that contains all the information, 'facts' and personal experiences of an individual. It contains all knowledge of self, based on memories of past events and experiences.
- *Declarative*
  Declarative memory is the memory storage system that contains declarative knowledge. It contains all knowledge that is concerned with an individual's conscious awareness and understanding of factual statements about the social world. It is concerned with facts about 'knowing that', rather than 'knowing how'. Certain conditions must be met to obtain declarative memory: the information must be true, the person must believe that the information is true, and the person must be in a position to know or confirm it is true.

  Examples of declarative memories are knowing the dates that J. F Kennedy, Marilyn Munroe or Princess Diana died. Such knowledge is understood to be true as the person has the opportunity to confirm the facts through reference material such as newspapers and books.
- *Echoic*
  Echoic memory is a type of short-term auditory memory which is concerned with the storage of all aspects of heard sound.
- *Episodic*
  Episodic memory is a form of long-term memory that preserves information about personal experiences and events, such as getting married a few years ago, being knocked over by a car a few months ago, listening to the radio yesterday, or drinking a coffee a few seconds ago.

  Episodic memory stores specific information about specific events and experiences that occur in particular times and places, allowing the individual to retain a sense of coherence and familiarity with the past.
- *Explicit*
  Explicit memory is a form of memory that is generated when performance on a task requires conscious recollection of previous

learnt information of knowledge. It allows learning to take place by consciously recalling previously learnt information.

* *Flashbulb*
A flashbulb memory is an unusually vivid, highly detailed and often long-lasting memory of any situation or experience in which important or dramatic events have occurred. Flashbulb memories can often be incorrect.

   An example of a flashbulb memory is that many people can recollect where they were and/or what they were doing at the time Neil Armstrong walked on the moon or the New York twin towers were destroyed.

* *Long-term (LTM)*
Long-term memory is a form of memory that can store information for a period ranging from 30 seconds up to many decades. It is also known as secondary memory. Long-term memory is often divided into semantic (information about the world) and episodic (information about experiences and events) memory.

* *Procedural*
Procedural memory contains all our information about how to do things (procedural knowledge). The knowledge contained within this memory has been gained through repetition and learning over a long period of time. Sometimes it has been gained without conscious awareness, through association, **reinforcement** and repetition and can become an **automatic response** to specific **stimuli**.

   An example is driving: after ten years of driving, an individual no longer has to think consciously about how to drive a car; the procedure or actions have become automatic.

* *Semantic*
Semantic memory is a form of long term memory in which factual information about the world, including about one's own experiences is contained. Examples include knowledge stored of the dates Marilyn Munroe and John Kennedy died. Tulving introduced this concept in 1972, thus identifying semantic memory as being different from episodic and procedural memory.

* *Short-term (STM)*
Short-term memory is a memory storage system that can hold a limited amount of information for a limited period of time, approximately 20–30 seconds. With rehearsal and repetition however, the information can be renewed and stored

M

indefinitely, until it is either lost (forgotten) or transferred to long-term memory storage. The **Atkinson and Shiffrin** (1968) model is a multistore model of the memory system that differentiates between the functions and processes of the short-term and long-term memory. Their model however views short-term memory as being a unitary short-term store, whereas Baddeley and Hitch (1974) view short-term memory (or working memory as they prefer to term it) as a complex system, consisting of a central control system aided by a variety of memory systems.

* *Working*
Baddeley and Hitch's (1974) view of the working memory, which was modified slightly following further studies by Baddeley (1986), suggested that the notion of a short-term memory should be replaced with the concept of a working memory system. A working memory is not just concerned with the temporary storage of information, but also with the functional and active processing of such information. Working memory can be seen as a complex, multi-component structure and processing system, as opposed to a single unitary store.
   The working memory is made up of three systems:
   * The central executive: this is the most important component of the model. It is responsible for monitoring and organizing the operations of the slave systems and plays a role in synthesizing information from the long-term memory also. It can process information from any **modality** and has some storage facility, although this is minimal.
   * The phonological loop: this component stores a limited number of sounds for a brief period of time. Gathercole and Baddeley (1993) suggest that this is made up of two components: the phonological store, which allows acoustically coded items to be stored briefly; and the articulatory control system, which enables speech-based repetition of items stored in the phonological store.
   * The visual–spatial scratch pad: this component stores visual and spatial information and has a limited capacity. This visual input can be either direct, via the visual sensory register, or in the form of visual images retrieved from long-term memory.

Because of the different focus of the phonological loop and visual-spatial components, each is known respectively as the 'inner ear' and 'inner eye'. Both of these components have limited capacity, but can work independently, so it is possible simultaneously to rehearse a set of numbers in the phonological loop while also making decisions about the spatial layout of the set of numbers in the visual–spatial scratch pad.

See **action slips, Atkinson and Shiffrin multi-store model of memory, automatic response, brain, modality effect, reinforcement, semantic coding, stimulus.**

Atkinson, R. C. and Shiffrin, R. M. (1968) Human memory: a proposed system and its control processes. In K. W. Spence and J. T. Spence (eds), *The Psychology of Learning and Motivation*, vol. 2. London: Academic Press.

Baddeley, A. D. (1986) *Working Memory*, Oxford: Clarendon.

Baddeley, A. D. and Hitch, G. J. (1974) Working memory. In G. H. Bower (ed.), *The Psychology of Learning and Motivation*, vol. 8. London: Academic Press.

Barsalou, L. W. (1988) The content and organization of autobiographical memories. In U. Neisser and E. Winograd (eds), *Remembering Reconsidered: Ecological and Traditional Approaches to the Study of Memory*. Cambridge: Cambridge University Press.

Gathercole, S. E. and Baddeley, A. D. (1993) *Working Memory and Language*. Hove, Erlbaum.

Robinson, J. A. (1992) Autobiographical memory. In M. M. Gruneberg, and P. Morris (eds), *Aspects of Memory. Vol. 1: The Practical Aspects.* 2nd edn. London: Routledge.

Tulving, E. (1972) Episodic and semantic memory. In E. Tulving and W. Donaldson (eds), *Organization of Memory*. Hillsdale, NJ: Lawrence Erlbaum.

www.memory-key.com/EverydayMemory/autobiographical_memory.htm (information from Capital Research Limited).

Memory buffer

A memory buffer is any memory system that retains incoming information for a period of time while it is being transferred to a long-term store, such as the phonological loop or short-term **memory**.

See **memory.**

M

Meta-analysis

This is a method of collecting and statistically measuring the findings of a large number of studies that have studied the same **hypothesis**, or very similar ones. Many consider it to be a statistical version of a literature review. Smith et al. (1980) undertook a meta-analysis to determine the effectiveness of different forms of therapy. They did this by combining the **data** of many studies to estimate the effectiveness of each form of treatment. **Beck** (1998) conducted a similar meta-analysis to determine the impact of mothers who experienced postnatal **depression** on the cognitive and emotional development of their child.

See **Beck Depression Inventory (BDI, data, depression, hypothesis.**

Beck, C. T. (1998) The effects of postpartum depression on child development: a meta-analysis. *Archives of Psychiatric Nursing*, **12** (1), 12–20.

Smith, M. L., Glass, G. V., and Miller, T. I. (1980) *The Benefits of Psychotherapy*. Baltimore: Johns Hopkins Press.

Sutton, A. J. (2000) *Methods for Meta-analysis in Medical Research*. Chichester: John Wiley.

Methodology

Methodology is concerned with the best 'ways' and methods to generate, collect and gain knowledge and understanding about human behaviour and the world. Such methods of investigation are derived from and informed by a particular theoretical approach and assumptions about the reality of the world (**ontology**) and the nature of knowledge (**epistemology**). For example, a behaviourist methodology will use **objective**, scientific methods of investigation, based on the assumption that behaviour is a product of environmental **cause and effect**. Such an approach is concerned with the production of 'testable' laws and facts, and focuses on methods of **objectivity**, as what individuals 'think' cannot be observed.

See **cause and effect, epistemology, objectivity, ontology, research.**

Milgram

Milgram, Stanley (1933–1984), undertook **research** that explored individuals' **obedience** to the authority of others. His work has always been regarded as controversial, due to what participants in his studies were asked to do. In his 1974 study, Milgram paired participants off into the roles of teacher and learner. The learner was always an associate of Milgram's. The teacher was asked to administer an electric shock to the learner each time he or she answered a question incorrectly, and to increase the intensity of the shock each time. The learner never received an actual shock but the teacher never was aware of this. Milgram found that 65 per cent of participants in this situation did administer the maximum electric shock, and in doing so acted in **obedience** to authority. Smith and Bond (1993) carried out cross-cultural variations of this study to test if Milgram's findings could apply across cultures; while the experiment was difficult to replicate in some cultures, figures of 80 per cent or higher (of participants willing to administer the electric shock) were found in Italy, Spain, Germany and Holland.

Milgram (1974) identified three main reasons why individuals acted **obediently** in the Milgram situation:

- Individuals have learned through experience that authorities can be trusted.
- The experimenter's requests moved gradually from the reasonable to the unreasonable and this made it difficult for the participants to notice the point at which this changed.
- The participants began to take less conscious responsibility for their actions as they viewed themselves as being ordered to do them.

See **conformity, Asch, obedience, research, social psychology.**

Milgram, S. (1974) *Obedience to Authority: An Experimental View*. New York: Harper and Row.

Smith, P. and Bond, M. H. (1993) *Social Psychology Across Cultures: Analysis and Perspectives*. New York: Harvester Wheatsheaf.

Minimal groups

This refers to a category of group whose members may have very little in common, and can display or engage in very little interaction with other members of the group. In experiments to understand whether group membership can increase liking among members of the same group, findings revealed that even in minimal groups whose members who do not engage in interaction, people still show 'in-group' favouritism compared with their treatment of members of 'out groups'.

See **Asch, majority influence.**

Minority group

M

A minority group is regarded as a group in society whose members share similar characteristics but are a minority of society as a whole. It is a term that is often used to refer to groups that are (or think they are) disadvantaged within society.

See **Asch, majority influence, social identity theory.**

Mitosis

This is a type of cell division within a body in which a cell divides into daughter cells and each of these 'new' cells receives an exact copy of the parent cells' **chromosomes**, a full set of **chromosomes**. Mitosis occurs again and again in development until the organism achieves **adulthood**.

> *See* **adulthood, chromosomes, gene, genotype, phenotype.**

Modality effect

Generally the modality effect refers to the difference in effect when the same information is presented in different modalities, or forms: for example, hearing, vision or touch. It particularly relates to how a subject is able to freely recall words more easily when provided with different information modality sources. Subjects are able to freely recall the last word or two more easily when provided with auditory information material than with visual information.

Mode

The mode is a **measure of central tendency**, and it refers to the value from a set of values that has the greatest frequency. For example, in the set 1, 2, 2, 2, 3, 3, 4, 4, 4, 4, 4, 4, 4, 5, 6, 7, 8, 8, 9, 9, 9, the mode is 4, as this is the value that is repeated more frequently.

> *See* **mean, median, measures of central tendency, descriptive statistics.**

Monozygotic twins

'Monozygotic twins' is another term for identical twins who share identical **genes**.

> *See* **gene, twin studies.**

Moral development

Moral development refers to how individuals come to understand and make sense of what they believe is right or wrong. It is the process by which individuals **internalize** the moral codes of right and wrong that are dominant within their society. There are many different views as to how moral development is achieved, varying in different psychological approaches.

- Cognitive development theorists, such as **Kohlberg**, view moral development as occurring in stages throughout childhood; moral development is reflective of a child's developing intellectual ability. Each child at a particular age and developmental stage needs to resolve specific moral conflicts before moving on to the next stage of moral development, which brings another unique moral conflict.

- **Behaviourists** view moral development as originating from social learning, conditioning and environmental factors. Moral behaviour is seen as a product of the **internalization** of morally acceptable behaviour, learnt and shaped through the imitation of others behaviours, and in **response** to **negative** or **positive reinforcements**, such as praise or punishment.
- Psychodynamic theorists such as **Freud** suggest that moral development and resulting behaviour occurs through the attempt to resolve the **Oedipus** and **Electra** psychological conflicts within the mind. Children identify with same-sex parents and **internalize** their moral values, which in turn creates the **superego**. The **superego** can be viewed as the moral guide that steers children into behaving in socially desirable ways and so steers them away from engaging in morally unacceptable behaviour.

See **behaviourism, Electra complex, Freud, internalization, Kohlberg's theory of moral development, negative reinforcement, Oedipus complex, positive reinforcement, response, superego.**

http://classweb.gmu.edu/awinsler/ordp/theory.html (links to particular theorists of moral development).

Motivation

Motivation is regarded as the driving force/s that elicits, perpetuates and maintains goal-directed behaviour, the reason that individuals do what they do. It is related to basic biological drives, such as thirst, hunger, love and sex, and to social aspects of motivation, such as the need for **affiliation**, belonging, reassurance and achievement. Motivation has tended to be explained in relation to physiological, psychological or behavioural determinants

M

- Physiological explanations focus upon the basic physical drives that motivate an individual's behaviour. For example, an individual who has spent a long time in the desert without water will be motivated to find water, to satisfy physical thirst. Such drive states as thirst, hunger and sex are termed 'primary' drives, as they are seen as being of primary importance to an individual.
- **Behavioural** explanations focus on drives and motivation sources acquired through social learning. For example,

individuals would be motivated to work and make money because of the learnt association that money can satisfy the primary drives for thirst and hunger, and possibly attract the opposite sex and thereby satisfy their sexual drives.

● Psychological explanations focus on the psychological, **instinctual** drives that motivate an individual to attempt to reduce psychological conflict by undertaking drive-reducing behaviour. For example, an individual who needs to have a sense of belonging or **affiliation**, or to move towards **self-actualization** will be motivated towards engaging in particular social situations.

See **affiliation, behaviourism, instinct, self-actualization theory.**

Motor neuron

See **efferent neurons.**

Motor skills

Motor skills are the skills and abilities an individual possesses that are dependent upon the regulation of muscular co-ordination and control. Such skills usually involve co-ordinating muscle control with the sensory information received via senses such as vision and sound. For example, children being given instructions on how to hold pencils and write their names need to be able to control their hand movements according to the instructions being given.

See **sensori-motor stage, efferent neurons.**

Muller–Lyer illusion

The Muller–Lyer illusion involves two vertical lines, one with arrows on each end pointing inward, and the other with arrows on the end pointing outward. The aim is to guess which of the lines is the longer. The line with the arrows pointing outward appears longer, but this is in fact a trick of **perception**. The lines are actually the same length; the arrows pointing outward just give the illusion that the line is longer. This is not really an illusion, just an error of **perception** in which our **perception** does not match the actual physical reality. The Muller–Lyer illusion demonstrates how individuals can make false predictions and decisions about what they believe to be real. There has been much debate about the reason for the 'faulty' processing of this illusion; some explanations include theories of errors in judging distance and depth to eye movement explanation. For a review of some of these debates please visit the website of the Rochester Institute of Technology.

See **field dependence, field independence, perception.**

www.langara.bc.ca/psychology/muller.htm (the Muller–Lyer illusion and other illusions from John Melville Harris).

www.rit.edu/~gssp400/muller/muller.html (information from Rochester Institute of Technology, NY, United States).

Multiple regression

See **regression.**

Multistore memory model

See **Atkinson and Shiffrin multi-store memory model.**

Mutation

A mutation occurs when there is a rapid change in the **genotype** of an organism that is not due to direct inheritance. As the process of **meiosis** occurs, a **chromosome** may separate from the **chromosome** pairs and instead join in a different formation. Such mutated changes in **genes**, may prove to have an adaptive value to the organism in evolutionary terms, if the change enables the organism to adapt better than others of its species to the environment. This process is known as **natural selection**.

See **chromosomes, gene, genotype, meiosis, theory of evolution.**

M

Nativism

Nativism is a psychological approach that stresses the importance of innate and inborn inherited factors for human behaviour and development. Nativism can be seen to strongly sit on the nature side of the **nature–nurture debate**, portraying innate characteristics of an individual as being the most influential factors underpinning human action and thought.

> *See* **genetic determinism, nature–nurture debate.**

Natural selection

The theory of natural selection attempts to explain why some individuals of the same species produce more offspring than others, and it forms part of **Darwin's theory of evolution.** Evolution theory suggests that individuals that adapt well to their environment will produce and leave behind more offspring than those that are less well suited and adapted to the environment. As time passes, the **traits** and characteristics that enable individuals to be more successfully adapted than others, in terms of survival and reproduction, will become more dominant within the species. The most successful and effective **traits** of any species are those that enhance its survival and reproduction chances within its particular environment.

> *See* **Darwinism, determinism, nature–nurture debate, theory of evolution, trait theories of personality.**

Nature–nurture debate

The nature–nurture issue is a major debate within psychology, and the positions theorists take on it depend on the psychological approach they are situated within. The debate is concerned with the degree to which aspects of behaviour are a product of inherited or learnt factors. Approaches such as biological psychology and **nativism** sit firmly on the nature side of the debate, viewing human behaviour as being primarily **motivated** and driven by innate and biological characteristics. For example, **depression** and **schizophrenia** are seen as the product of genetic or physiological factors. In contrast behaviourists sit on the nurture side of the debate, regarding human behaviour as being primarily driven by environmental influences, such as the imitation of others' behaviour, **reinforcement** and conditioning. Others, such as psychodynamic theorists and social constructivists, tend to adopt a mid-way position, viewing human behaviour as occurring via the interactive processes occurring between nature and nurture factors.

See **addiction, depression, motivation, nativism, reinforcement, schizophrenia, social constructionism, theory of evolution.**

Necker cube

This is an example of an **ambiguous figure**, in which an individual can view the cube from two different perspectives that can continuously change. Its appearance depends upon the point the viewer is fixating on. The 3-D cube spontaneously appears to changes from rear to front and back again; such perceptory illusions are used to provide evidence of the **top-down** view of **perception**.

See **ambiguous figures, perception, top-down processing.**

www.bbc.co.uk/science/humanbody/mind/surveys/neckercube/index.shtml (the Necker cube test, courtesy of BBC's Science and Nature site).

Negative reinforcement

Negative reinforcement can be seen as the strengthening of a **response** or behaviour through the elimination and termination of an unpleasant or aversive **stimulus** or situation after the **response**/behaviour has been made. For example if a dog constantly barks, the dog's behaviour produces an aversive, unpleasant situation for the owner. If the owner then responds by taking the dog for a walk, he or she is negatively reinforcing the dog's behaviour (barking behaviour equals reward/walk). The dog is therefore likely to carry out the behaviour again in the future as it has learnt to associate barking with going for a walk. Negative reinforcement contrasts with punishment, as punishment decreases the **response** that led to it while negative reinforcement increases it.

See **classical conditioning, conditioned stimulus, operant conditioning, reinforcement, response, stimulus.**

N

Neural network

This is a system of connected **neurons** within the **brain** and **central nervous system** that transmit information via electrical impulses.

See action potential, brain, neurotransmitter, neuron.

Neuron

A neuron is a nerve cell and the network and connection of neurons make up the nervous system. Neurons send information within the nervous system by means of changes in electrical impulses. A neuron is normally made up of **dendrites** that receive information, **axons** that transmit information, and the cell body. There are three types of neuron: receptors, **efferent** or motor neurons and interneurons.

See action potential, axon, dendrite, afferent neurons, efferent neurons.

Neuroses

Neurosis is a term used to describe a wide range of mental disorders that are milder than those associated with psychosis. Neurotic individuals do not lose contact with reality. They may however experience characteristics such as:

- Unacceptable levels of **anxiety**. These can often be associated with other issues, such as **phobias**, **addictions** or compulsions.
- The behaviours and actions of the individual may fall within socially expected norms of behaviour, but the neurotic individual may still find his or her own behaviour and actions unacceptable.

See addiction, anxiety, depression, DSM IV.

N

Neurotransmitter

A neurotransmitter is a chemical that is released by a **neuron** and crosses the synaptic gap to be received by the receptor sites on another **neuron**. The neurotransmitter enables **neurons** to communicate and transmit information throughout the **neural network**. Dopamine, **serotonin** and adrenalin are types of neurotransmitters.

See action potential, brain, depression, neural network, neuron, serotonin.

Nominal measurements

Nominal measurements are categorical, frequency, or count **data**. Objects are distinguished from each another by a name. Such categories have no **ranking**. For example, children at school can be placed into the nominal categories of visual, auditory or kinaesthetic learners.

> See **data, descriptive statistics, interval measurements, measures of central tendency, measures of dispersion, ordinal measurements, rank, ratio measurements.**

Nomothetic psychology

Nomothetic is a term that simply means 'generally applied', in the case of generating nomothetic 'laws', 'truths' or in terms of investigating **personality** 'traits'. Studies would be concerned with generating findings that can be universally applied to society. Nomothetic psychology is therefore concerned with understanding the similarities across societies and cultures, in contrast to **idiographic psychology**, which focuses on understanding individual differences.

> See **idiographic psychology, individualism, personality, social psychology, trait theories of personality.**

Non-conformity

This refers to an individual's ability to reject the temptation to adopt and **conform** to the values, beliefs or behaviours of the **majority** group. The process of 'self-categorization' is often used to explain non-conformity, as individuals tend to describe themselves in terms of belonging to a particular group or category, for example, being football fans or art students. If 'self-categorization' and group belonging form a crucial part of an individual's self-concept then that person would be more likely to conform. This would be due to normative influences, as individuals want to be seen as part of the group, rather than deviating from it. If however, 'self-categorization' within that group does not form an important part of a person's self-concept, then the individual will not feel 'pressured' to conform to the norms of the group.

> See **Asch, conformity, majority influence, Milgram.**

Non-parametric tests

Non-parametric tests, such as the **Wilcoxon test**, **Mann-Whitney U test** and **Friedman test** use either **ranks** or ordered scores.

They provide methods of testing **hypotheses** or producing **confidence intervals** that are not dependent on the assumptions made about the form of the population distributions.

> *See* **confidence interval, Friedman test, hypotheses, Mann-Whitney U test, parametric tests, rank, Wilcoxon test.**

Normal distribution

This refers to the representation of a set of scores that might be displayed on a frequency graph as producing a symmetrical **bell-shaped curve**. When measuring different **variables** that are normally distributed in the population as a whole, scores are supposed to form a **bell-shaped curve**. **Variables** such as intelligence and height are commonly identified as being normally distributed. When scores are normally distributed, the majority of scores are clustered around the central point with higher and lower scores being distributed towards the relevant ends of the curve. Mathematically, different normal distributions only differ in the values of the **mean** of scores and **standard deviation** of the scores.

> *See* **Bell-shaped curve, ceiling effect, kurtosis, mean, skewed distribution, standard deviation, variables.**

Norms

> *See* **social norms.**

Null hypothesis

> *See* **hypothesis.**

N

Obedience

Obedience is an action in which an individual succumbs to external pressure, to the explicit instructions of others, or to an authorative figure; it is a form of **conformity** to social influence. **Milgram** (1933–1984) conducted experiments (1974, 1963) into obedience, in which participants administered what they believed to be painful electric shocks to other individuals when told to do so by an authorative figure.

See **Asch, conformity, Milgram, social impact theory, social psychology.**

Milgram, S. (1963) Behavioural study of obedience. *Journal of Abnormal and Social Psychology*, 67, 371–8.

Milgram, S. (1974) *Obedience to Authority: An Experimental View*. New York: Harper and Row.

Objectivity

Objectivity can be viewed as an individual's decision and ability to undertake a **research** study or experiment and to collect **data** without allowing his or her own personal bias, experiences and interpretations to influence the process. Objectivity is regarded as an absolute imperative in conducting traditional, scientific, experimental **research**, in which the acquisition of objective truths and facts is striven for. In attempting to collect **data**, researchers who reflect upon their own **subjective** beliefs or interpretations of the event or situation may find it difficult to remain objective about the participants and **variables** under study. Depending on the nature and theoretical standpoint of the **research** study however, a researcher may strive to make (and value) an objective or **subjective** interpretation of the objects under study, or indeed incorporate both methods to provide contrasting **data** and viewpoints.

See **data, subjectivity, quantitative research, qualitative research, research, variables.**

Object permanence

This is an understanding that objects when hidden have a continued 'real' physical presence in the world, even though one has no physical evidence that they actually exist. **Piaget** suggested that children under the ages of eight months could not create a mental image of an object when it was not in their sight. This suggests that from a child's perspective, any object that disappears from view, such as toys or even their mother, seems to mysteriously vanish and later reappear when seen again. Children, according to **Piaget's theory of cognitive development**, acquire object permanence in the early part of the **sensori-motor stage** through actively exploring their environment.

See **Piaget's theory of cognitive development, sensori-motor stage.**

Object recognition

This refers to an individual's ability to identify three-dimensional structures as belonging to specific individual objects or classes of objects. This can usually be done regardless of an individual's position and relation to the object, and this allows people to negotiate their **response** and reactions to objects. Object recognition goes beyond basic visual **perception** and there are a many theories that attempt to explain how object recognition occurs:

- *Marr's model*
  Marr's (1982) approach is a **bottom-up processing** approach as object recognition begins through input from the external world into the visual perceptual system, and processes then take place to transform this information into an image. It is a stage model of object recognition.
     The processes are:
  - Grey level description
    The initial stage of measuring the intensity of light at individual points of the image is to generate the grey level description.
  - Primal sketch
    This contains two main modules:
    a) Raw primal sketch
    Gaining from the grey level description a description of the more significant areas of the object, such as lines and contours that may aid in recognizing the shape of the object.

b) Full primal sketch
This examines how the significant areas may go together and form structures.

* 2.5D sketch
Gaining an understanding of how the structures gained in the last stage relate to each other and the viewer helps to contextualize the object.

* Object recognition
This stage is concerned with recognition by extracting descriptions of the appearance of objects in the scene. Earlier information is converted into descriptions which are independent of viewpoint-object centred descriptions.

* *Biederman's components theory*
In contrast Biederman (1987) offered a recognition by components theory in an attempt to explain object recognition. The main claim of this theory is that the foundations of object recognition are based upon a small set of (around 36) volumetric shapes, such as cylinders, blocks, cones and wedges, known as *geons*. Geons, Biederman suggested can be put together in numerous ways to produce structural descriptions for most objects. He claimed that we match in parallel the geons extracted from any given object against our stored representations of object descriptions to make sense of and recognize an object.

See **bottom-up processing, pattern recognition, perception, response.**

Biederman, I. (1987). Recognition-by-components: a theory of human image understanding. *Psychological Review*, 94, 115–47.

Kirkpatrick-Steger, K., Wasserman, E. A. and Biederman, I. (1998). Effects of geon deletion, scrambling, and movement on picture recognition in pigeons. *Journal of Experimental Psychology: Animal Behavior Processes*, 24, 34–46.

Marr, D. (1982) *Vision: A Computational Investigation into the Human Representation and Processing of Visual Information*. San Francisco: W. H. Freeman.

www.pigeon.psy.tufts.edu/avc/kirkpatrick/ (information from K. Kirkpatrick, University of York, UK).

O

Observation

Observation is a term used to describe any event or situation in which an observer monitors, views or records behaviours, actions or speech exhibited by the observed participant. Observation can be used to define the design and approach of a study or the actual technique to collect and gather **data**. It is the use of observation as a **research** approach that leads to a variety of forms of observation.

In observation, unlike experimental studies, there is no attempt to manipulate an independent **variable (IV)** to affect the behaviour. Types of observational studies are:

* Controlled observations: while the behaviour of the participants is not under the influence of the manipulation of the IV, the environmental conditions are controlled to some extent by the researchers. Participants' behaviours are observed within the confines of this environment.
* Naturalistic observation: in naturalistic approaches, participants' behaviours are observed within a natural context, such as students at college.
* Participant and non-participant observation: in participant observation the researcher/observer participates within the group being observed. In non-participant observation the researcher observes the group from outside the situation, while attempting to be as detached and as non-intrusive as possible.
* Structured observation: the collection of **data** and recording of behaviour in structured observations is guided by observational categories. For example, a child's behaviour may only be recorded each time he or she repeats the same behaviour, such as hitting a doll (event **sampling**); or the number of times the child hits the doll, repeats the behaviour within a given time slot may be recorded (time **sampling**).

See **data, ethnography, fieldwork, qualitative research, research, sampling, variables.**

Sanger, J. (1996) *The Compleat Observer? A Field Research Guide to Observation*. London: Falmer.

Observational learning

Observational learning, also known as imitation, is the copying of another individual's behaviour. Imitating the behaviours of others is a powerful form of social learning, and the **reinforcement** parents provide their children via reward and praise as their children imitate 'grown up' and morally acceptable behaviour, ensures children develop many aspects of their behaviours in this manner. **Piaget** suggested that children in the latter part of the **sensori-motor stage**, towards the age of two, show evidence of deferred imitation; the ability to imitate behaviours that they have seen before.

See **gender development, Piaget's theory of cognitive development, reinforcement, sensori-motor stage, social learning theory.**

Occupational psychology

Occupational psychology is a branch of psychology concerned with how organizations function, how individuals and small groups behave at work, and the performance of people at work. Occupational psychologists attempt to increase the effectiveness and efficiency of organizations, and to enhance the individual's job satisfaction. This branch covers a variety of areas and interests such as ergonomics, personnel management, staff recruitment and selection and time management. Work can also be in advisory, teaching and research roles, and even extend to technical and administrative roles. Occupational psychologists can work for large companies, in government and public services, in private consultancies and management training centres.

Occupational psychologists are employed by the Civil Service, in settings such as the prison service, the Home Office, the Employment Department Group, the Ministry of Defence and the Civil Service Commission.

To become an occupational psychologist, an applicant will need an undergraduate degree in psychology that confers GBR (graduate basis for recognition) with the British Psychological Society. This should be followed by an MSc in occupational psychology and two years supervised practice under the supervision of a chartered occupational psychologist. It is also advisable to gain some experience in a relevant setting either before or in the course of MSc studies.

www.bps.org.uk (further career details from the British Psychological Society).

Oedipus complex

The Oedipus complex of **psychoanalytic** theory relates to the inner mental conflict that **Freud** suggests men experience as they journey through the **psychosexual stages** of development. **Freud** suggests that a son will experience a sexual desire for his mother (from about the ages of three to five years of age), which is accompanied by a deep jealousy and hatred for his father. There is a female equivalent which is named the **Electra complex.** Failure to resolve such conflicts, according to **Freud,** may lead to **neuroses** in later life.

See defence mechanism, Electra complex, Freud, neurosis, psychoanalysis, psychosexual stage, regression.

One-tailed hypothesis

See **hypothesis.**

O

One-tailed test

A one-tailed test is used when conducting a test for **significance** for a given set of **data** when the researcher is convinced (usually based on prior **research** findings) that the findings could only go in one direction. For example, **research** predicts that men will be faster in running two miles than women.

See **data, hypothesis, research, significance levels.**

Ontology

Ontology is an area of philosophy that is concerned with attempting to understand what things 'are' and the nature and reality of these 'things' in the social world. Each particular philosophical approach has its own set of ontological assumptions that attempt to define how individuals make sense of the social world around them. For example, experimental **social psychology** suggests that the social world is quite separate from people, it is simply an arena in which we exist and operate; in contrast **critical social psychology** suggests that the reality and understanding of the world is brought into being by the meaning making and social interactions of humans.

See **critical social psychology, social psychology.**

Robson, C (2002) *Real World Research*. Oxford: Blackwell.

Open-ended questions

Open-ended questions contrast with **closed questions**; as the name suggests, such questions leave the end of the question – the answer – open. They are designed to draw information or opinions from an individual. Open-ended questions do not request a simple 'Yes' or 'No' reply; instead they are designed to open up debates and discussions on a particular subject or area. Open-ended questions are often used in undertaking interviews, especially in **qualitative research** studies. Examples of open-ended questions are:

'How could we improve maternity services?'
'What could be done to help the elderly in your neighbourhood?'
'Where is good to go on holiday?'

Open questions are often known as the 'where, when, what and how' questions, designed to make interviewees think about their replies rather than simply state facts or answer 'Yes' or 'No'.

See closed questions, qualitative research, questionnaire.

Operant conditioning

Operant conditioning was first theorized by B. F. **Skinner** (1904–90), who suggested that almost all behaviour was under the control of reward and **reinforcement**. Behaviour that was followed by reward would increase in frequency and behaviour not '**reinforced**' with reward would naturally decrease in frequency. **Skinner** undertook many experiments to demonstrate the effects of operant conditioning on behaviour and developed the **Skinner box.**

See behaviourism, classical conditioning, Pavlov, reinforcement, Skinner, Skinner box.

Skinner, B. F. (1971) *Beyond Freedom and Dignity*. New York: Knopf.
Skinner, B. F. (1980) *The Shaping of a Behaviourist*. Oxford: Holden.

Oral stage

In **Freud**'s theory of **psychosexual** development, this is the first of five libidinal stages. It lasts from birth to approximately 18 months, in which time sexual **instincts** are concentrated on the area of the mouth. The stage is split into two phases:

- Passive oral phase: this lasts from birth to approximately eight months and is when a child passively takes milk from the mother's breast.
- Aggressive oral phase: in this phase children express anger by biting or chewing as they begin to become independent.

See Freud, instinct, psychosexual stages.

O

Ordinal measurements

These are measurements that have been categorized and **ranked** according to the relative amounts of some characteristic the objects possesses. Any differences between the **ranks** are meaningless, as such measurements are simply a rating score. For example, swimmers involved in a national swimming competition receive ratings of 1, 2, 3 or 4. These scores are simply based on performance characteristics.

> See **nominal measurements, rank, ratio measurements, interval measurements.**

Organizational psychology

This is another name for the branch of psychology known as **occupational psychology** that is concerned with the structures and functions of organizations and the behaviours of the individuals within them.

> *See* **occupational psychology.**

O

Paired comparison test

In statistics, these **significance** tests take two sets of scores that can be grouped into pairs. For example, if the same participants have performed in two **conditions**, their scores can be paired. These tests can show whether the differences between the paired scores, the performance in each **condition**, are significant.

> *See* **control condition, experimental condition, significance levels.**

Paradigm

In psychology the term 'paradigm' has two particular meanings. A paradigm can refer to a particular theoretical viewpoint, model, approach or general conceptual framework that is underpinned by specific assumptions about how knowledge is produced and the reality of the world. Such paradigms lead to specific approaches and techniques that suggest how best to understand and research human behaviour and **attitudes**. Science can be seen as a specific paradigm in which theories such as **behaviourism** and experimental methods have been constructed. The term 'paradigm' is also used to define a particular experimental procedure, such as the **classical conditioning** paradigm.

> See **attitude, behaviourism, classical conditioning.**

Parallel play

This is the type of play engaged in by two or more children who are using the same objects or materials within the same context but who do not interact together.

Parametric tests

These tests, also known as distribution dependent tests, are tests of **significance** that make assumptions about the characteristics of the population. They are considered quite powerful, as in such tests the probability is of not making a type II **error**. In using parametric tests certain requirements need to met:

* The **data** should be **interval** or **ratio** and normally distributed.
* The **variances** in the two conditions should be reasonably similar.

See **data, errors, interval measurements, non-parametric tests, ratio measurements, significance levels, variances.**

Parapsychology

This is a branch of psychology that is concerned with investigating and attempting to explain the paranormal, (events or experiences that cannot be explained in terms of a normal sensory occurrence). Clairvoyance (the **perception** of objects and events not available to normal sensory **perception**), telepathy (thought transference) and precognition (the **perception** of events yet to occur) are all examples of paranormal phenomenon.

See **perception.**

www.parapsychology.org/ (Paranormal Psychology Foundation).

Pattern recognition

Pattern recognition is a function or process of visual **perception** that enables individuals to recognize and identify two-dimensional **stimuli** (such as the numbers on a calendar) and three-dimensional objects, such as objects in our environment. There are a number of theories that attempt to explain how individuals can achieve such recognition. These include:

* Prototype theories: individuals are seen as comparing incoming **stimuli** to 'typical' images on the basis of past experience and knowledge of that class of **stimuli**. For example, if I asked you to imagine a car, you would probably have a similar image in your mind to that of most individuals from a Western society. Anything you then perceive that has similar features to that image you will then recognize and identify as a car.
* Template theories: individuals are seen as comparing incoming **stimuli** to stored images or templates within their **brain** and **memory** systems. If the **stimulus** matches the stored template image, a match is made and the individual recognizes it.

See **brain, memory, perception, stimulus.**

Pavlov

Pavlov, Ivan Petrovich (1849–1936), was a Russian psychologist who undertook a range of experiments in the 1920s that led him to devise the theory of **classical** (or Pavlovian) **conditioning.** Pavlov is famous for the experiments in which he conditioned dogs to salivate in **response** to hearing the noise of a bell.

> *See* **classical conditioning, Skinner, response.**

Perception

Perception is the act or process by which individuals are able to translate information from the external world into an experience of objects, sound, events, conversation and so on. Perception can be seen as the dual effect of the physiological processes that occur within biological sensory **responses** combined with the functioning within the **brain** that enables interpretation to be made of those senses. The two main attempts to explain perception focus particularly on one particular side of these processes, creating **top-down** theories (focusing on cognitive functioning in perception) or **bottom-up** theories (focusing on sensory, physiological input).

> *See* **bottom-up processing, brain, object recognition, pattern recognition, response, top-down processing.**

Perceptual constancy

This refers to how objects tend to still be perceived in the same form even when the environmental viewing conditions may change. For example, a brick will still be viewed as a brick whether it is on the top of a wall or at the bottom of a bucket of water; the perceptual properties of an object will still be viewed the same in terms of size (constancy), shape (constancy) and colour (constancy).

Personal construct theory

George Kelly (1906–1967) suggested the theory of personal constructs, which he viewed as representing the 'ways' in which individuals 'construct' their understanding and view of the world around them. A personal construct is an individual's **perception** of the common factors existing between two objects or events, which can separate and distinguish them from a third object or

P

event. For example, one might see two of one's colleagues as understanding and a third as aloof. This would then create a personal construct of 'understanding versus aloof' to group those individuals into categories. Individuals would then use such categories from their personal construction of the world around them to attempt to predict events in the social world. Personal constructs can be individual to the person or can be shared with others. They can remain stable and constant through time, but if an individual receives information or experiences that conflict with the category of constructs, such constructs can be changed. The repertory grid test and role construct repertory test were created to assess an individual's personal constructs.

See **Cattell, Eysenck personality questionnaire, five-factor model of personality, perception, social representations.**

Kelly, G. (1955) *The Psychology of Personal Constructs.* 2 vols. New York: Norton.

Maher, B. (1969) *Clinical Psychology and Personality: The Selected Papers of George Kelly.* New York: John Wiley.

Personality

Personality is a term used to describe the **traits** and stable characteristics of an individual that are viewed as determining particular consistencies in the manner in which that person behaves in any given situation and over time. It is suggested that differences in individual character **traits** are the reason why different people will behave differently in the same situation. Personality is differentiated from temporary states such as moods, as it is seen as stable over time. For example an introverted individual will act in an introverted manner consistent with his or her personality in a wide range of situations. There are critiques from a situationist perspective of this **trait** view that suggest that an individual's behaviour does not remain consistent over time and across situations.

See **Cattell, big five model of personality, Freud, trait theories of personality.**

Phallic stage

In psychodynamic theory, the phallic stage is the third of **Freud**'s suggested libidinal stages, occurring from the age of three to seven years. In the phallic stage the libido (sexual **instinctual** drive) is concentrated on the child's own sexual organs, as masturbation is seen as occurring. Within the phallic stage the child is also seen to go through the **Oedipus/Electra complex**, becoming sexually attracted to the parent of the opposite sex and hostile to and jealous of the parent of the same sex.

See **Electra complex, Freud, instinct, Oedipus complex, psychosexual stages.**

Phenomenology

Phenomenology is a philosophical doctrine proposed by Edmund Husserl (1859–1938) that focuses on the study of conscious human experience in which **objective** preconceptions, understandings and interpretations of reality are not taken into account. It can be regarded as a **qualitative research** method that is concerned with the study and analysis of mental experience and not behaviour.

See **humanistic psychology, objectivity, qualitative research, Rogers.**

Phenotype

The phenotype incorporates the outward, observable characteristics of an organism. It consists of physical parts such as molecules, cells, structures, metabolism, tissues and organs, and also of reflexes and behaviours. The phenotype can be seen as a product of the interaction of the **genotype** with the environment.

See **genotype.**

Phobia

A phobia or phobic disorder is a type of **anxiety** disorder in which there is a persistent and irrational fear of an object or situation. An individual with an intense phobia will experience extreme **anxiety** and fearfulness, and to reduce this **anxiety** will attempt to avoid the object or situation at all costs. Phobias can in their most intense forms interfere with the normal functioning of an individual so that a person may find it impossible to lead a normal life. There are three categories of phobia listed in the **DSM IV**, which are:

- Social phobias: fear of engaging in social situations and interactions that may be seen as potentially embarrassing, such as presenting a speech or eating in public or talking to new people.
- Agorophobia: fear of open or public places.
- Specific phobias: there are literally thousands of specific

phobias, such as a fear of spiders (arachnobia) and a fear of flying (aerophobia).

See **anxiety, DSM IV, list of phobias.**

Phoneme

This is the smallest unit of speech or sound that enables the user or the listener to differentiate one word from another. For example the sound (h) and (b) allow the words 'hit' and 'bit' to be differentiated.

See **language development.**

Piaget's theory of cognitive development

Piaget, Jean (1896–1980), began his interest in **cognitive psychology** in the early 1920s when he worked alongside Binet on the early intelligence tests. Through working with children, Piaget realized that children of similar ages made the same kind of errors when answering questions. From this, he argued that younger children might use different rules of logic or thought processes than older children.

Piaget proposed a stage theory of cognitive development that attempted to explain at what stage of **maturation** children would make particular kinds of errors. He hypothesized that children passed sequentially through a series of cognitive development stages. In each stage he depicted children's thoughts and cognitive skills as being qualitatively different to those of the prior stage.

Key aspects of Piaget's theory:

- Children are born with similar biological structures, senses, reflexes and **brains**.
- Babies are born with an innate set of reflexes that allow them to interact with the environment.
- Babies possess an innate **schema** (a knowledge structure) that can contain information gained from interacting with the world and information yet to be gained.
- A baby's **schema** can develop through interacting with the environment and can lead to new experiences and in turn to development of a new **schema**.

Piaget proposed two ways in which **schema** can develop: **assimilation** and **accommodation**. He proposed a four-stage theory of children's cognitive development:

1. **Sensori-motor stage** (0–2 years).

2. **Preoperational stage** (2–7 years).
3. **Concrete operational stage** (7–11 years).
4. **Formal operational stage** (11+ years).

> *See* **accommodation, assimilation, brain, cognitive psychology, concrete oper-ational stage, conservation, decentration, egocentrism, formal operational stage, maturation, preoperational stage, schemas, sensori-motor stage.**

Donaldson, M. (1978) *Children's minds.* London: Fontana.
Piaget, J. (1955) *The Child's Construction of Reality.* Routledge and Kegan Paul.
www.piaget.org/index.html (Information from the Jean Piaget Society).

Placebo

In drug trials or experimental **research**, a placebo is a substance known not to have any medicinal properties that is given to the **control group**. The **experimental** group can then be given the medicinal substance and each group's **responses** can be observed and recorded to distinguish the medicinal effects of the substance itself from the psychological effects of individuals thinking they are receiving it.

> *See* **control condition, control group, experimental condition, placebo effect, research, response.**

Placebo effect

This is the effect or improvement witnessed in a patient's or partic-ipant's condition caused by simply receiving a **placebo**. The placebo effect can be seen as a psychological effect: a change in the individual's thinking that is eliciting changes in behaviour.

> *See* **placebo.**

Pleasure principle

In **psychoanalysis**, this is viewed as the pleasure-seeking and impulsive characteristics that are inherent in each individual, usually associated with the **id**. Individuals are seen as being driven by the **id** to gratify its urges and needs regardless of the moral or real consequences.

> *See* **Freud, ego, id, psychosexual stages, superego.**

Positive reinforcement

This is the use of something that strengthens (reinforces) the action or behaviour that occurred before it. Positive reinforcers are usually

P

things that an individual finds attractive or rewarding and can be defined as drive reducers. An example is the gold star given to a child who gets ten out of ten in a maths test. The gold star is a reward and serves to reinforce repetition of this behaviour. A positive reinforcer always strengthens the **response**, making the behaviour more likely to occur in the future. In contrast, aversive or unpleasant **reinforcers** have the opposite effect as it serves to decrease the likelihood of that action recurring in the future. An example is when a child has a favourite toy taken away for misbehaving or ignoring the parents' requests.

See **operant conditioning, classical conditioning, negative reinforcement, reinforcement, response.**

Prejudice

Prejudice in psychology refers to the way a person can be judged simply on his or her membership of a particular group or category. Prejudices are prejudgements that are resistant to change and the influence of 'new' knowledge; they go deeper than just being preconceived ideas about other individuals, as they involve making evaluations of them. While prejudice can be either positive or negative in psychology, it usually refers to the negative **attitudes** held towards individuals. **Stereotyping** helps to sustain prejudices, maintaining the belief that all members of a group share the same characteristics. There are many theories that attempt to explain prejudice:

- Cognitive theories: these stress that it is important for individuals to **stereotype** and categorize people because of the need to simplify in order to make sense of the world (see **attributional biases**).
- Personality theories: the authoritarian personality theory views prejudice as a product of an individual's style of upbringing.
- Sociocultural theories: these view prejudice as evolving through the sharing and **assimilation** of cultural beliefs to which an individual is subject. People's association with a particular group may lead them to develop prejudices that are concurrent with those of other group members about other groups, created through competition or conflict. The person's own group is viewed as the 'in group' and the other as the 'out group'.

See **assimilation, attitude, attributional biases, majority influence, social identity theory, social representations, stereotyping.**

P

Preoperational stage

In **Piaget's theory of cognitive development**, this is the second stage that children are seen to pass through, at approximately two to seven years of age. In this stage children are seen going beyond the ability to undertake only direct action in the **sensori-motor stage**, and becoming capable of symbolic functioning. Children can now think about objects that are not present. They are still, however, greatly influenced by their own **perceptions** of the environment. Children are seen within **conservation** tasks as focusing on only one aspect of the whole event, which leads to errors. In these **conservation** tasks children do not realize that the visual display is still the same despite changes in the way it appears. Children's **language development** skills are also seen to advance throughout this stage.

> *See* **conservation, language development, perception, Piaget's theory of cognitive development, sensori-motor stage.**

Primacy effect

In studies of free recall, the primacy effect refers to the way individuals are more able to recall the first items presented to them than items from the middle or end of a list. In **social psychology** the primacy effect relates to the way first impressions of meeting people tend to play a major role in how we perceive them. Simply, material or **stimuli** that is presented to individuals earlier exert a stronger effect on their thoughts and views than material presented later; so first impressions really do count!

> *See* **recency effect, social psychology, stimulus.**

Prisoner's dilemma

> *See* **game theory.**

Procedural memory

> *See* **memory.**

Pro-social behaviour

This is a positive type of helping behaviour, a behaviour that an individual elicits and offers that is seen to be socially desirable and benefits the social group or society in which the individual exists.

> *See* **altruism, antisocial behaviour.**

Psychoanalysis

Psychoanalysis, based upon psychoanalytic theory developed by **Freud**, is a complex theory of human emotional development and the formation of **personality**. Psychoanalysis can be seen as the practical application of psychoanalytic theory in a form of treatment. It has been used to address a number of client issues, such as **phobias**, **anxiety** and sexual problems. It attempts to provide clients with an insight into the working of their unconscious minds via **dream analysis** and the interpretation of fantasies, **attitudes** and the process of **free association**.

> *See* anxiety, attitude, dream analysis, ego, free association, Freud, id, personality, phobia, psychosexual stages, superego.

Psychometric testing

Psychometric tests are forms of psychological test that attempt to measure an aspect of the functioning of an individual's mind. Psychometry is a branch of psychology that is solely concerned with the measuring and testing of mental functions. Examples are aptitude, intelligence and personality tests designed to assess whether a person will be suited for a particular type of career, such as the army or police force. Alfred Binet at the turn of the twentieth century was the first person to create an intelligence test; tests that are in use today include the Wechsler intelligence test for children **(WISC-III)** and the Wechsler intelligence test for adults **(WAIS-III).**

> *See* **WAIS-III, WISC-III.**

Kaufman, A. S. and Lichtenberger, E. O (1999) *Essentials of WAIS-III Assessment* (Essentials of Psychological Assessment Series). London: Wiley.
Kaufman, A. S. and Lichtenberger, E. O. (2000) *Essentials of WISC-III and WPPSI-R Assessment*. London: Wiley.

Psychosexual stages

Freud's theory of psychosexual development was one of the first theories to highlight and examine how studying child development can help to understand adult behaviour, **attitudes** and thinking. Freud was also one of the earliest thinkers to put forward a stage theory, which suggests that development occurred gradually as humans move through a set of particular developmental stages.

    Freud argued that **personality** developed through an individual moving through five psychosexual stages. In each of these stages the driving force or **motivation** is to express innate sexual energy in the area of the body relevant to the stage being experienced. The stages are:

1. The **oral stage** (0–2 years).
2. The **anal stage** (2–3 years).
3. The **phallic stage** (3–6 years).
4. The **latency stage** (6–12 years).
5. The **genital stage** (12+ years).

Freud viewed individuals as developing into particular **personality** types, such as oral, anal or genital, according to how they progress through each of the stages. Each **personality** type, **Freud** suggested, had specific **traits** and characteristics relevant to that particular type. For example, anal personalities tend to be mean, obstinate and orderly.

> See **anal stage, attitude, ego, Freud, genital stage, id, latency stage, motivation, oral stage, personality, phallic stage, superego, trait theories of personality,**

Psychosocial stages

> See **Erikson's psychosocial development stages.**

Q-sort

This is a technique that is designed to identify patterns in **subjectivity**; it is used in therapy to determine the progress that clients are making towards their goals. Clients choose – from a set of cards that have statements about them, about the ideal self, relationships and so on – the statements that are most like or least like themselves. They then place these statements into a variety of categories, ranging from most characteristic to least characteristic. A study of people's choice of cards can show how they view themselves and whether they have positive or negative self-images. Q-sort is also used as a **research methodology** within social and **critical social psychology**.

> *See* **critical social psychology, methodology, research, subjectivity.**

Brown, S. R. (1996) Q methodology and qualitative research. *Qualitative Health Research*, **6** (4), 561–7. Available online at: www.rz.unibw-muenchen.de/ ~p41bsmk/qmethod/srbqhc.htm.

Brown, S. R. (no date) *The History and Principles of Q Methodology in Psychology and the Social Sciences.* From the Q Archive Website: facstaff.uww.edu/cottlec/Qarchive/Bps.htm.

Dennis, K. E. (1986). Q methodology: relevance and application to nursing research. *Advances in Nursing Science*, **8** (3), 6–17.

Stainton Rogers, R. (1995). Q methodology. In J. A. Smith, R. Harre and L. Van Langenhove (eds), *Rethinking Methods in Psychology*. Thousand Oaks, CA: Sage.

Qualitative research

Qualitative research is an approach that sits in direct contrast to **quantitative research**; it attempts to offer an alternative approach to the traditional scientific methods used within experimental approaches. Many different researchers use qualitative research methods and there is no one theoretical **epistemological** position; such methods are usually used to understand how people make sense of the world. Qualitative research therefore, in contrast to experimental approaches that examine **cause and effect** relationships, tends to be

Interested in the quality and nature of individual's experience. Such an approach attempts to understand and explain experiences and events rather than make and test predictions.

Two types of qualitative research that can be distinguished:

- Big Q: this term refers to the open-ended and inductive **research** methodologies that focus upon the generation of theories and meanings.
- Little q: this type of research begins with a **hypothesis** and specific categories of interest chosen by the researcher. Little q can be seen to work from the top down (as opposed to big Q, which works from the bottom up), as it does not engage with the **data** to create new insights of the world; rather it seeks to ask specific questions of the world.

Qualitative research is largely concerned with meaning, and explores the use and interpretation of language through research methods such as interviews, diaries and methods of analysis such as **discourse analysis** and interpretive **phenomenological analysis.**

Many feminist researchers use qualitative research methods, as they feel this approach makes it possible to address the particular **gender bias** that has occurred within quantitative studies that have neglected to comprehend women's experiences.

In contrast to **quantitative research** methods, which focus on predicting and measuring, qualitative research incorporates both the participant's and researcher's **subjective** knowledge. Such knowledge or reflexivity enables the researcher to understand how the interaction with 'others' within the research process has contributed to the meaning-making process and the knowledge produced.

> *See* **cause and effect, research, hypothesis, data, discourse analysis, phenomenological analysis, gender bias, quantitative research, subjectivity, feminist psychology, social psychology.**

Ribbens, J. and Edwards, R. (2000) *Feminist Dilemmas in Qualitative Research*. London: Sage.

Silverman, D. (2001) *Interpreting Qualitative Data*. London: Sage.

Willig, C. (2001) *Introducing Qualitative Research in Psychology*. Buckingham: Open University Press.

www.nova.edu/ssss/QR/web.html (online journal dedicated to qualitative research).

Quantitative research

Quantitative research is mainly concerned with predicting possible outcomes by testing **hypotheses** and measuring **variables**. It attempts to identify and generate real 'facts' about the nature of the world and of human behaviour, through the use of **objective** methods of investigation. In quantitative research, the researcher is ideally an **objective** observer who does not participate in or influence what is being studied. Quantitative research is synonymous with the experimental, scientific approach and emphasizes the importance of measuring **variables**, using statistics **objectivity** and the **reliability** and **validity** of research findings.

> See **experimental condition, control condition, experimental psychology, hypothesis, objectivity, reliability, validity, variables.**

Quasi-experiment

This is a type of research in which full control over all the **variables** is not possible, for example in naturalistic and **ethnographic research**.

> *See* **ethnography, observation, variables.**

Questionnaire

A questionnaire is a set of questions that is specifically designed to elicit information from individuals about a particular topic or area. It can also be used to reveal something about an individual's **personality** or **attitude**.

> *See* **attitude, Likert scale, personality, reliability.**

> Foddy, W (1994) *Constructing Questions for Interviews and Questionnaires: Theory and Practice in Social Research*. Cambridge: Cambridge University Press.
>
> Parahoo, K (1997) *Nursing Research: Principles, Process and Issues*. Hampshire: Palgrave.
>
> Oppenheim, A. N. (2000) *Questionnaire Design, Interview and Attitude Measurement*. London: Continuum International Publishing group.

Quota sampling

> *See* **sampling.**

Randomized control trial

This is a type of controlled experiment in which individual's **responses** are tested to determine the success of a therapy or treatment. Individuals who are experiencing the same disorder or condition (such as **schizophrenia** or **depression**) are divided into two groups, the **experimental** and **control condition**; those in the **control condition** are given a **placebo** treatment, and those in the **experimental condition** are given the actual treatment. By contrasting the findings of each group, the study can determine the actual effectiveness of the treatment upon the disorder or condition.

> *See* **control condition, depression, experimental condition, placebo, response, schizophrenia.**

Range

In statistics, the range is the difference between the highest score and the lowest score in a distribution, the range by which the scores vary.

> *See* **descriptive statistics.**

Rank

This means placing scores, items or values into an order according to their position from first to last. For example:

Name	Time taken to run 1 km	Rank
Jane	8 minutes	3
Susan	20 minutes	4
Karen	5 minutes	1
John	6 minutes	2

Rating scale
This refers to the assessment of an individual according to some standard rating criteria. An example is rating a person's exam grade

according to an achievement level of: A = excellent, B = very good, C= good, D = pass, E = fail.

See **Likert scale.**

Ratio measurements

Ratio **data** have the highest level of measurement as they can measure ratios between **data** as well as intervals, because there is a starting point (zero).

See **data, interval measurements, nominal measurements, ordinal measurements.**

Raw score

A raw score is the actual score/s derived from an experiment or test that has not been modified into another format such as a percentage or measure of **standard deviation.**

See **standard deviation.**

Reality principle

In **psychoanalytic** theory, it is through this principle that individuals become aware of the demands of the external world and modify their behaviour accordingly. As they adapt their behaviour so as to **conform**, the **instinctual** urges and desires of the **id** are suppressed. The reality principle is seen as governed by the **ego.**

See **conformity, ego, Freud, id, instinct, psychoanalysis.**

R

Recency effect

In free recall studies in the field of learning, the term 'recency effect' refers to how participants are more likely to recall the items presented at the end of a list than items in the middle of the list. In **social psychology**, it is a term that defines how recent events and experiences will have a greater influence on an individual's **attitudes**. For example if your friend is late and you have recently heard on the radio that there has been a car accident on the road into town, you may assume that your friend is late as he is stuck in traffic on this road. This contrasts with the **primacy effect.**

See **attitude, primacy effect, social psychology.**

Reciprocal altruism

This is a form of **altruism** that is based on a shared understanding that individuals will mutually help each other.

See **altruism.**

Reductionism

In psychology this term refers to how human behaviour and the social world can be best understood by reducing the phenomenon into its most basic constituents. It is a view that maintains that psychology is best understood within the framework of science, and adopts an experimental approach. Approaches such as biological and **cognitive psychology** and **behaviourism** are examples of reductionist approaches that adopt a **cause and effect** model. Biological and **cognitive** approaches attempt to explain human behaviour in terms of the underlying constituents of cognitive processes and/or human biology and physiology. **Behaviourists** break human behaviour down into the basic constituents of **stimulus response**. Reductionism is strongly critiqued however, as such an approach takes no account of human action and **free will** as possible causes of human behaviour.

See **behaviourism, cause and effect, cognitive psychology, free will, response, stimulus.**

Brown, T. and Smith, L. (2003) *Reductionism and the Development of Knowledge.* Mahwah, NJ: Lawrence Erlbaum.

Regression

Regression refers to an individual returning to an earlier, usually childish, way of thinking and behaving. In **psychoanalysis** it relates to how an individual loses his or her grip on reality and returns to earlier ways of coping with **instinctual** sexual urges. It is thought to be a **defence mechanism** that enables an individual to avoid current **anxiety** by returning to earlier, childlike behaviour patterns.

Regression also refers in statistics to any method that enables an individual to make predictions about the value of one **variable** on the basis of knowledge about the values of another **variable**/s. Two types of regression are:

- Linear regression: this involves predicting the value of a **variable** by drawing a line of 'best fit' through the x- and y-plotted **data** values on a graph.

* Multiple regression: this involves predicting the value of one **variable** based on the knowledge of the values of several other **variables**.

See **anxiety, data, defence mechanism, instinct, psychoanalysis, variables.**

Reinforcement

This refers to the process by which a behavioural **response** is strengthened. When a **response** is followed by a pleasant event, such as the receiving of a reward such as praise, this motivates a repetition of the **response**; the **response** is viewed as having been reinforced. There are two types of reinforcement:

* **Positive reinforcement**: the **response** is followed by something that an individual wants and enjoys receiving.
* **Negative reinforcement**: the **response** is followed by the removal of something unpleasant

Reinforcement always strengthens the tendency of an individual engaging in a particular **response**, making the behaviour more likely to be repeated in the future.

See **classical conditioning, negative reinforcement, positive reinforcement, operant conditioning, response, secondary reinforcer.**

Relationship theories

There are many theories that have explored the processes that underpin the formation of and changes that take place in a variety of types of interpersonal relationships. Theories include:

* *Biological theories*
  These theories have examined social relationships from a biological and evolutionary standpoint. The key aspect of this approach is that all individuals are **motivated** to form and engage in interpersonal relationships to enable them to sexually reproduce and ensure the survival of their **genes**. In terms of the development of non-romantic and non-sexual relationships, relationships with family members are viewed as **motivated** to perpetuate the survival of their **genes** (genetic characteristics shared and contained in other family members' **genes**) through helping other family members to survive to reproduce. Such a theory, while able to account for relationship formation and maintenance within families, does not offer explanations for

R

interpersonal non-sexual relationships with individuals outside of the family system.

- *Reinforcement and needs satisfaction theory*
  This theory suggests that individuals are **motivated** to form and maintain interpersonal relationships because of the rewards and **reinforcement** they receive from others. Rewards can be things such as smiles, love, sex, praise, reassurance, status, help or money. They serve to **motivate** individuals to engage in certain relationships so that they can meet their social needs. For example, praise and reassurance may serve to meet our need to be accepted by others and increase our **self-esteem**, while love may meet our sexual needs. While this theory does offer an account of why people form relationships it does not provide reasons for why individuals would stay in relationships that are low in rewards, such as abusive relationships.
- *Exchange and equity theories*
  These theories follow on from the **reinforcement** theories to examine how the formation of and engagement in relationships are **motivated** by an individual's need to **maximize** personal rewards and minimize costs.

See **equity theory, gene, kin selection, maximizing (game theory), motivation, natural selection, reinforcement, self-esteem, social exchange theory, theory of evolution.**

Fellner, C. H. and Marshall, J. R. (1981) Kidney donors revisited. In J. P. Rushton and R. M. Sorrentino (eds), *Altruism and Helping Behaviour*. Hillsdale, NJ: Erlbaum.

Reliability

If the findings of a study or test can be repeated on any other occasion and yield the same findings, then the study/test is deemed reliable.

A **research** study's findings can be defined as reliable if the same findings can be gained in repeated investigations that have adhered to the same conditions.

Psychometric tests can be regarded as reliable if they have internal and external reliability. Measuring internal reliability means that the **questionnaire** is checked to see if the participants answer the questions in the same way each time. Measuring external reliability means that the answers to the questions can be checked over a period of time to ensure that the findings are stable over time. If the participant's answers are found to be consistent over time, then the **questionnaire** is said to have external reliability.

See **research, psychometric tests, questionnaire.**

REM sleep

REM is an abbreviation for 'rapid eye movement'; this type of sleep is characterized by dreaming and quick, jerky eye movements. It occurs periodically throughout the night, lasting up to one hour, although usually for about 20 minutes. REM sleep is usually accompanied by a faster breathing pace and increased heart rate and pulse.

Repertory grid test

See **personal construct theory.**

Repression

Freud suggested in his psychodynamic theory that repression is the process by which any **anxiety** or guilt-provoking thoughts or memories are removed from conscious thought. It is a **defence mechanism** that blocks such thoughts and material originating in the **id** from reaching a person's conscious mind. These repressed thoughts and material are blocked but, as **Freud** suggests, are not deactivated. Instead they affect a person's behaviour and are manifest mainly in the form of symbolic imagery in dreams or within neurotic behaviour.

See **anxiety, defence mechanism, dream analysis, Freud, id, psychoanalysis.**

Research

R

Research is a general term used to describe any attempt or method that is used with the aim of collecting and analysing **data** and generating findings. There are many different approaches to research, depending upon the researcher's philosophical position and theoretical viewpoint, as seen within the experimental approach in contrast to the critical approach. Such a theoretical position would inform the choice and range of research methods used in undertaking research. Two types of research are **qualitative** and **quantitative**, with **quantitative** types being traditionally associated with experimental research and **qualitative research** associated with critical research.

See data, qualitative research, quantitative research.

Denzin, N. K. and Lincoln Y. S. (2005) *The Sage Handbook of Qualitative Research*. London: Sage.
Bryman, A. (2004) *Social Research Methods*. Oxford: Oxford University Press.

Resistance

Generally, resistance refers to an individual's reluctance to take part in something or to follow orders. In **psychoanalysis** however, it refers to an individual's unconscious thoughts and experiences that are prevented or blocked from entering the conscious mind. It is also used in **psychoanalysis** to define the way in which the analysand (client in therapy) resists accepting the interpretations made by the analyst.

See **Freud, psychoanalysis**.

Response

This term generally means the reactive behaviour of an organism or individual to, or in the presence of, a **stimulus**.

See **stimulus**.

Reticular activating system (RAS)

RAS stands for ascending reticular activating system. It is a system of the **brain** located in the **brain** stem, thalamus and cortex that has inputs from the senses. It is responsible for arousal from sleep, wakefulness, and **attention**.

See **attention, brain**.

Retrieval

This refers to the accessing and collection of any information from **memory**, whether this is in an organism, individual or computer.

See **Atkinson and Shiffrin, memory**.

Rogers

Rogers, Carl (1902–1987), was instrumental in the development of non-directive **psychotherapy** (*Rogerian psychotherapy*). The basic assumptions underpinning such therapy was the acceptance of

unconditional positive regard and empathic understanding within the therapeutic relationship, which Rogers believed was necessary and sufficient to create a space conducive to enabling the client to fully experience and understand his or her self. Rogers views are generally located within the areas of **humanistic psychology** and **phenomenology**, as he particularly focused upon examining and understanding the **subjective** experience of human beings.

See **humanistic psychology, phenomenology, psychotherapy, subjectivity, unconditional positive regard.**

Rogers, C. (2004) *On becoming a person*. London: Constable and Robinson.
www.mywiseowl.com/articles/Carl_Rogers (information from MyWiseowl. com).

Rosenthal effect

This refers to how the results of an experiment can be distorted because of the effect of the researcher's expectations and beliefs. Rosenthal demonstrated this effect in studies (1966, 1982); the effect is a form of **self-fulfilling prophecy** as what you expect to happen under the influence of the researchers own expectations has a tendency to actually happen.

See **self-fulfilling prophecy.**

Rosenthal, R. (1966) *Experimenter Effects in Behavioural Research*. New York: Appleton-Century-Crofts.
Rosenthal, R. and Rubin, D. B. (1982) A simple general purpose display of magnitude of experimental effects. *Journal of Educational Psychology*, 74, 166–169.

Rumination

Rumination is the dwelling upon and preoccupation with past thoughts and experiences that are usually traumatic, distressing and emotionally charged for the individual. Rumination, continuing to linger in the past rather than look towards the future, has been linked to conditions such as **depression**. Therapies such as **cognitive behaviour therapy** attempt to challenge such negative 'thinking' patterns by focusing on the development of more positive ways of thinking.

See **cognitive behaviour therapy, depression.**

Ss

Sample

A sample is a group of individuals who are representative of the general population or the group that the **research** is concerned with studying. Examples of sample groups are:

- *Matched sample*
  A sample group is chosen on the basis of each participant possessing a particular characteristic, other than those under investigation, so that it can be compared against another sample group.
- *Representative sample*
  These sample groups are selected because they are representative of the population in general. An attempt is made to ensure that no members of the population are more likely than others to get into the sample; in other words everyone has an equal chance.
- *Random sample*
  This is the most common form of sampling in which each participant is given a particular number and all have an equal chance of being selected. For example, participants are given a number and all numbers are placed in a hat and numbers are drawn, one at a time, until the sample size is reached. This style of sampling is most suitable for a homogenous sample and where the sample is unlikely to be seriously biased.

See **research, sampling.**

Sampling

This is the method in which you gain a **sample** group that is representative of the whole population on which the **data** is to be gathered. Methods of sampling are:

- *Biased sampling*
  Biased sampling occurs when participants from one particular

category or group (females, males, people of a certain age, culture or race) are over-represented within a **sample** group. This would then indicate that the **sample** group fails to accurately represent the population from which it was derived. Sampling bias may occur in many ways:

- only using volunteers; are people who volunteer for **research** representative of the population?
- only using student volunteers for a **research** project because they are a convenient or a purposeful sample group (simply because they were there and met the purpose of the study); are they representative of the population?
- not thinking carefully about your sample technique, for example only picking participants who just happen to be hanging around campus; are they really representative of the population when all other students are in lectures?

- *Stratified sampling*
This involves gaining a **sample** group by taking a specified number of participants systematically from each section of the population.
- *Quota sampling*
This occurs when a particular quota or number of participants in a **research** study are selected on the basis of their frequency or occurrence within the given population; for example a quota of particular age groups.

See **research, sample, snowball effect.**

Scaffolding

See **zone of proximal development.**

S

Schema

In **social psychology**, a schema is a store that contains all the information about previous events and experiences. Schemas or schemata are **retrieved** to make decisions about future experiences and evaluate the possible outcomes of engaging in certain events. For example, you are asked to babysit for your sister's newborn baby. Your previous experience of babysitting involved hours of listening to a screaming baby, sickness and nappy changing, and having to resort to calling your sister (to your embarrassment) to come back early. This previous schema influences the way in which you would perceive the possible events and outcomes of babysitting in the future.

According to **Piaget's cognitive theory of child development**, a schema is an organized structure of skills and knowledge that alter and change with a child's age and experience.

> *See* **accommodation, assimilation, memory, Piaget's cognitive theory of child development, retrieval, social psychology.**

Schizophrenia

Schizophrenia is a severe mental disorder and is marked by a range of serious and diverse symptoms and disruptions in mental functioning. Symptoms include:

* perceptual disturbances such as hearing voices, experiencing **hallucinations** and not being able to understand other people's emotional states
* emotional disturbances on either side of the spectrum, from exhibiting no emotions at all to exhibiting inappropriate or excessive emotional **responses**
* thought disturbances, such as illogical reasoning, delusions and making sense of events in a manner that has no bearing on reality
* physical disturbances, such symptoms as inappropriate physical actions, excessive giggling or laughing
* social functioning disturbances, such as poor social skills and an inability to form or maintain social relationships.

There are many explanations for schizophrenia, including:

* medical evidence that suggests schizophrenia is associated to actual **brain** damage that leads to enlargement of the **brain** ventricles
* biochemical explanations that emphasize the role of the **neurotransmitter** dopamine in triggering the disorder
* genetic explanations that suggest there is a genetic vulnerability that may lead some individuals, given a particular set of social environmental conditions, into developing schizophrenia.

The treatment of schizophrenia usually involves anti-psychotic drugs that aim to eliminate the main symptoms of the disorder, and psychotherapies such as family therapy.

> *See* **abnormal behaviour, abnormal psychology, brain, diathesis-stress model, DSM IV, hallucination, neurotransmitters, response.**

S

Bentall, M. (2004) *Models of Madness: Psychological, Social and Biological Approaches to Schizophrenia*. London: Bruner-Routledge.

Scientific method

The scientific method is an experimental, **objective research** method traditionally associated with **behaviourism**. The scientific method is based on the assumption that stringent **objective** testing can generate facts about the reality of the world and of human behaviour.

See **behaviourism, experimental condition, objectivity, Skinner, research.**

Secondary reinforcer

A secondary reinforcer (in behaviourist theories of **operant** and **classical conditioning**) is a **stimulus** that reinforces/strengthens a behaviour that has already been followed by a reinforcer on a previous occasion.

See **classical conditioning, operant conditioning, reinforcement, stimulus.**

Selective attention

This refers to the focus of concentration upon one **stimulus** or **stimuli** to the exclusion of all others.

See **attenuator model of attention, Broadbent, stimulus.**

Self-actualization theory

A theory developed by Maslow (1954) that attempts to explain human **motivation** in terms of attempting to become, to achieve or grow into a higher self; to self-actualize. Maslow theorized two processes that humans must undergo to achieve self-actualization: self-exploration and action; the deeper the self-exploration the greater the personal growth and development. The closer we come to self-actualization the nearer we are to reaching our potential.

After a study of persons both living and dead (Maslow 1954), Maslow concluded that people had reached self-actualization when they displayed certain characteristics that include:

- an efficient **perception** of reality and being comfortable in relating to it
- possessing an acceptance of self, others and nature

- the ability to act spontaneously and not to be restricted by convention, but not to flout it
- not being **egocentric**, instead focusing on issues outside oneself
- being able to enjoy one's own company, solitude and silence
- being able to remain calm in the face of things and events that have a tendency to upset other people
- being independent and autonomous, not dependent on society or culture
- not being dependent on others for satisfaction, although perhaps being dependent on others for the satisfaction of the basic needs such as love, safety, respect and belongingness
- being able to continuously see the beauty and good in the world
- feeling that life holds limitless possibilities
- being able to empathize with other people and their situations in life
- being able to relate easily and deeply to other people
- being non-judgemental and tolerant of others
- being creative.

Eysenck (2000) suggests that the strengths of Maslow's theory lie in it being a more comprehensive account than other approaches in attempting to explain human **motivation**. However, Eysenck suggests that the concept of self-actualization is a very difficult one to measure, and suggests that not everyone has the **motivation** for personal growth. As evidence for this, he points out that some people spend 20 hours or more in front of the television each week, seemingly uninterested in reaching their potential. He also criticizes Maslow's theory for its lack of emphasis on the possible effects of environmental factors in facilitating personal growth and self-actualization, such as a person having supportive friends and family, good education opportunities and financial security.

See **egocentrism, motivation, perception.**

Eysenck, M. W. (2000) *Psychology: A Student's Handbook*. Hove: Psychology Press.
Maslow, A. H. (1954) *Motivation and Personality*. New York: Harper.
Maslow, A. H. (1970) *Toward a Psychology of Being*. New York: Van Nostrand.

S

Self-efficacy

This refers to people's belief that they can perform adequately in any given situation, and specifically focuses on what individuals believe they can do with the skills they possess. Self-efficacy beliefs are important when attempting to understand and predict individuals' **attitudes** to health, and in turn changing unhealthy behaviours. For example, if people believe that they have no will-power, they may believe that dieting would be too difficult for them. An individual's self-efficacy in any situation is likely to be affected by four key factors:

- the person's history of previous successes and failures within that situation
- **observational learning** having observed somebody else in the same situation succeeding or failing
- support from others who persuade the person that he or she can do it
- the individual's emotional state (feelings of **anxiety** and negativity can reduce self-efficacy).

See **anxiety, attitude, observational learning, self-esteem.**

Bandura, A. (1977) Self-efficacy: toward a unifying theory of behaviour change. *Psychological Review*, 84, 191–215.

Bandura, A. (1986) *Social Foundations of Thought and Action: A Social Cognitive Theory*. Englewood Cliffs, NJ: Prentice Hall.

Self-esteem

Self-esteem is the way in which individuals evaluate their understanding of self and the value that they place upon self. It affects how worthwhile, confident and valued individuals feel about themselves. In childhood, children have a tendency to judge themselves according to four key areas:

- Social competence: how well they can get along with other children.
- Cognitive competence: how good are they at solving problems.
- Physical competence: how good they are at running, playing and other physical activities.
- Behavioural conduct: whether they view themselves as good or naughty.

As individuals grow older, there are more judgements to be made in valuing self, in areas such as attractiveness, ability at work, relationships and sense of humour. There are suggestions that it is individuals' self-perceptions of their abilities in all of these areas that create their self-esteem. Other theorists take the view that our self-esteem is affected by the judgements of others on our abilities, and that we base our own self-evaluation upon these external judgements.

See **looking-glass self.**

Self-fulfilling prophecy

This relates to the fact that individuals are likely to behave in a manner that others expect them to. Simply put, this means that what you expect to happen will more than likely come true. For example, if a parent expects a child to misbehave when they go shopping, the parent may treat the child in a manner that may lead the child into behaving in the expected way.

Selfish gene theory

This is a sociobiological theory proposed by British ethologist Dawkins (1978, 1989) that suggests that any behaviour of an organism is designed to specifically **maximize** the survival of its genes. This theory suggests that the actual survival of any organism is of secondary importance to the primary goal of survival and perpetuation of its genes.

See **genetic determinism, maximizing (game theory), theory of evolution.**

Dawkins, R. (1978) *The Selfish Gene*. Oxford: Oxford University Press.
Dawkins, R. (1989) *The Selfish Gene*, 2nd edn. Oxford: Oxford University Press.

Self-perception theory

This theory suggests that our **attitudes** and characteristics can be shaped by our evaluation and **observations** of our own behaviour. For example, if we find ourselves often taking the lead in meetings we may see ourselves as natural leaders. Similarly if we find ourselves shrinking into the background at meetings, we may see ourselves as unassertive or shy.

See **attitude, observation, social psychology, social identity theory.**

Self-serving attributional bias

This refers an individual's tendency to attribute positive outcomes to **dispositional** factors (personal characteristics or **traits**) and negative outcomes to **situational** factors (environment, other people). It is typified in the proverbial worker who blames the tools when a job is badly done.

See **attribution, dispositional attributions, situational attributions, trait theories of personality.**

S

Semantic coding

This refers to how information about objects and events is processed in the form of mental concepts that are listed according to their properties, instead of being classified according to their visual image or by forming a prototype.

Semantic differential

This is technique developed by Osgood (1957), in which individuals are asked to rate an item according to a seven-point rating scale. Each scale indicates a **range** on a dimension of polar opposites such as 'hard–soft', where one indicates very hard and seven very soft. The results gained from such ratings, Osgood claimed, could be explained in relation to three underlying dimensions: activity, potency and value.

See **range.**

Osgood, C. E., Suci, G. J. and Tannenbaum, P. H. (1957) *The Measurement of Meaning*. Chicago, IL: University of Illinois Press.

Semantic memory

See **memory.**

Sensitization

In psychology, sensitization can be viewed as the process of becoming highly sensitive to specific events or situations, especially to emotional events or situations, without any external **reinforcement**. With repeated exposure to the fearful situation or **stimuli**, the **anxiety response** will increase and become sensitized. Sensitization can create a strong fearful **response** to similar **stimuli** or situations that are not threatening or dangerous in any way, if they have been previously preceded by a painful experience.

See **aversion therapy.**

Sensori-motor stage

The sensori-motor-stage is the first developmental stage in **Piaget's theory of cognitive development.** During this stage, which **Piaget** identifies as occurring approximately from birth to 18 months of age, children explore and interact with objects within their social world and begin to recognize objects through their senses.

In interacting with the world, children are able to **accommodate** and **assimilate** patterns of actions and interact with objects to form cognitive **schemas** (representations and knowledge of objects), so that they can build upon existing knowledge.

> *See* **accommodation, assimilation, concrete operational stage, formal operational stage, Piaget's theory of cognitive development, preoperational stage, schema.**

Separation anxiety

This is the anxiety experienced by young children, or indeed anyone, when they are separated from their loved ones. In the case of children, it is a particular anxiety that stems from the separation from their primary caregiver, who is often the mother. There have been many studies that have revealed the detrimental effects of separation on children's social, emotional and psychological development.

> *See* **Ainsworth, anxiety, attachment, Bowlby, maternal deprivation.**

Serotonin

Serotonin, whose alternative name is 5–hydroxytryptamine (5–HT), is a **neurotransmitter**, a chemical that exhibits an **inhibitory** action within the body and **brain**. It is one of the major **neurotransmitter** substances found in the **central nervous system**, particularly the raphe nucleus area, which is involved in regulating functions such as sleep, arousal, **attention**, and mood and **depression**. Serotonin levels are believed to play a crucial role in the onset of **bipolar disorder** and mood disorders.

> *See* **attention, bipolar disorder, brain, central nervous system, depression, inhibitor, neuron, neurotransmitter.**

S

Sex characteristics

These are regarded as genetically determined physical **traits** that differentiate the sexes. Characteristics such as genitalia and mammary glands that are directly associated with reproduction are known as primary sex characteristics, while characteristics that play no specific role in this (shape of buttocks, thickness of hair) are known as secondary sex characteristics.

> *See* **chromosomes, gender development, genotype, phenotype, trait theories of personality.**

Shaping

Shaping is a process used in **operant conditioning** in which an animal is conditioned to elicit a particular **response** that it would not otherwise naturally produce. Reward and **reinforcement** of any action that leads towards the desired **response** will change an animal's behaviour slowly and gradually towards the desired pattern.

> *See* **operant conditioning, reinforcement, response, Skinner.**

Short-term memory

> *See* **memory.**

Sign test

The sign test can be used to assess the results of a matched participant design (using different but similar subjects) or repeated measures design (using the same subjects in each **experimental condition**). It is a **non-parametric test** and is best used with **ordinal data**; if **data** is **interval** or **ratio** it is best to use the **Wilcoxon** matched pairs signed rank test as it usually more sensitive than the sign test.

> *See* **data, experimental condition, interval measurements, non-parametric tests, ordinal measurements, ratio measurements, Wilcoxon**

> Coolican, H. (2004) *Research Methods and Statistics in Psychology*. Bristol: Hodder and Stoughton.

S

Significance level (p)

In statistical analysis, a significance level is used to determine the likelihood of the **research** study's findings having occurred due to chance, or to the **variables** under study. The significance level indicates the probability level (p) at which the null **hypothesis** and the making of a type 1 **error** can be rejected.

In psychological **research**, the significance or probability level is usually set at 0.05 or 0.01, indicating that at 0.05 there is a 5 per cent (5 in 100) likelihood that the findings are due to chance (or some other factor not under study) and at 0.01 there is a 1 per cent (1 in 100) likelihood that it is due to chance.

> See **errors (type I, type II), hypotheses, tables of significance, research, variables.**

Situational attribution

This is a term used in attribution theory and refers to individuals attributing their own or other people's behaviour to situational and external factors (such as weather, time, work, social pressures and so on) rather than internal **traits** or characteristics.

> See **attribution, dispositional attribution, situational attribution, trait theories of personality.**

Sixteen-personality factor questionnaire (16PF)

> See **Cattell.**

Size constancy

This refers to the tendency for objects to still be perceived, according to their actual size, regardless of changes in their distance, which are registered on the retina of the eye.

> See **object permanence, object recognition.**

Skewed distribution

A skewed distribution reveals a population whose values/scores are not distributed around the **mean** when plotted on a graph. If scores reveal a left skew, then this would indicate a negative skew and a concentration of lower scores. If scores reveal a right skew, then this would indicate a positive skew and a concentration in higher scores. Two forms of skewed distribution are **ceiling effect** and **kurtosis**.

> See **ceiling effect, kurtosis, measure of central tendency, mean, measures of dispersion, normal distribution, standard deviation.**

Skinner

Skinner, B. F. (1904–90), was one of the founders of **behaviourism**; he suggested that the laws of **cause and effect** could explain all human behaviour and that behavioural **responses** were simply a reaction and **response** to environmental factors. He believed that this meant there was no need to study unobservable mental processes. Skinner is known primarily for his theory of **operant conditioning**, in which the future re-occurrence of an organism's **responses** is determined by the consequences associated with that **response**. He is famous for his experiments on rats in which he developed the **Skinner box**.

See **behaviourism, cause and effect, classical conditioning, operant conditioning, response, Skinner box.**

Slater, L. (2005) *Opening Skinner's Box: Great Psychological Experiments of the Twentieth Century*. London: Bloomsbury.

Skinner box

The Skinner box, named after its designer, was developed to reveal the various mechanisms and processes involved in **operant conditioning**. The box was a small enclosed cage in which an animal, such as a rat, had to learn to manipulate a mechanism for delivering reinforcers, such as food. Reinforcers (the food) are delivered after the animal has engaged in the action needed to undertake the mechanism, such as pressing a lever, which then leads to continuance of the action.

See **classical conditioning, operant conditioning, reinforcement.**

Slater, L. (2005) *Opening Skinner's Box: Great Psychological Experiments of the Twentieth Century*. London: Bloomsbury.

Snowball effect

This is said to occur when members of a group hold conflicting views; if one member changes his or her expressed beliefs, a knock-on effect occurs as other members also change their views.

Social comparison theory

This theory suggests that individuals compare their own behaviour, emotions and **attitudes** with those of other individuals to determine how they should behave. If individuals are uncertain as to how to behave in a situation, they will look at others and modify their behaviour to match what they view as the prevalent 'norm' of behaviour.

See **attitude, social norms.**

Ruble, D. N., Boggiano, A. K., Fieldman, N. S. and Loebl, J. H. (1980)

A developmental analysis of the role of social comparison in self-evaluation. *Developmental Psychology*, 16, 105–15.

Social constructionism

Social constructionism is a psychological approach that is based upon the assumptions that 'knowledge' and an individual's experience and understanding of the world and 'self' are the products of social constructions. This approach suggests that there are no universal 'truths' that can be identified by **objective**, scientific methods. Knowledge instead is seen as being continuously created, modified and constructed according to the social, cultural and historical location of the individual.

A key feature of social constructionism is the use of discourse. Discourse can be regarded as the method and form in which individuals', groups' or societies' views, beliefs and understanding of the world are represented and transmitted. Discourses are contained within language and visual imagery, and there are a variety of methods of **discourse analysis** that attempt to understand the role of discourse in human behaviour and understanding. Dominant discourses of childhood are **tabula-rasa**, puritan and romantic, each of which represents a particular notion of what childhood is.

See **discourse analysis, objectivity, tabula-rasa.**

Burr, V. (2003) *Social Constructionism*. Routledge: London.

Social exchange theory

The social exchange theory (Thibaut and Kelley 1959) offers an explanation of the factors that could underpin interpersonal attraction. The key assumptions of this theory are that individuals attempt to **maximize** the rewards (**attention**, affection) they gain from a relationship, while minimizing the losses (time and effort invested in the other person). It also assumes that an individual expects the other person in the relationship to mutually reciprocate factors such as affection, time and **attention**, so that each gives and receives in equal measure. In this theory, how satisfied an individual is with the gains and losses experienced in the relationship will depend upon past relationship experiences. In having such a comparison level, individuals will decide whether they believe that they deserve the gains and losses experienced in the existing relationship on the basis of experience of past relationships. People will also compare gains and losses of the existing relationship with the potential gains

S

(sex, affection) and losses (arguments, loss of control) if they developed a relationship with someone else. The assumptions of this theory have been further extended in **equity theory**.

See **attention, equity theory, maximizing (game theory).**

Thibaut, J. W. and Kelley, H. H. (1959) *The Social Psychology of Groups*. New York: John Wiley.

Social identity theory

Tajfel developed the social identity theory (1978, 1981), which argues that individuals possess a need to understand and evaluate themselves. To do this they use a process named self-categorization, in which they perceive themselves as being members of a number of categories and social identities. Such social identities originate from the particular groups that people associate with and categorize themselves within. These social identities can include racial group, gender, social group and nationality, and an individual can identify with many groups at the same time; for example, being female, British and a student. Another important aspect of social identity theory is that of self-enhancement: individuals attempt to enhance their self-esteem by viewing the group/s they belong to as superior to other groups. A key feature of this theory is that the self-image of individuals depends upon how positively they view the groups to which they belong.

See **in groups, out groups.**

Hirt, E. R., Zillman, D., Erickson, G. A. and Kennedy, C. (1992) Costs and benefits of allegiance: changes in fans' self ascribed competencies after team victory versus defeat. *Journal of Personality and Social Psychology*, 63, 724–38.

Tajfel, H. (1978) Intergroup behaviour. 1: Individualistic perspectives. In H. Tajfel, and C. Fraser (eds), *Introducing Social Psychology*. Hammondsworth: Penguin.

Tajfel, H. (1981) *Human Groups and Social Categories*. Cambridge: Cambridge University Press.

Social impact theory

The social impact theory is a theory of social influence that was first suggested by Latane (1981). The key propositions of this theory are:

- When there are large numbers of people (audience), or when the audience includes people of higher social status, and when their impact is closer and more immediate, the social influence upon an individual to act or feel in a particular way will be greater. For example, a person is likely to experience more nervousness when presenting a speech in front of the town mayor and 80 invited members, than in front of four family members.

● The greater the number of people who are subject to the particular influence, the more important these people are, and the less immediate the effect, then the less impact social influence will have. For example, a person is likely to experience less nervousness when performing as a member of a dance team than when he or she is to perform a dance solo.

See **audience effect.**

Latane, B. (1981) The psychology of social impact. *American Psychologist*, 36, 343–56.

Socialization

Socialization refers to the way in which individuals acquire particular views, belief systems and forms of behaviour from the social world and significant others. This process is believed to commence in infancy, and such social factors as culture, family, religion, education and economics are seen as **shaping** and moulding the child's behaviour and understanding.

Theorists, such as **Bowlby** have claimed that if an infant fails to form an **attachment** with a significant other, such as a mother or mother figure, socialization may be marred and never be fully recovered.

See **attachment, Bowlby, shaping.**

Schaffer, R. (1996) *Social Development.* Oxford: Blackwell.

Social learning theory

Social learning theories depict individuals as learning not through direct **reinforcement**, but through observing the behaviour of others and modelling their own behaviour in accordance with this. This learnt behaviour, they suggest, occurs through the process of imitating others' modelled actions. **Bandura** and Walters (1963) suggested that the majority of a person's behaviour is shaped by imitating the behaviour of role models whom that person respects. The role of social learning can be evidenced within the **shaping** of children's behaviour, as in **Bandura's** famous Bobo doll experiment (1973).

Social learning can provide explanations for the acquisition of many complex social behaviours, such as moral behaviour and

S

gender role behaviour that simple **reinforcement** models of learning cannot account for.

See **Bandura, reinforcement, shaping.**

Bandura, A. (1973) *Aggression: A Social Learning Analysis*. London: Prentice hall.

Bandura, A. and Walters, R. H. (1963) *Social Learning and Personality Development*. New York: Holt, Rinehart and Winston.

Pajares, F. (2004) *Albert Bandura: Biographical Sketch*. Retrieved 20 June 2005, from: www.emory.edu/EDUCATION/mfp/bandurabio.html

Social norm

A social norm is a view, belief, **attitude** or **perception** that is dominant and perpetuated within a particular group, culture or society. Social norms such as moral codes of behaviour and etiquette can guide and shape an individual's behaviour and thinking within particular social groups and contexts. An individual who does not **conform** to the dominant social norms is said to be **antisocial**.

See **antisocial behaviour, Asch, attitude, conformity, majority influence, Milgram, non-conformity, perception.**

Social psychology

Social psychology is a branch of psychology that is concerned with the study of social behaviour in all its forms. Such areas of study include **obedience** to authority, **conformity**, social compliance, interpersonal attraction, **attitudes**, **attribution** processes, group processes, non-verbal communication and helping behaviour. Culturally there has been a slightly different approach to psychology within the United States from that in Europe. The United States has focused more upon experimental **social psychology**, using more **objective quantitative methods** of investigating the social aspects of human behaviour, whereas Europe has predominantly taken a more **critical social psychology** approach, that attempts to incorporate **qualitative methods** and **subjective** accounts of human experience and behaviour.

See **attitude, attribution, conformity, critical social psychology, obedience, objectivity, social psychology, subjectivity, qualitative research, quantitative research.**

Tuffin, K. (2004) *Understanding Critical Social Psychology*. London: Sage.

Stainton Rogers, W. (2003) *Social Psychology: Experimental and Critical Approaches*. Buckingham: Open University Press.

S

Social representations

Social representations can be viewed as shared social beliefs, concepts, ideas and explanations that originate and are continuously passed between individuals, in the course of social interaction. For example, we may have developed an understanding of what 'Disneyland' is like, not because we have first-hand experience of going there, but because we have heard of others' experiences of going.

Social representations enable individuals to transform unfamiliar objects or events into something more familiar that can make sense. It is the tendency for individuals to name, categorize and classify unfamiliar events and objects, by comparing and contrasting these with familiar categories of events and objects that they already know about. Individuals simply look for similarities between the familiar and unfamiliar, and attempt to **accommodate** the unfamiliar to the constraints of the familiar object or event. Moscovici (1961) has suggested that the reason individuals process information in this way is because when they make sense of an unfamiliar object or event, it becomes less threatening and frightening.

For example, you may be asked to be 'best man' at your sister's wedding; you have never been 'best man' before, so this is an unfamiliar event. To enable you to make sense of what your social role may be as 'best man', you look towards existing knowledge you have acquired, perhaps from television and listening to other friends' experiences. Such knowledge enables you to make sense of what is expected of a 'best man' and is appropriate behaviour in that role.

Researchers such as Carugati (1990), Herzlich (1973) and Jodelet (1991) have undertaken studies in the areas of representations of intelligence, health and mental illness. Such studies support the theory that individuals do make sense of 'new' concepts and ideas on the basis of already existing knowledge and categories.

See **accommodation, anchoring, heuristics, memory.**

Carugati, F. (1990) Everyday ideas, theoretical models and social representations: the case of intelligence and its development. In G. R. Semin and K. J. Gergen (eds), *Everyday Understanding: Social and Scientific Implications*. London: Sage.

Herzlich, C. (1973) *Health and Illness: A Social-psychological Analysis*. London: Academic Press.

Jodelet, D. (1991) Representation sociale: phenomenes, concept et theorie. In S. Moscovici (ed.) *Psychologie sociale*. Paris: Presses Universitaires de France.

Moscovici, S. (1961) *La psychoanalyse: son image et son public*. Paris: University of France Press.

Moscovici, S. (1976) *Social Influence and Social Change*. London: Academic Press.

S

Moscovici, S. (2000) *Social Representation: Studies in Social Psychology*, London: Polity.

Spearman rank order correlation (rho coefficient)

The correlation coefficient is sometimes known as the Spearman rank correlation coefficient. It mathematically represents the relationship or correlation between two sets of measurements to see if a trend or pattern exists. A correlation coefficient of $+1$ indicates a perfect positive correlation, which is extremely rare, and a correlation coefficient of -1 indicates a perfect negative correlation. A coefficient of 0 would indicate no relationship at all between two sets of measurements. The strength and direction of the correlation coefficient indicates (from **-1**, -0.9, -0.8, -0.7, -0.6, -0.5, -0.4, -0.3, -0.2, -0.1, **0**, $+0.1$, $+0.2$, $+0.3$, $+0.4$, $+0.5$, $+0.6$, $+0.7$, $+0.8$, $+0.9$, **$+1$**) the type of correlation between the **variables**.

See **correlation coefficient, variables.**

Coolican, H. (2004) *Research Methods and Statistics in Psychology*. Bristol: Hodder and Stoughton.

Eysenck, M. W. (2000) *Psychology: A Student's Handbook*. Hove: Psychology Press.

Split-brain studies

Studies of split-brain patients (individuals who have usually been suffering severe epilepsy that can often cause loss of consciousness and elicit collapse) have provided valuable insights into how the two hemispheres of the **brain** work. The corpus callosum, the bridge between the two hemispheres of the **brain**, would be surgically cut to restrict epileptic seizures within one hemisphere of the **brain** only. Problems however arose in split-brain patients' ability to transfer information from one hemisphere to the other, although they could receive visual **stimuli** in both hemispheres by simply rolling their eyes around. Studies revealed that in right-handed people, speech is situated in the left hemisphere; this created difficulties in split-brain patients, as information presented to the right hemisphere could not be discussed, because the speech ability is located in the left hemisphere. The right hemisphere contains and controls visuo-spatial activities and the left hemisphere can reflect upon such activities via speech. Such studies suggest that the corpus callosum enables each hemisphere to be aware of the other's activities.

See **brain, Brocha's aphasia, stimulus, Wernicke's aphasia.**

Levy, J., Trevarthen, C. and Sperry, R. W. (1972) Perception of bilateral chimeric figures following hemispheric deconnection. *Brain*, 95, 61–78.

Split span procedure

See **Broadbent.**

Standard deviation

This is the most generally used **measure of dispersion**; it is more difficult to calculate than the **range** but can provide a more accurate measure of the spread of the scores. It reveals the average amount that all scores deviate from the **mean**.

See **mean, measures of dispersion, normal distribution, range.**

Standardization

This refers to how tests are standardized, given to a large **sample** group that is representative of the group that the test is designed for. Individuals' scores can then be compared against the scores of other individuals. This establishes the population norms for the test, which can ensure that the test is reliable and **validity**.

See **reliability, sampling, validity.**

Stereotype

A stereotype can be regarded as a static **generalization**, or an over-simplified classification made about any group of class of people. Stereotypes are used to aid individuals in making quick and easy judgements about other people, so that they can predict possible behaviour. These individuals can be seen as cognitive misers as they attempt to process cognitive information in the easiest, quickest way possible. There are a variety of **heuristics** that enable people to take shortcuts in how they come to understand and stereotype people.

Stereotypes are generally negative (for example, all football fans are hooligans) and are intertwined with **prejudices** and discrimination. Not all stereotypes, however, are necessarily always false assumptions, as some may be underpinned with some elements of truth.

A stereotype portrays a widely held set of beliefs, which serves to reinforce within individuals the feeling that there must be

S

some form of 'truth' within this view. Stereotypes can shift and change with time, but it is difficult to change a particular stereo-typical view once it is engrained within an individual's belief systems.

See **anchoring, attributional biases, generalization, heuristics, prejudice, social representations, social constructionism.**

Stereotyping

This is seen as the act or process of forming or using a **stereotype**. Examples are categorizing all women with blonde hair as stupid, or all women in the army as 'butch'.

See **stereotype.**

Stimulus

A stimulus is regarded as any internal or external event, action, agent or influence that can elicit a reaction in any organism. Stimuli usually have the following features:

- They have some form of physical characteristic that is able to arouse a reaction in an organism, such as smell, taste or sound.
- They must be able to stimulate some form of a reaction in the organism.
- They must be able to excite the organism's sensory organs.

See **classical conditioning, operant conditioning, positive reinforcement.**

Stimulus–response learning

This is a term used to describe any type of learning that takes place following an association being made between a stimulus and response. In **classical conditioning**, this type of learning can elicit a response by simple presentation of the stimulus. Take the example of a dog that starts to jump around with excitement when its owner picks up the dog lead. It has learnt to associate the owner picking up the lead with going for a walk, and the response is excitement.

See **classical conditioning, negative reinforcement, operant conditioning.**

Strange situation task

See **Ainsworth.**

S

Stratified sampling

See **sampling.**

Stress

Psychological and physical stress can be triggered by a variety of factors that are difficult to endure or cope with, such as emotional, social, physical, occupational or economic events, experiences and circumstances. Stress can be understood in a variety of ways, as:

- A **stimulus** or trigger, also known as a 'stressor': these are identified as social stressors, such as job-related stress, child-care pressures and family pressures.
- A **response** or reaction: how an individual reacts to the stressor.
- An individual's perceived inability to cope. This is posited in a particular psychosocial view of stress known as the transactional model, in which the interaction between an individual's perceived demands and perceived ability are psychologically appraised by the individual concerned. If he or she perceives that the demands are too great to cope with, this will create an imbalance between the perceived demands and the perceived ability to cope, and this will result in the stress **response**. For example, if a student has to complete an assignment for tomorrow (demand) but feels unable to do it in the time available (appraisal of ability), he or she will experience the stress **response**.

Excessive or prolonged stress can affect mental, emotional and physical functioning, and can trigger a variety of effects such as:

- physiological effects such as raised blood pressure, heart arrhythmia, sweating, blushing, increased blood glucose levels and breathing difficulties
- behavioural effects such as excessive eating, drinking, loss of appetite and an inability to sleep
- cognitive effects such as **memory** loss, concentration difficulties and hypersensitivity to criticism
- health effects such as headaches, ulcers and coronary heart disease
- subjective effects such as decreased **self-esteem**, lethargy, lack of **motivation** and fatigue

See **anxiety, depression, fight–flight response, memory, motivation, self-esteem, stimulus, response.**

S

Field, T. M., McCabe, P. M. and Schneiderman, N. (1985) *Stress and Coping*, Hillsdale, NJ: Lawrence Erlbaum
www.stress.org/ (The American Institute of Stress).

Stroop task

See **automatic processing.**

Subjectivity

Subjectivity can be viewed as an individual's unique and personal understanding and experience of 'self' and the world. In approaches such as experimental and behavioural psychology, researchers have striven to understand human behaviour via **objective** methods. In contrast, approaches such as **humanistic psychology** and **phenomenology** have focused upon emphasizing the value of listening and gaining access to individuals' subjective experiences. Subjectivity is particularly valued in **qualitative research** methods of **data** collection and analysis.

See **critical social psychology, data, feminist psychology, humanistic psychology, objectivity, phenomenology, qualitative research.**

Superego

The superego is a concept introduced by **Freud** within his psycho-dynamic theory of the mind and human behaviour. **Freud** suggested that the human mind or psyche is made up of three components, **id**, **ego** and superego, and human behaviour is determined by the intra-psychic conflicts that take place between these three.

The superego is defined as the component of the mind that contains all moral understanding and codes of appropriate behaviour that are gained through socialization and interaction with the social world.

See **ego, Electra complex, Freud, id, Oedipus complex, psychoanalysis, psychosexual stages.**

Synapse

A synapse is a minute gap, a junction that exists between **neurons** or between a **neuron** and a muscle or a gland, where nerve impulses can be relayed. The nerve impulses cannot cross the synapse alone and so travel across through the use of a **neurotransmitter** (spherical structures that contain molecules of chemicals).

See afferent neurons, action potential, efferent neurons, neural network, neuron, neurotransmitter.

Syntax

Syntax refers to the branch of **linguistics** that is concerned with the study of grammatical arrangement, and the rules that govern the legitimate sequence and use of words and morphemes within sentences.

See **language development, linguistics.**

S

Tables of significance

In statistics, tables of significance are used to determine, for each particular statistical test used, whether the **research** findings are significant at a variety of levels of **significance**. The standard level of **significance** used within psychological **research** is usually 5 per cent or $p < 0.05$; this means that the likelihood of the findings occurring due to chance is 5 in 100. If the tables reveal findings are significant, then the experimental **hypothesis** has been supported and the null **hypothesis** can be rejected.

See **hypotheses, research, significance level.**

Clegg, F. (1982) *Simple Statistics*. Cambridge: Cambridge University Press.
Coolican, H (2004) *Research Methods and Statistics in Psychology*. Bristol: Hodder and Stoughton.
Eysenck, M. W. (2000) *Psychology: A Student's Handbook*. Hove: Psychology Press.

Tabula-rasa

Tabula-rasa is a particular way (or **discourse**) of viewing childhood that particularly focuses on the nature and innate characteristics of a child at birth. Locke's essay of 1690, which examined human understanding, suggested that a child's mind at birth is a tabula-rasa: a blank slate upon which knowledge would be imprinted upon through interaction and experience with the social world. Such a portrayal of humankind views humans as inherently good, being all born equal and independent, and regards any abnormal or 'wicked' behaviour as being socially learnt.

See **discourse analysis, social constructionism, social learning theory.**

www.philosophypages.com/locke/g0.htm (a guide to John Locke's Essay concerning human understanding).

Theory of evolution

The theory of evolution was theorized by Charles Darwin

(1809–1882) in his book *On the Origin of Species* (1859). Darwin suggested that the development of any organism occurs over time, through a process named '**natural selection**', which is the way that any species evolves and changes through time, so becoming more adaptive to its environment. Key aspects of **natural selection** are:

- Organisms each have their own unique genetic characteristics.
- Some organisms' genetics are better suited and adapted to the environment, so they survive and reproduce while others die before they reproduce.
- The genetic characteristics of the survivors are retained and reproduced in their offspring.
- The genetic characteristics of those that die and were less well adapted are lost.

The theory of evolution simply suggests that individuals and organisms evolve and develop according to the success of their genetic characteristics. Those that have genetic characteristics that enable them to adapt better to the environment will survive and reproduce, and are more likely than those with less well-adapted genetic characteristics to pass their **genes** on to the next generation. The species then passes through what can be viewed as selective breeding: the continued survival of those with the most successful **genes**, which are selected and determined by their suitability to the environment.

See **gene, natural selection, selfish gene theory.**

Barret, L., Dunbar, R. and Lycet, J. (2001) *Human Evolutionary Psychology.* Hampshire: Palgrave.

Darwin, C. (1859) *The Origin of Species*. London: Macmillan.

www.pbs.org/wgbh/evolution/ (information on evolution from Clear Blue Sky Productions).

T

Theory of mind

Most people have what is referred to as a theory of mind, which means that they intuitively understand their own and other individuals' mind and mental states. These mental states include beliefs, **attitudes** and thoughts, and individuals can use their understanding to make sense of and interpret other people's actions, intentions and behaviours. This understanding also helps people to communicate their own needs and intentions within various social interactions, through both verbal and non-verbal (such as facial gestures, body language) cues.

Research (Wimmer and Perner 1983) has revealed that the majority of young children have developed a theory of mind by the age of three to four years. Frith (1989) suggested that for children to develop a theory of mind, they need to experience frequent social interactions and should be able to 'mentalize'; it is the ability to cognitively process a vast amount of information gained from the social world that enables them to make sense of their own experiences.

Baron-Cohen (1995) and Baron-Cohen, Leslie and Frith (1985) have suggested that individuals with autism have a poorly developed theory of mind, as they have difficulty understanding mental states and how mental states affect behaviour. Without this theory of mind, social interaction and communication appears to be disrupted and negatively affected.

See **attitude, research.**

Baron-Cohen, S. (1995) *Mindblindness*. Cambridge, MA: MIT Press.
Baron-Cohen, S., Leslie, A. and Frith, U. (1985) Does the autistic child have a theory of mind? *Cognition*, 21, 3–46.
Frith, U. (1989) *Autism: Explaining the Enigma*, Oxford: Basil Blackwell.
Wimmer, H. and Perner, J. (1983) Beliefs about beliefs: representation and constraining function of wrong beliefs in young children's understanding of deception. *Cognition*, 13, 103–28.
www.autism.org/mind.html (information by S. Edelson of the Center for Autism, Salem, United States).

Theory of planned behaviour

This theory was developed by Ajzen (1991) to take account of the limitations identified within the **theory of reasoned action**. The theory of planned behaviour adds a third determinant of behavioural control: perceived behavioural control.

Perceived behavioural control is posited as people's **perceptions** and beliefs of how likely it is that they will have the resources and opportunities around them to undertake a particular behaviour. This leads to a person's **motivation** for undertaking a course of action being determined by how successfully the person can (or cannot) perform the behaviour

If an individual holds intense control beliefs around the existence of factors that will aid in engaging in a behaviour, then the individual will experience high-perceived control over that behaviour. However, if the person possesses a low **perception** of control over the behaviour, then he or she will experience a strongly negative control belief that will impede the behaviour.

See **motivation, perception, social psychology, theory of reasoned action.**

Ajzen, I. (1991) The theory of planned behavior. *Organizational Behavior and Human Decision Processes*, 50, 179–211.

Beck, L. and Ajzen, I. (1991). Predicting dishonest actions using the theory of planned behaviour. *Journal of Research and Personality*, 25, 285–301.

Theory of reasoned action

Ajzen and Fishbein (1980) developed the theory of reasoned action, suggesting that by understanding people's **attitudes** and behavioural intentions, one could understand, explain and predict individuals' actions.

This theory determines that there is a relationship between the **attitudes** people hold and their behaviour, suggesting that people self-evaluate their behavioural intentions in relation to **social norms** and **attitudes** before deciding whether or not to engage in particular kinds of behaviour.

As people tend to evaluate their behavioural intentions in relation to their **attitudes**, a person would determine and reason whether the likely outcome of undertaking the action would be good or bad. People also evaluate their behavioural intentions in relation to **social norms** and the perceived social pressure that would be exerted upon them from significant others if they were to undertake or not undertake that action.

Consequently, if an individual believes that there will be a positive outcome from undertaking the behaviour, he or she will be more likely to engage in it. This theory however places greater emphasis for predicting human behaviour on behavioural intentions than on the **attitudes** people hold.

There have been criticisms of this theory. Godin and Kok (1996) have suggested that it cannot account for those individuals who experience or feel that they have little control over their own behaviours and **attitudes**. This led to the development of the **theory of planned behaviour**.

See **attitude, social norms, theory of planned behaviour.**

Ajzen, I. (1998). *Attitudes, Personality and Behavior*. Chicago, IL: Dorsey Press.

Ajzen, I. and Fishbein, M. (1980) *Understanding Attitudes and Predicting Social Behavior*. Englewood Cliffs, NJ: Prentice-Hall.

Godin, G. and Kok, G. (1996). The theory of planned behavior: a review of its applications to health-related behaviors. *American Journal of Health Promotion*, **11** (2), 87–98.

Madden, M. J., Ellen, P. S. and Ajzen, I. (1992). A comparison of the theory of planned behavioral and the theory of reasoned Action. *Personality and Social Psychology Bulletin*, **18** (1), 3–9.

hsc.usf.edu/~kmbrown/TRA_TPB.htm (information by K. McCormack Brown, University of South Florida, United States).

Therapy

Therapy is a general term for any type of treatment for a disorder or condition by any method (except surgery) that has been designed with the aim of curing or alleviating the experience.

Many different types of therapy are used within the sphere of psychology, depending upon psychological perspective and theories. These include **Rogers'** 'person-centred' therapy, psychotherapy/ **psychoanalysis**, **behaviour modification**, **cognitive behaviour therapy** and **hypnotherapy**.

> See **behaviour modification, cognitive behaviour therapy, hypnotherapy, psychoanalysis, Rogers.**
>
> www.babcp.co.uk (The British Association for Behavioural and Cognitive Psychotherapies).

Three-mountain task

Piaget designed the three-mountain task specifically to identify and reveal how children's cognitive ability and thinking capacities are limited, depending on and according to their stage of cognitive development. Experiments such as the three-mountain task and the **conservation** task were designed to determine the limitations in children's thinking, by revealing what children could not do.

Piaget suggested that children in the **preoperational stage** of cognitive development, usually before the age of seven, were **egocentric**: that they could only view things, emotions and physical settings from their own point of view.

In the three-mountain task, children are shown a 3-D model of three mountains, with various objects placed within the model. At the other side of the model sits a toy doll that looks down on the model, but from a different perspective. The child is asked what the toy doll can see and asked to choose the doll's view from photographs. **Piaget** found that children under seven chose the photograph of the view of the three mountains from their own point of view, revealing that children under this age had not yet developed an understanding of other viewpoints. **Piaget** concluded that children under the age of seven could only think about the world from their own perspective.

There are criticisms of **Piaget**'s work however, as Donaldson (1978) found that children could undertake such tasks when the task made more sense in the real world. For example, a child could hide a doll successfully from a policeman in a maze constructed for the task.

See centration, cognitive stages of development, concrete operational stage, conservation, egocentrism, formal operation stage, Piaget's theory of cognitive development, preoperational stage, sensori-motor stage.

Donaldson, M. (1978) *Children's Minds*. London: Fontana.
www.psy.pdx.edu/PsiCafe/KeyTheorists/Piaget.htm (information on Piaget from the PSI café).

Threshold

A threshold is referred to as the lowest intensity, point or value (pitch of a tone or colour of a line) at which a **stimulus** or object provides a **response** that can be detected. A threshold is also seen as the point at which two **stimuli** or objects can be discriminated against each other.

See **absolute threshold, stimulus, response.**

Token economy

Token economy is a technique frequently used in **behaviour modification** therapy to reinforce, elicit and shape socially desirable behaviour. Token economy systems are often used within educational and hospital settings. Tokens are given to individuals when they have demonstrated desirable behaviour; the individual can then exchange these tokens for a reward or privileges. For example, children in school may be given a gold star each time they hand their homework in on time; when they reach 10 gold stars, they receive a special certificate of merit that is given in assembly. The desirable behaviour has been positively reinforced with rewards designed to elicit positive behaviour/s.

See **behaviour modification (therapy), cognitive behaviour therapy, classical conditioning, negative reinforcement, positive reinforcement.**

Top-down processing

Top-down processing is a term used within **cognitive psychology** to explain how individuals can recognize, process and perceive information. In contrast to **bottom-up processing, perception** and recognition begins with the individual's cognitive processes, such as prior knowledge of the object and event, rather than external sensory factors. In this approach information flows top-down.

Goodman's (1967) portrayal of reading as a 'psycholinguistic guessing game' is a classic top-down theory. Goodman noted that individuals do not read each and every word; instead they **sample** the text, making **hypotheses** about the next word to be met, they then **sample** the text again, to verify their predictions, repeating this process again and again. Individuals therefore, Goodman suggested, need only to view enough of the text to enable them to predict the meanings of the following words or sentences. His theory would suggest that when an individual reaches the final word in the last sentence, he or she may already know what the word will be, and would not need to process all its letters; just the first two or three letters would be enough to confirm the prediction.

> See **bottom-up processing, cognitive psychology, hypotheses, perception, sampling.**

Goodman, K. S. (1967). 'Reading: a psycholinguistic guessing game'. *Journal of the Reading Specialist*, 4, 126–35.

Goodman, K. S. (1970). Reading: a psycholinguistic guessing game. In H. Singer and R. B. Ruddell (eds), *Theoretical Models and Processes of Reading*. Newark, DE: International Reading Association.

www.psy.pdx.edu/PsiCafe/Areas/Developmental/InfoProcessView/index.htm (information on information processing from PSI café).

Towers of Hanoi

This is a transformational, problem-solving experiment designed by the mathematician Eduord Lucas in 1883. It is sometimes known as the Tower of Brahma or the End of the World puzzle. It is used by cognitive psychologists to enable understandings to be gained of the role of cognitive representations and processes in learning to solve problems.

It is classified as a transformational problem because it involves events that transform one situation into another and, as is typical of such problems, asks the participant to solve the problem of how to transform one state into something else.

The Towers of Hanoi puzzle starts with three rings of different sizes on peg A. The task is to move all the rings to peg B in the fewest possible moves, subject to the following restrictions.

- You may only move one ring at a time.
- You cannot place a ring on top of a smaller ring.
- You can only place rings on one of the three pegs, not on the table or floor.

In setting such a problem, researchers are able to observe the actual stages each individual goes through in solving this task. Adding more rings can further complicate the task and allow researchers to

a) Initial situation

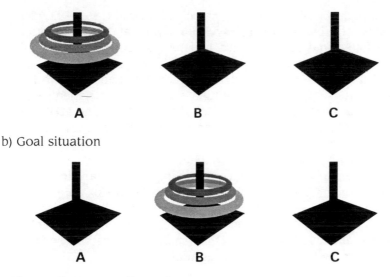

b) Goal situation

Figure 6 Towers of Hanoi

explore more deeply the role of experience on individual's learning and problem solving abilities.

Play the Towers of Hanoi online at:
www.lhs.berkeley.edu/Java/Tower/tower.html.
Want to know the quickest way to solve the problem?
www.dcs.napier.ac.uk/a.cumming/hanoi/rechelp.html

Trait theories of personality

See **Cattell, five-factor model of personality, Eysenck personality questionnaire, Freud.**

Transcription

This usually means changing a message from one code into another. Transcription is often used within **qualitative research** to change verbal interview **data** and audio language into 'transcribed' written speech. This allows the researcher to analyse and code the **data**/speech. Transcription can be a lengthy, time-consuming process.

See **data, qualitative research.**

Transference

The concept of transference originated with **Freud** (1856–1939) and is commonly referred to in **psychoanalysis** and psychotherapy. **Freud** found that some patients undergoing psychotherapy would respond to him as though they were a child, and he the parent, and that female patients would often became infatuated or fall in love with him. He suggested that during therapy sessions, patients were unconsciously transferring or shifting their emotions and **attitudes** derived from their original experiences with early significant figures in their lives onto the analyst.

   Freud argued that working through these transference issues is a critical aspect of the therapeutic process in **psychoanalytic** therapy through which aspects of past relationships are examined and resolved. He believed that the transferential relationship experienced between analyst and patient acted as the curative factor in **psychoanalysis**, and made interpreting the transference the pinnacle factor of the theory and practice of **psychoanalysis**.

> *See* **attitude, Freud, psychoanalysis, repression, regression.**

> Freud, S. (1914) Remembering, repeating and working-through. *Standard edition*, XII, pp. 147—56
> www.du.edu/~psherry/transferlec.html (information from the University of Denver, United States).

Transformational problem

> *See* **Towers of Hanoi.**

Trend analysis

Throughout human history, people have been preoccupied with attempting to forecast or predict the future. Methods such as trend analysis have been designed to help people better understand future possibilities in order to make better decisions today. Trend (or extrapolative) analysis is a type of statistical analysis which attempts to describe **objectively** what the future will be or could be. It is used to determine consistent trends in **data**, and findings can sometimes be used to predict possible events. For instance, through analysing a present trend, information can be gained about the possible and the probable outcomes, as we analyse what will happen if the trend continues, or what may cause the trend to change.

> *See* **data, Jonckheere test, objectivity.**

T-test

The t-test is a type of **parametric test** (a test that bases its calculation on an estimate of the population). It should be used when **data** is at an **interval** level and **samples** are taken from a normally distributed population. Types of t-tests are:

- Related t-test: designed to test the differences between pairs of **data**, usually taken from two repeated experiment conditions. For example, the dependent **variable** is measured before and after some form of treatment.
- Unrelated t-test: designed to test the differences between the **means** of unrelated groups, such as when each participant has only been involved in one of two conditions of an experiment.
- Single-sample t-test: designed to establish whether a single **sample** has been taken from a different population.

See **data, interval measurements, parametric tests, sampling, variables.**

Coolican, H. (2004) *Research Methods and Statistics in Psychology*. Bristol: Hodder and Stoughton.

Twin studies

Twin studies are used to understand the roles of heredity (**genes**) and environment (culture) in producing individual differences in human behaviour. Such studies compare **monozygotic** (MZ) identical twins with **dizygotic** (DZ) fraternal twins. Identical twins share identical **genes**, whereas fraternal twins are no more alike than normal siblings.

By contrasting identical twins with fraternal twins, environmental causes of behaviour can be ruled out if there is a high correlation of a measurable **trait** between identical twins. The higher the correlation between identical twins and the more that this differs from the correlation between fraternal twins, then the greater influence on behaviour of **genetic**, **heritability** factors that is indicated. Twin studies have been particularly used to examine the role of genetics in disorders such as anorexia nervosa, bulimia nervosa, **schizophrenia**, cancer, arthritis and diabetes.

See **addiction, adoption studies, dizygotic twins, gene, heritability, monozygotic twins, nature–nurture debate, schizophrenia, trait theories of personality.**

Segal, N. L. (1993). Implications of twin research for legal issues involving young twins. *Law and Human Behavior*, 17, 1.
Segal, N. L. (1997). Same-age unrelated siblings: a unique test of within-family

environmental influences on IQ similarity. *Journal of Educational Psychology*, **89** (2), 381–90.
www.ists.qimr.edu.au/ (International Society for Twin Studies).
twins.usc.edu/what.htm (University of California Twin Programme).

Two-tailed hypothesis

See **hypothesis**.

Type I error

See **errors**.

Type II error

See **errors**.

U u

Unconditional positive regard

Theorized by Carl **Rogers** (1959), unconditional positive regard is referred to as the therapist's expression or **attitude** of acceptance and warmth towards a client. **Rogers** believed this was an essential aspect of the therapeutic process and of a successful outcome, and he believed that it could and should be offered regardless of how nasty or distasteful the client was.

Rogers suggested that individuals experienced problems as a result of parents and others setting 'conditions of worth', such as: 'I will love you if clean your bedroom'. Individuals respond to this by **internalizing** and adopting the standards of others. This can lead them to set and expect high standards of themselves that they find hard to fulfil, thus causing low **self-esteem**. **Rogers** suggested that if unconditional positive regard was offered from an early age, individuals could develop a positive self-image or concept that is not distorted by the beliefs of others. Unconditional positive regard is a key feature of Roger's person-centred therapy, a popular form of counselling.

See **attitude, internalisation, Rogers, self-actualization theory, self-esteem.**

Mearns, D. and Thorne, B. (2000) *Person-centred Therapy Today: New Frontiers in Theory and Practice*. London: Sage.

Rogers, C. R. (1959) A theory of therapy, personality, and interpersonal relationships as developed in the client-centred framework. In S. Koch (ed.), *Psychology: A Study of Science*. New York: McGraw Hill.

www.pce-europe.org/nidxengl.htm (network of the European associations for person-centred and experiential psychotherapy and counselling).

Unconditioned response (UCR)

In **classical conditioning** the UCR is a natural, innate **response** to an **unconditioned stimulus** (UCS).

See **behaviourism, classical conditioning, conditioned response, conditioned stimulus, Pavlov, response, Skinner, unconditioned stimulus.**

Unconditioned stimulus (UCS)

In **classical conditioning**, the UCS is an object or event, a stimulus that elicits a natural, innate **response** in an individual.

See **behaviourism, classical conditioning, conditioned response, conditioned stimulus, Pavlov, response, Skinner.**

Unstructured interview

This is a type of interview used in **research** in which the topics or interview questions have not been planned or created in advance. It can be regarded as a naturalistic interview in which **open-ended questions** are favoured rather than **closed questions**.

See **closed questions, open-ended questions, research.**

Silverman, D. (2004) *Doing Qualitative Research, A Practical Handbook*. London: Sage.

Wilig, C. (2001) Introducing Qualitative Research in Psychology: Adventures in Theory and Practice. Milton Keynes: Open University Press.

U

Validity

Validity is the most important consideration in test evaluation. It refers to the appropriateness, meaningfulness and effectiveness of the specific deductions achieved from the test results. Test validation is the process of gaining evidence to sustain the test findings.

Some types of validity are:

- Content: this refers to the extent to which the questions in a test or in a **questionnaire** can appropriately measure everything that they have been designed to measure. For example, a test used in employment selection to measure abilities, skills and competencies specific to performance in the job is said to require high content validity.
- Ecological: this refers to the extent to which the **research** findings can be applied and generalized, not just to the **research** situation but also to ordinary, natural life.
- Face: this refers to the extent that a test based on **subjective** interpretation, estimated or intuitively judged (not based on **objective** evidence), appears to measure what is has been designed to measure.

See **objectivity, questionnaire, reliability, research, subjectivity.**

www.burns.com/wcbcontval.htm (information on validity by W. Burns).

Variables

Variables are items of **data** that values can be assigned to, which can be observed and measured.

There are two specific types of variables:

- Dependent variables (DVs) are one or more variables that may be influenced in some manner by the independent variable/s (IV). DVs are seen to be the result of the manipulation of the independent variable (IV).
- Independent variables (IV) are the **data** that are controlled by

the experimenter, such as the time allowed (say 10 minutes) for a participant to answer questions. The DV in this situation would be the number of questions answered. In laws of observable **cause and effect**, the IV is the cause and the DV is the effect. The purpose of an experimental study is to test the prediction made by a **hypothesis** that determines that an IV will generate a particular effect upon the DV.

See **cause and effect, data, experimental condition, control condition, hypotheses.**

Variance

Variance refers to the degree of variability, dispersion or scatter amongst a set of scores. It is used in **descriptive statistics** and is sometimes called the **mean** square, as it is calculated as the square of the **standard deviation**.

See **descriptive statistics, homogeneity of variance, mean, measures of dispersion, standard deviation.**

Vygotsky

Vygotsky, Lev (1896–1934), was a Russian psychologist who emphasized the importance of the role of social and cultural contexts on child development. He placed specific emphasis on the importance of the role of the adult in the transmission of knowledge, culture and language to children. Vygotsky theorized that interaction with others was vital in enabling learning to occur and to be extended. He suggested (1978) that children's development and learning could be extended by operating in the presence of more able individuals within the **zone of proximal development (ZPD).**

See **zone of proximal development.**

Vygotsky, L. S. (1978) *Mind in Society: The Development of Higher Psychological Processes*. Cambridge, MA: MIT Press.
www.kolar.org/vygotsky/ (information on Vygotsky and his work by S. Kolar and L. D'Ambrosio).

V

WAIS-III

The WAIS-III, the Wechsler Adult Intelligence Scale, is a general test of intelligence, designed as a comprehensive test of cognitive ability for people aged 16 and over. The tests are divided into two parts: verbal and performance. Verbal subtests include information, comprehension, arithmetic, digit span, similarities and vocabulary. The performance subtests include picture arrangement, picture completion, block design, object assembly and digit symbol. A version of the WAIS is also available for children, the **WISC-III** (Wechsler Intelligence Scale for Children). Such psychological tests are used specifically within areas such as **educational** and **clinical psychology**.

See **clinical psychology, educational psychology, WISC-III, psychometric tests.**

Kaufman, A. S. and Lichtenberger, E. O. (1999) *Essentials of WAIS-III Assessment,* (Essentials of Psychological Assessment Series), London: John Wiley.

Kaufman, A. S. and Lichtenberger, E. O. (2000) *Essentials of WISC-III and WPPSI-R Assessment*, London: John Wiley.

Wernicke's aphasia

This is experienced when damage has occurred to the temporal lobe, the part of the **brain** located near the ears which is situated in the language-governing hemisphere. Such damage can occur through head trauma or when an individual experiences a stroke, brain haemorrhage or tumour. In contrast to **Broca's aphasia**, individuals have no difficulty with fluency of speech; however patients with Wernicke's aphasia have trouble understanding and comprehending language. Their sentences are often long, with the addition of unnecessary, made-up or meaningless words, and they do not recognize the mistakes they make in speech.

See **brain, Broca's aphasia.**

Wilcoxon (matched pairs signed ranks) test

The Wilcoxon matched pairs signed ranks test is a test of difference and can be used to test whether the differences between two conditions or **sample** groups are **significant**. This test is used when a matched participant design (with different but similar subjects) or repeated measure design (where the same subjects take part in all **experimental conditions**) has been used and the **data** are **interval** or **ratio** as it is thought to be more sensitive than the **sign test**. If the **data** were **ordinal** it would be better to use the **sign test**. It is a **non-parametric test**.

> See **data, experimental condition, interval measurements, non-parametric tests, ordinal measurements, ratio measurements, sample, sign test, significance level.**
>
> Coolican, H. (2004) *Research Methods and Statistics in Psychology.* Bristol: Hodder and Stoughton.

WISC-III

A (Wechsler) intelligence scale for children, designed to test their cognitive ability, relative to age and stage of development.

> See **WAIS-III, psychometric tests.**

Wish-fulfilment

In **psychoanalytic** theory, wish fulfilment is a theory of dreaming developed in 1900 by **Freud**, who suggested that all dreams symbolize wish fulfilment, predominantly of repressed unconscious desires of the **id**, such as sexual desires. These desires are often unacceptable to the dreamer, due to the conflict created between the **id** and the moral nature of the **superego**. Gratification of these desires therefore, is undertaken in a disguised format, such as in dreams, fantasy or projection, which enables conflict with the punitive **superego** to be resolved. The actual dream and its meaning are known as the latent content, but by the time the dreamer awakes and can consciously recall some aspects of the dream, this has been distorted into manifest content, a more acceptable form.

> See **dream analysis, Freud, id, psychoanalysis, superego.**
>
> Freud, S. (1900) *The Interpretation of Dreams* (translated by J. Strachey). London: Allen and Unwin.
> Freud, S. and Tridon, A. (2003) *Beginner's Guide to Dream Analysis.* London: Standard Publications.

W

www.freud.org.uk/index2.html (Information on Freud and dreams from the Freud museum).

Within-subjects design

This is a **research** method in which each individual participant engages in each and all of the **experimental conditions**. The advantage of this design over a between-subjects design is that it reduces the effects of differences between the subjects. The disadvantage is that if subjects take part in all conditions, this may affect their performance in later conditions.

See **experimental condition, research.**

Working memory

See **memory.**

W

X chromosome

See chromosomes.

Y-axis

This is the vertical axis on a graph.

> *See* **regression (linear)**.

Y chromosome

> *See* **chromosomes**.

Yates' correction

In statistics, this is a correction that is made when calculating the chi-square in a 2-by-2 contingency table for small samples, in an attempt to provide a better estimate of the significance level. Where figures exceed the expected value, 0.5 is deducted, and 0.5 is added to figures that are less than the expected values. Some suggest that the correction should be used when at least one of the expected cell values of the table is less than five, others suggest less than ten.

> *See* **chi-square, sample, significance level**.

Zeitgeist

Zeitgeist refers to the general intellectual, moral and **social** cultural **norms** that are characteristic of a particular period or era of time. Zeitgeist is taken from the German words *'zeit'*, which means time, and *'geist'*, meaning spirit or ghost. It can be defined therefore, as the 'spirit of the time'. Characteristics that reflect the zeitgeist of twenty-first-century Western nations could be viewed as materialism, consumerism and 'celebrity'.

> *See* **social norms.**

Zener cards

These are a set of 25 cards with one of five symbols (a circle, star, square, cross or wavy lines) printed upon the face of each card. They are used in **research**, particularly by **parapsychologists**, to test for extrasensory **perception** or psychic ability in an individual. They are named after the US psychologist Karl Zener (1903–1964), who developed them. They are also known as ESP cards.

> *See* **parapsychology, perception, research.**
>
> www.scientificpsychic.com/esp/esptest.html (take the ESP test now courtesy of A. Zamora).

Zollner illusion

This is a geometric illusion in which lines placed vertically parallel are crossed by short oblique lines, running in the opposite direction to each other. The lines appear to be moving away from each other and seem to tilt. This is an example of the simultaneous tilt effect.

> www.questacon.edu.au/html/zollner_illusion.html (an example of the illusion from Questacon).

Zone of proximal development (ZPD)

The zone of proximal development is a term introduced by **Vygotsky** (1896–1934). He suggested (1978) that children function at two different levels:

- the child's actual level
- the child's potential level.

Children can learn with the help of a knowledgeable other, for example an adult who can aid learning through scaffolding (a process in which learning is viewed as built and developed through the interaction between child and 'other'). Through the use of scaffolding and interaction, a child is seen to progress from working within his or her actual level to working within the potential level of development.

Vygotsky theorized that the ZPD exists at the interchange between these two levels, thus allowing children to function to the utmost of their ability. The ZPD can be seen as the difference between what the child can do with the help and guidance of another individual, and what he or she can do alone.

See **Vygotsky.**

Daniels, H. (1996) *An introduction to Vygotsky*. London: Routledge.

Doolittle, P. (1997) Vygotsky's zone of proximal development as a theoretical foundation for cooperative learning. *Journal on Excellence in College Teaching*, **8** (1), 83–103.

Penuel, W. R., Wertsch, J. V. and Hiatt, F. L. (1995) Vygotsky and identity formation: a sociocultural approach. *Educational Psychologist*, **30** (2), 83–92.

Vygotsky, L. S. (1978) *Mind in Society: The Development of Higher Psychological Processes*, Cambridge, MA: MIT Press.

www.kolar.org/vygotsky/ (information on Vygotsky and his work).

Z

Revision lists

Key statistical concepts

ANOVA
Chi-square (χ^2)
Descriptive statistics
Errors
  Type I error
  Type II error
Friedman test
Goodness of fit
Inferential statistics
Jonckheere test
Kruskal-Wallace test
Mann-Whitney U test
Non-parametric tests

Parametric tests
Repertory grid test
Skewed distribution
Sign test
Spearman rank order correlation
  (rho coefficient)
Standard deviation
t-test
Variance
  Homogeneity of variance
Wilcoxon test
Yate's correction

Key theorists

Ainsworth
Ajzen and Fishbein
Anderson
Asch
Atkinson and
  Shiffrin
Baddeley
Bandura
Bem
Bowlby
Broadbent
Bruner
Camus
Cattell
Chomsky

Darwin
Erikson
Eysenck
Festinger
Freud
Gilligan
Gould
Heider
Heidegger
Husserl
Jung
Kelly
Kierkegaard
Kohlberg
Levinson

Maslow
Mead
Milgram
Nietzsche
Pavlov
Piaget
Rogers
Sartre
Skinner
Thorndike
Triesman
Vygotsky
Watson

Key theories

ACT* system
Attachment theory
Attenuator model of attention
Attraction theories
Causal schemata model
Classical conditioning
Correspondent inference model
Co-variation theory
Cue arousal theory
Diathesis-stress model
Disengagement theory
Electra complex
Equity theory
Erikson's psychosocial
development stages (Eight ages
of man)
Evolutionary theory
Exchange theory
Expectancy theory
Filter model of selective
attention
Frustration-aggression
hypothesis
Gain and loss theory of
attraction
Game theory
Genetic determinism
Gould's theory of adult
development
Hassles and uplifts
Implicit personality theory

Kohlberg's theory of moral
development
Law of effect
Levinson's seasons of a man's
life
Looking-glass self
Maternal deprivation theory
Multistore memory model
Oedipus complex
Operant conditioning
Personal construct theory
Piaget's theory of cognitive
development
Reticular activating system
Self-actualization theory
Self-perception theory
Social adjustment theory
Social comparison theory
Social learning theory
Social learning theories
Social exchange theory
Social identity theory
Social impact theory
Strange situation technique
Theory of mind
Theory of planned behaviour
Theory of reasoned action
Trait theories of personality
Zone of proximal development
(ZPD)

Key psychological approaches

Abnormal psychology
Applied psychology
Behaviourism
Biopsychology
Clinical psychology
Coaching psychology
Cognitive psychology
Comparative psychology
Counselling psychology
Critical social psychology
Developmental psychology
Educational psychology
Ego psychology
Empiricism
Evolutionary theory

Existentialism
Experimental psychology
Feminist psychology
Forensic psychology
Gestalt psychology
Health psychology
Humanistic psychology
Nativism
Occupational psychology
Occupational psychology
Organizational psychology
Parapsychology
Phenomenology
Social psychology

Key research concepts

Case study
Closed questions
Coding
Control condition
Double-blind procedure
Experimental condition
Fieldwork
Likert scale
Longitudinal study
Meta-analysis
One-tailed test
Open-ended questions
Paired comparison test

Randomized control trial
Research
Qualitative research
Quantitative research
Quasi-experiment
Q-sort
Questionnaire
Ranking scale
Rating scale
Two-tailed test
Unstructured interview
Within-group design
Within-subjects design

Key psychological acronyms

ACT*	Adaptive control of thought system	ICD	International classification of diseases
APA	American Psychological Association	IPA	interpretive phemenological analysis
BPS	British Psychological Society		
BAL	blood alcohol level	IV	independent variables
CDA	Critical discourse analysis	MZ	monozygotic
CNS	Central nervous system	NS	neutral stimulus
DA	Discourse analysis	RAS	reticular activating system
df	Degrees of freedom		
DSM	Diagnostic Statistical Manual	REM	rapid eye movement
		UCR	unconditioned response
DV	dependent variable		
DZ	Dizygotic	UCS	unconditioned stimulus
ECT	electroconvulsive therapy	WAIS-III	Wechsler Adult Intelligence Scale
ESP	extrasensory perception		
FAE	fundamental attribution error	WISC-III	A (Wechsler) intelligence scale for children
FDA	Foucauldian discourse analysis		
		ZPD	zone of proximal development
GBR	Graduate basis for recognition		

List of phobias

This list gives you an idea of the many diverse phobias in existence, but this is only a brief selection (believe it or not, there are many more).

A
Abuse, sexual: Contrellophobia
Accidents: Dystychiphobia
Air: Anemophobia
Air swallowing: Areophobia
Airsickness: Aeronausiphobia
Alcohol: Methyphobia or potophobia
Alone, being: Autophobia or monophobia
Amnesia: Amnesiphobia
Anger: Cholerophobia
Animals: Zoophobia
Animals, wild: Agrizoophobia
Ants: Myrmecophobia
Anything new: Neophobia
Automobile, being in a moving: Ochophobia
Automobiles: Motorphobia

B
Bacteria: Bacteriaphobia
Bald people: Peladophobia
Becoming bald: Phalacrophobia
Bathing: Ablutophobia
Beards: Pogonophobia
Beautiful women: Caligynephobia
Beds or going to bed: Clinophobia
Bees: Apiphobia or Melissophobia
Bicycles: Cyclophobia
Birds: Ornithophobia
Black: Melanophobia
Blood: Hemophobia,
hemaphobia or hematophobia
Blushing or the colour red: Erythrophobia
Body odours: Osmophobia
Bogeyman: Bogyphobia
Books: Bibliophobia
Bound or being tied up: Merinthophobia
Bulls: Taurophobia
Burglars: Scelerophobia

C
Cancer: Cancerophobia
Car, riding in: Amaxophobia
Cats: Aclurophobia or felinophobia
Cemetries: Coimetrophobia
Chickens: Alektorophobia
Childbirth: Maleusiophobia, tocophobia or parturiphobia
Children: Pedophobia
Chins: Geniophobia
Church: Ecclesiophobia
Clocks: Chronomentrophobia
Cold: Frigophobia
Computers: Cyberphobia
Criticism: Enissophobia

D
Dampness: Hygrophobia
Dancing: Chorophobia
Dark or night: Nyctophobia
Death or dying: Necrophobia
Decisions, making: Decidophobia

Deformity, poor body image:
Dysmorphophobia
Dentists: Dentophobia
Dinner conversations:
Delpnophobia
Dirt: Molysmophobia
Disease: Nosophobia
Doctors: Tatrophobia
Dolls: Pediophobia

E
Eating: Phagophobia
Eight, the number: Octophobia
Electricity: Electrophobia
Englishness: Anglophobia
Erect penis: Medorthphobia

F
Failure: Atychiphobia
Fainting: Asthenophobia
Fatigue: Kopophobia
Feathers: Pteronophobia
Female genitals: Kolpophobia
Fire: Pyrophobia
Food: Cibophobia
Friday the 13th: Paraskavedeka-
triaphobia
Frogs: Batrachophobia

G
Garlic: Cherophobia
Germs: Verminophobia
Ghosts: Phasmophobia
Girls or virgins: Parthenophobia
Gods: Zeusophobia

H
Halloween: Samhainophobia
Handwriting: Graphophobia
Heat: Thermophobia
Hell: Hadephobia
Home: Ecophobia

Horses: Equinophobia
Hospitals: Nosocomephobia

I
Ice or frost: Pagophobia
Ideas: Ideophobia
Imperfection: Atelophobia
Injections: Trypanophobia
Insects: Entomophobia

J
Japanese culture: Japanophobia
Jealousy: Zelophobia
Justice: Dikephobia

K
Kissing: Philemaphobia
Knowledge: Gnosiophobia

L
Lakes: Limnophobia
Laughter: Geliophobia
Lawsuits: Liticaphobia
Learning: Sophophobia
Lice: Pediculophobia
Light: Photophobia
Love: Philophobia

M
Machines: Machanophobia
Marriage: Gamophobia
Meat: Carnophobia
Men: Androphobia
Mice: Musophobia
Mirrors: Catoptrophobia
Mother-in-law: Prentheraphobia

N
Names: Nomatophobia
Narrow places: Stenophobia
Needles: Aichmophobia or
belonephobia

Noise: Acousticophobia
Nudity: Gymnophobia
Number 13: Trisadekaphobia

O
Ocean: Thalassophobia
Old people: Gerontophobia
Outer space: Spacephobia

P
Pain: Algiophobia
People: Anthropophobia
Phobias: Phobophobia
Pins and needles: Belonephobia
Pope: Papaphobia
Poverty: Peniaphobia

R
Rain: Ombrophobia
Rape: Virginitiphobia
Relatives: Syngenesophobia
Religion: Theophobia
Reptiles: Herpetophobia

S
Satan: Satanophobia
School: Scolionophobia
Sex: Genophobia
Sin: Hamartophobia
Sleep: Somniphobia
Snow: Chionophobia

T
Taking tests: Testophobia
Thinking: Phronemophobia
Thunder: Ceraunophobia
Trees: Dendrophobia

U
Ugliness: Cacophobia
Undressing in front of someone:
    Dishabillophobia
Urine: Urophobia

V
Vaccination: Vaccinophobia
Vegetables: Lachanophobia
Vomiting: Emetophobia

W
Washing: Abultophobia
Wasps: Spheksophobia
Water: Hydrophobia
Work: Ergophobia
Wrinkles: Rhytiphobia

X
X-rays: Radiophobia

Y
Yellow colour: Xanthophobia

Key psychology weblinks

www.bps.org.uk (British Psychological Society)
www.bps.org.uk/careers/careers_home.cfm (British Psychological Society Careers Service)
Contains a wide range of information on careers, courses and accredited training courses in areas of psychology.

www.bps.org.uk/conferences-%26-events/events-home.cfm
(British Psychological Society Conferences and events)
Includes details of events and conferences in all areas relevant to psychology.

www.apa.org (American Psychological Association)
Provides access to a wide database of research and publications in the sphere of psychology.

www.apa.org/psycinfo/
Gain access to psychological abstracts relevant to your research or studies.

www.psychology.org (Encyclopaedia of Psychology website)
Simply type in a keyword such as cognitive and this site will link to relevant information.

www.questia.com
Provides access to reference material in a wide range of areas.

www.linkspider.org.uk/index.cgi/Science/Social_Sciences/Psychology
Provides links to a wide range of academic areas of psychology.

www.sosig.ac.uk (Social Science Information gateway)
Provides access to invaluable psychology resources.

Index